The Future of Work in Africa

The Future of Work in Africa

Harnessing the Potential of Digital Technologies for All

Jieun Choi, Mark A. Dutz, and Zainab Usman, Editors

A copublication of the Agence française de développement and the World Bank

Africa Development Forum Series

The **Africa Development Forum Series** was created in 2009 to focus on issues of significant relevance to Sub-Saharan Africa's social and economic development. Its aim is both to record the state of the art on a specific topic and to contribute to ongoing local, regional, and global policy debates. It is designed specifically to provide practitioners, scholars, and students with the most up-to-date research results while highlighting the promise, challenges, and opportunities that exist on the continent.

The series is sponsored by Agence française de développement and the World Bank. The manuscripts chosen for publication represent the highest quality in each institution and have been selected for their relevance to the development agenda. Working together with a shared sense of mission and interdisciplinary purpose, the two institutions are committed to a common search for new insights and new ways of analyzing the development realities of the Sub-Saharan Africa region.

Advisory Committee Members

Agence française de développement
Thomas Mélonio, Executive Director, Research and Knowledge Directorate
Hélène Djoufelkit, Director, Head of Economic Assessment and Public Policy Department
Marie-Pierre Nicollet, Director, Head of Knowledge Department on Sustainable Development
Sophie Chauvin, Head, Edition and Publication Division

World Bank
Albert G. Zeufack, Chief Economist, Africa Region
Markus P. Goldstein, Lead Economist, Africa Region
Zainab Usman, Public Sector Specialist, Africa Region

IBRD 39088 | MAY 2019

Source: World Bank (IBRD 39088, May 2019).

Titles in the Africa Development Forum Series

2020

The Future of Work in Africa: Harnessing the Potential of Digital Technologies for All (2020), Jieun Choi, Mark A. Dutz, and Zainab Usman (eds.)

2019

Electricity Access in Sub-Saharan Africa: Uptake, Reliability, and Complementary Factors for Economic Impact (2019), *Accès à l'électricité en Afrique subsaharienne : adoption, fiabilité et facteurs complémentaires d'impact économique* (2020), Moussa P. Blimpo, Malcolm Cosgrove-Davies

The Skills Balancing Act in Sub-Saharan Africa: Investing in Skills for Productivity, Inclusivity, and Adaptability (2019), Omar Arias, David K. Evans, Indhira Santos

All Hands on Deck: Reducing Stunting through Multisectoral Efforts in Sub-Saharan Africa (2019), Emmanuel Skoufias, Katja Vinha, Ryoko Sato

2018

Realizing the Full Potential of Social Safety Nets in Africa (2018), Kathleen Beegle, Aline Coudouel, Emma Monsalve (eds.)

Facing Forward: Schooling for Learning in Africa (2018), *Perspectives : l'école au service de l'apprentissage en Afrique* (2019), Sajitha Bashir, Marlaine Lockheed, Elizabeth Ninan, Jee-Peng Tan

2017

Reaping Richer Returns: Public Spending Priorities for African Agriculture Productivity Growth (2017), *Obtenir de meilleurs résultats : priorités en matière de dépenses publiques pour les gains de productivité de l'agriculture africaine* (2020), Aparajita Goyal, John Nash

Mining in Africa: Are Local Communities Better Off? (2017), *L'exploitation minière en Afrique : les communautés locales en tirent-elles parti?* (2020), Punam Chuhan-Pole, Andrew L. Dabalen, Bryan Christopher Land

2016

Confronting Drought in Africa's Drylands: Opportunities for Enhancing Resilience (2016), Raffaello Cervigni and Michael Morris (eds.)

2015

Safety Nets in Africa: Effective Mechanisms to Reach the Poor and Most Vulnerable (2015), *Les filets sociaux en Afrique : méthodes efficaces pour cibler les populations pauvres et vulnérables en Afrique subsaharienne* (2015), Carlo del Ninno, Bradford Mills (eds.)

Land Delivery Systems in West African Cities: The Example of Bamako, Mali (2015), *Le système d'approvisionnement en terres dans les villes d'Afrique de l'Ouest : L'exemple de Bamako* (2015), Alain Durand-Lasserve, Maÿlis Durand-Lasserve, Harris Selod

Enhancing the Climate Resilience of Africa's Infrastructure: The Power and Water Sectors (2015), Raffaello Cervigni, Rikard Liden, James E. Neumann, Kenneth M. Strzepek (eds.)

Africa's Demographic Transition: Dividend or Disaster? (2015), *La transition démographique de l'Afrique : dividende ou catastrophe ?* (2016), David Canning, Sangeeta Raja, Abdo Yazbech

The Challenge of Fragility and Security in West Africa (2015), Alexandre Marc, Neelam Verjee, Stephen Mogaka

Highways to Success or Byways to Waste: Estimating the Economic Benefits of Roads in Africa (2015), Ali A. Rubaba, Federico Barra, Claudia Berg, Richard Damania, John Nash, Jason Russ

2014

Youth Employment in Sub-Saharan Africa (2014), *L'emploi des jeunes en Afrique subsaharienne* (2014), Deon Filmer, Louise Fox

Tourism in Africa: Harnessing Tourism for Growth and Improved Livelihoods (2014), Iain Christie, Eneida Fernandes, Hannah Messerli, Louise Twining-Ward

2013

The Political Economy of Decentralization in Sub-Saharan Africa: A New Implementation Model (2013), Bernard Dafflon, Thierry Madiès (eds.)

Empowering Women: Legal Rights and Economic Opportunities in Africa (2013), Mary Hallward-Driemeier, Tazeen Hasan

Les marchés urbains du travail en Afrique subsaharienne (2013), *Urban Labor Markets in Sub-Saharan Africa* (2013), Philippe De Vreyer, François Roubaud (eds.)

Securing Africa's Land for Shared Prosperity: A Program to Scale Up Reforms and Investments (2013), Frank F. K. Byamugisha

2012

Light Manufacturing in Africa: Targeted Policies to Enhance Private Investment and Create Jobs (2012), *L'Industrie légère en Afrique : politiques ciblées pour*

susciter l'investissement privé et créer des emplois (2012), Hinh T. Dinh, Vincent Palmade, Vandana Chandra, Frances Cossar

Informal Sector in Francophone Africa: Firm Size, Productivity, and Institutions (2012), *Les entreprises informelles de l'Afrique de l'ouest francophone : taille, productivité et institutions* (2012), Nancy Benjamin, Ahmadou Aly Mbaye

Financing Africa's Cities: The Imperative of Local Investment (2012), *Financer les villes d'Afrique : l'enjeu de l'investissement local* (2012), Thierry Paulais

Structural Transformation and Rural Change Revisited: Challenges for Late Developing Countries in a Globalizing World (2012), *Transformations rurales et développement : les défis du changement structurel dans un monde globalisé* (2013), Bruno Losch, Sandrine Fréguin-Gresh, Eric Thomas White

2011

Contemporary Migration to South Africa: A Regional Development Issue (2011), Aurelia Segatti, Loren Landau (ed.)

L'Économie politique de la décentralisation dans quatre pays d'Afrique subsaharienne : Burkina Faso, Sénégal, Ghana et Kenya (2011), Bernard Dafflon, Thierry Madiès (eds.)

2010

Africa's Infrastructure: A Time for Transformation (2010), *Infrastructures africaines, une transformation impérative* (2010), Vivien Foster, Cecilia Briceño-Garmendia (ed.)

Gender Disparities in Africa's Labor Market (2010), Jorge Saba Arbache, Alexandre Kolev, Ewa Filipiak (eds.)

Challenges for African Agriculture (2010), Jean-Claude Deveze (ed.)

All books in the Africa Development Forum series that were copublished by Agence française de développement and the World Bank are available for free at https://openknowledge.worldbank.org/handle/10986/2150 and https://www.afd.fr/fr/collection/lafrique-en-developpement.

Contents

Figures

Maps

Tables

Foreword

The digital revolution is transforming industries and changing the nature of work across all regions of the world, including in Sub-Saharan Africa. Amidst this ongoing change, there are fears that automation and other digital innovations will lead to large-scale job displacement in manufacturing, retail services, and other industries. In developing countries where a large share of the labor force is in informal employment, there are fears that automation could close the traditional industrial pathway to economic transformation through low-wage factory employment. Across low-, middle-, and high-income countries, digital solutions have allowed fortunate workers in some industries to quickly adapt to working from home during the COVID-19 pandemic. What will be the future of work in Africa?

The reality for African countries is rather complex and likely to be more positive going forward. As this companion report to the *World Development Report 2019* finds, African countries have the potential to take advantage of the digital revolution in varied ways. To begin with, African countries have a smaller manufacturing base, at less than 10 percent of gross domestic product (GDP), than other regions. Therefore, automation is not likely to instantly replace as many African jobs as in more industrialized regions of the world, though robotization in other countries could slow down some local job opportunities. Innovations in digital financial services and logistics are proving to be game changers across the region: Kobo360 and Lori Systems have each invested in cashless, paperless, mobile-based on-demand trucking logistics technologies that have created new and better-functioning markets. Mobile technologies are allowing young entrepreneurs to use various digital platforms to access larger markets. Of course, the risk of large sections of the poor, the low-skilled, and the uneducated being left behind in a so-called digital divide looms large as more than 60 percent of the labor force is made up of ill-equipped adults and almost 90 percent of total employment is in the informal sector.

To harness the full potential of digital technologies, African governments and other crucial stakeholders, including the private sector and development partners, should prioritize investments in several important areas. These priorities are even more important as Africa addresses the humanitarian, economic, and social implications of the COVID-19 global pandemic and sets the foundations for the needed recovery afterward.

The first priority is to improve the availability of digital technologies across the region to help increase the productivity of workers and businesses. It will be important to close the current gap in digital infrastructure by enhancing affordable broadband access with improved regulatory frameworks.

Secondly, boosting human capital in African countries is crucial to enable broader participation of all segments of the population in the digital economy. This will entail supporting a critical mass of inventors and entrepreneurs in developing and scaling digital technologies to boost the productivity of low-skilled workers and should complement increased investments in early childhood education and health care service delivery. Investments in digital infrastructure and solutions, facilities, and personnel for health and education are even more consequential as the region adjusts to COVID-19 and develops resilience to possible future pandemics.

The third priority is to create a business environment that helps increase the productivity and upgrade the skills of informal businesses and workers— including by leveraging worker-enhancing digital solutions for low-skilled workers. This is a more effective approach to addressing informality in African countries than an exclusive focus on formalization policies. Although much of the business focus during the relief period of the COVID-related health crisis needs to protect existing formal sector jobs and the incomes of informal workers, a better business environment coupled with support of new, more productive investments in technology adoption will be needed to create and sustain the foundations of future growth recovery and prosperity.

Finally, African governments should strengthen and expand social protection systems to help workers manage risks in the formal and informal economy in a changing world of work. Increasing investments in social protection will entail greater efforts both to mobilize revenue from domestic sources and to improve the efficiency of current social expenditures. The message of expanding social protection systems and strengthening their governance is even more critical to ensure that livelihoods are protected during the COVID-related health crisis relief period and to support the entrepreneurial risk taking needed to underpin the vibrant recovery moving forward.

The challenge of creating more, better, and inclusive jobs for African countries is not in doubt. In this daunting task for policy makers, businesses, and development partners, the digital revolution presents vast opportunities as well as risks. The task will be even more daunting in a post-COVID-19 world—though if there is a silver lining, it may be linked to broader and more effective use of digital solutions. *The Future of Work in Africa* helps all stakeholders to navigate this transformation. Its lessons are powerful during periods of both relief and recovery.

Hafez M. H. Ghanem

Vice President, Africa Region
World Bank

Acknowledgments

This volume is part of the African Regional Studies Program, an initiative of the Africa Region Vice Presidency at the World Bank. This series of studies aims to combine high levels of analytical rigor and policy relevance, and to apply them to various topics important for the social and economic development of Sub-Saharan Africa. Quality control and oversight are provided by the Office of the Chief Economist of the Africa Region.

This book was prepared by a team led by Jieun Choi, Mark A. Dutz, and Zainab Usman under the guidance of Albert Zeufack, Chief Economist for the Africa Region at the World Bank. The main author of chapter 1 was Jieun Choi, with contributions from César Calderón and Catalina Cantú on digital infrastructure–related analyses; Jan Orlowski on LinkedIn data analysis, with support from Mar Carpanelli, Alan Fritzler, and Di Mo, all of LinkedIn; and Jakob Engel and Girum D. Abate on global value chain integration and foreign direct investment. The main authors of chapter 2 were Moussa P. Blimpo and Solomon Owusu. The main authors of chapter 3 were Pierre Nguimkeu and Cedric Okou, with contributions from Jeehye Kim on disruptive agricultural technologies. The main author of chapter 4 was Zainab Usman, with contributions from Jan Loeprick on revenue mobilization and Woubet Kassa and with comments from Dhushyanth Raju and Indhira Vanessa Santos.

The book benefited from useful guidance and advice from Haroon Bhorat, Mary Hallward-Driemeier, Jacques Morisset, Philip Schellekens, and others present at the book's inception and decision meetings or who separately provided helpful suggestions—including Diego Arias, Kathleen Beegle, and Ejaz Ghani. The team also benefited from discussions with Federica Saliola, task team leader of the 2019 *World Development Report*, and Ian Walker about the scope and main storyline of the book. The team thanks them for their helpful suggestions.

Maura Leary provided superb communications support. Sandra Gain provided timely editorial assistance. Production of the book was managed by Susan Mandel of the World Bank's formal publishing program; Jewel McFadden, of the Development Economics unit, was the acquisitions editor. Yaneisy Martinez, also with the World Bank publishing program, was the print coordinator.

About the Contributors

Girum D. Abate is an Economist in the Country Credit Risk Department at the World Bank. He holds a PhD in economics from Aarhus University in Denmark. He contributed to chapter 1.

Moussa P. Blimpo is a Senior Economist in the Office of the Chief Economist for the Africa Region at the World Bank. He holds a PhD in economics from New York University. He is co-author of chapter 2.

César Calderón is a Lead Economist in the Office of the Chief Economist for the Africa Region at the World Bank. He holds a PhD in economics from the University of Rochester. He contributed to chapter 1.

Catalina Cantú is a Consultant in the Office of the Chief Economist for the Africa Region at the World Bank. She holds a PhD in public policy from Tecnológico de Monterrey in Mexico. She contributed to chapter 1.

Mar Carpanelli is a Data Scientist and Economist with LinkedIn's Economic Graph initiative. She holds a master of public administration in international development from the Harvard Kennedy School and a master of science in economics from Universidad Torcuato Di Tella in Argentina. Mar developed the LinkedIn methodology and data sets used to measure digital skills in chapter 1.

Jieun Choi was a Senior Economist in the Office of the Chief Economist for the Africa Region at the World Bank at the time this book was prepared. She is currently the Senior Country Economist for the People's Republic of China. Jieun holds a DPhil (PhD) from the University of Oxford. She is one of the book's main editors as well as lead author of chapter 1 and co-author of the Overview. She also contributed to the other chapters.

Mark A. Dutz is a Lead Economist in the Office of the Chief Economist for the Africa Region at the World Bank. He holds a PhD in economics from Princeton University. He is one of the book's main editors and co-author of the Overview. He also contributed to the other chapters.

Jakob Engel is an Economist working on trade and regional integration in the Macroeconomics, Trade and Investment Global Practice at the World Bank. He is currently finalizing his DPhil (PhD) on trade and economic geography at the University of Oxford. He contributed to chapter 1.

Alan Fritzler is a Senior Data Scientist with LinkedIn's Economic Graph initiative. He received his master's degree from Northwestern University. Alan advised on the measurement of digital skills in chapter 1.

Woubet Kassa is a Research Analyst in the Office of the Chief Economist for the Africa Region at the World Bank. He holds a PhD in economics from American University. He contributed to chapter 4.

Jeehye Kim is an Agriculture Economist in the Africa Region of the World Bank. She holds a master of science degree in economics from the University of Glasgow. Jeehye contributed to chapter 3.

Jan Loeprick is a Senior Economist in the Fiscal Policy and Sustainable Growth Unit at the World Bank. He holds a PhD in economics from Vienna University of Business and Economics in Austria. He contributed to chapter 4.

Di Mo is an Economic Researcher and Senior Data Scientist on the Economic Graph team at LinkedIn. She received her PhD in economics from University of Leuven in Belgium. Di advised on the measurement of digital skills in chapter 1.

Pierre Nguimkeu is an Associate Professor of Economics at Georgia State University. He holds a PhD in economics from Simon Fraser University in Canada. He is co-author of chapter 3.

Cedric Okou is an Economist in the Development Prospects Group at the World Bank. He holds a PhD in financial economics from HEC Montréal. He is co-author of chapter 3.

Jan Orlowski is a Quantitative Economist consultant at the World Bank. He holds a PhD in economics from the University of Sydney. Jan contributed to the LinkedIn skills analysis in chapter 1.

Solomon Owusu is a PhD Fellow in economics at the United Nations University–Maastricht Economic and Social Research Institute on Innovation and Technology in the Netherlands. He is co-author of chapter 2.

Zainab Usman is a Public Sector Specialist in the Office of the Chief Economist for the Africa Region at the World Bank. She holds a DPhil (PhD) in international development from the University of Oxford. She is one of the book's main editors as well as lead author of chapter 4 and co-author of the Overview. She also contributed to the other chapters.

Executive Summary

The *World Development Report 2019: The Changing Nature of Work* highlights that the future of work, at the global level, will be determined by the tension between job losses in "old" manufacturing sectors that are susceptible to automation and job gains driven by product innovation in "new" sectors. Is this what the future of work looks like in Africa? The short answer is no. On the contrary, the region—given where it is today—has an opportunity to forge a different path from the rest of the world. Digital technology adoption has the potential, if harnessed effectively, to transform the nature of work for all Africans.

Sub-Saharan Africa is unlike other regions in several ways, including lower levels of technology adoption. It has a much smaller manufacturing base, so automation is not likely to displace many workers in the coming years—though adoption in other countries could slow down local job growth or foreclose some new job opportunities. Most African economies still have low levels of demand for products that are commonplace elsewhere, such as processed food and tourism, retail, and hospitality services. In the region, therefore, the greater consumer responsiveness to the cost and price reductions from technology adoption are likely to help firms grow, create more jobs for all, and produce more affordable products—to the extent that production takes place in African countries. Finally, because most African workers have limited education and tend to do informal work, usable technologies designed to meet their productive needs have the potential to help them learn more and earn more. In most African economies, there is no "old" or "new" sector—there is, however, enormous scope for innovation and growth across all sectors.

Why focus on digital technology adoption in Africa? Because digital technologies have the potential to help build skills not just for a privileged few but for all workers—including those with low education and limited opportunities—and to boost productivity and create better jobs in all enterprises, including informal ones. A recent study has found that the arrival of faster internet in Africa increased jobs not only for workers who had attended university, but also for those whose highest level of education was primary school.

Turning the promise of digital technology into reality depends on putting the right supportive policies in place—what this book and others refer to as "analog complements." These complements include competition, capital, and capacity—Africa's "three Cs." Governments need to ensure that market competition is sufficient to spur and enable rival businesses to adopt new technologies and expand output at affordable prices, thereby generating demand for jobs of most skill types. Businesses need more than money to expand in existing markets and to enter new markets. They need better entrepreneurial and worker human capital and better physical infrastructure capital—reliable electricity and transport as well as digital infrastructure. Finally, countries need stronger capacity to increase public investment in social protection. Such protection will help support greater risk taking by entrepreneurs and workers and support workers in their transitions between jobs. This is no small feat: the challenge of expanding social protection is more daunting in Africa than elsewhere because of low initial coverage, huge needs, and limited fiscal resources.

How should African countries start on their path toward digital transformation? They need to prioritize "three Es." First, enable entrepreneurship: let good ideas flourish no matter where they come from—so that African entrepreneurs build technology solutions that enable Africa's workers to build their skills as they work. Second, enhance the productivity of the informal sector: create a business environment that helps boost the productivity of informal businesses and workers—rather than focusing only on trying to formalize them. Third, extend social protection coverage: improve revenue collection, rebalance government spending, and more effectively coordinate development assistance.

The future of work in Africa could be bright. It is up to government policy makers and businesses to make bold choices and investments today that will pave the way for the next generation of African workers, inventors, and entrepreneurs to innovate and thrive.

Abbreviations

ACE	African Center of Excellence
AfCFTA	African Continental Free Trade Area
ALE	adult learning and education
ALMPs	active labor market policies
AML	anti-money laundering
ASPIRE	Atlas of Social Protection Indicators of Resilience and Equity
ATM	automated teller machine
C	Celsius
CFT	combating the financing of terrorism
CSR	corporate social responsibility
DAC	Development Assistance Committee
DHS	Demographic and Health Survey
DRM	domestic revenue mobilization
ECD	early childhood development
EMDEs	emerging markets and developing economies
FDI	foreign direct investment
GDP	gross domestic product
GNI	gross national income
GVC	global value chain
ICBT	informal cross-border trade

ICLS	International Conference of Labour Statisticians
ICT	information and communication technology
IT	information technology
NCEs	Networks of Centres of Excellence
ODA	official development assistance
OECD	Organisation for Economic Co-operation and Development
OJT	on-the-job training
PAM	Mathematics Adaptive Platform
PASET	Partnership for Skills in Applied Sciences, Engineering and Technology
PPP	purchasing power parity
R&D	research and development
RSR	Rapid Social Response
SPL	social protection and labor
SSN	social safety net
STEM	science, technology, engineering, and mathematics
TVET	technical and vocational education and training
UBI	universal basic income
UNESCO	United Nations Educational, Scientific and Cultural Organization
VAT	value added tax
WAEMU	West African Economic and Monetary Union
WDR	*World Development Report*
WTO	World Trade Organization

Overview

Jieun Choi, Mark A. Dutz, and Zainab Usman

In 2013, a hospital in Ogun State in southwest Nigeria asked Paga, a local start-up company, for help with its payment collection system. In the new system, instead of handing cash to administrative staff, patients used a mobile payment system. Transactions were recorded immediately, avoiding any corruption regarding quoted price or whether payments had been made. The hospital's revenues rose sixfold in two months. Today, Paga has almost 13 million customers and a nationwide network of more than 21,500 mobile payment agents to serve payment systems like the one at the Nigerian hospital. In the process of expanding, Paga has directly created these additional low-skill jobs at mom-and-pop stores, pharmacies, and grocery stores where people can access additional financial services. As Paga has grown, it continues training workers on the job, improving their skills for existing jobs, and preparing them for new jobs in more senior roles (see Kordunsky 2017).[1]

Clementina Achieng, a fishmonger in rural Kenya, used to walk half a day to the nearest local bank to transfer money to her husband, who buys fish in Lodwar, a small town near Lake Turkana. Since she started using M-Pesa mobile money, she can transfer money more frequently at much lower cost, which has enabled her husband to send more and fresher fish each day, and the expansion of her business. Clementina also uses M-Pesa to send tuition to her children's school. Such stories are common in Kenya, with M-Pesa now used by at least one individual in over 95 percent of Kenyan households outside Nairobi and over 50 percent of the population now using the system at least once a month. Although rapid adoption of mobile payments such as M-Pesa led to the loss of roughly 6,000 bank jobs between 2014 and 2017 in Kenya, the number of mobile payment agents increased by almost 70,000, resulting in a direct net positive job effect. Other kinds of jobs have been created indirectly—not only for hospital workers and fishmongers but also for workers at other informal and formal farms and firms—through access to credit for the previously unbanked, investments, cost reductions, and increased output from the use of digital financial services. Although the use of M-Pesa has been shown to reduce poverty and increase per capita consumption levels of Kenyan households, its impacts appear to be larger for female-headed households. M-Pesa has enabled more than 185,000 women to move out of subsistence farming and into business or sales occupations—or, like Clementina, to grow their existing businesses.

These are just two examples of how digital technologies are transforming the nature of work in Sub-Saharan Africa and providing a counterpoint to global fears that technology will only suppress job creation. Box O.1 summarizes the main findings and recommendations of the *World Development Report 2019: The Changing Nature of Work*, to which this book is a companion report. Using available evidence, this book finds that the global future of work outlined in the 2019 *World Development Report* (WDR 2019) is likely to play out differently in Sub-Saharan Africa than in the rest of the world. This difference is in large part due to underlying conditions in the region, including persistently low levels of human capital, a particularly large informal sector, and insufficient and inefficient social protection systems. Against this backdrop, the adoption of digital

---

BOX O.1

World Development Report 2019: The Changing Nature of Work

The 2019 *World Development Report* (WDR 2019) examines how technological advances are disrupting the nature of work. Five elements characterize these changes:

1. Technology is disrupting the nature of firms such that platform-based businesses like Amazon and Airbnb outcompete traditional brick-and-mortar companies such as retail stores and hotels. Platform companies create a network effect that connects customers, producers, and providers; and the companies facilitate interactions through multisided business models.

2. Technology is reshaping the skills needed for work. Although the demand for less advanced skills is declining, demand for advanced cognitive, socio-behavioral, and adaptable skills is rising. As a result, it is not just that new jobs are replacing old jobs but also that existing jobs increasingly require a different set of skills.

3. Threats to jobs from technology are exaggerated and not uniform across income groups. Although developed economies have shed industrial jobs, industrial employment is rising in some developing countries (for example, parts of East Asia) and stable in others.

(continued next page)

Figure BO.1.1 How Societies Can Benefit from the Potential of Technology

Effects of technology

Policy

Social inclusion

Goal

Source: World Bank 2019.

4. In many developing countries, about two-thirds of workers remain in low-productivity jobs, often in informal sector firms with poor access to technology. Informality has remained remarkably stable despite economic growth and the changing nature of work. Addressing informality and the absence of social protection for workers is a pressing concern for emerging market economies.

5. Technology, especially social media, affects perceptions of rising inequality that are often not corroborated by the data on income inequality. Increased exposure through digital communications to higher quality of life, different lifestyles, and opportunities heightens expectations, creates frustrations, and can lead to migration or societal fragmentation.

WDR 2019 recommends three policy directions for societies to benefit from the potential of digital technology (see figure BO.1.1):

1. Invest in human capital, particularly early childhood education, to develop higher-order cognitive and socio-behavioral skills in addition to foundational skills.

2. Strengthen social protection with a solid guaranteed social minimum and strengthened social insurance, complemented by reforms in labor market rules in some emerging market economies.

3. Create fiscal space for investments in human capital development and social protection by strengthening underused tax instruments, combined with eliminating tax avoidance and improving tax administration.

technologies may have a more positive and jobs-creating impact on less skilled and less educated workers in Sub-Saharan Africa than it does in higher-income regions.

Not surprisingly, the changing nature of work in the context of digital technologies and other global trends is high on the agenda of policy makers and researchers alike. Several studies have been published and more are in the pipeline; they use different methodologies to address various aspects of the future of work, especially on the African continent. For instance, a 2017 report by the World Economic Forum used LinkedIn data to conclude that the greatest long-term benefits of information and communication technology–intensive jobs in the region are likely to be in digital design, creation, and engineering (WEF 2017). The report suggests that, to build a pipeline of future skills, Africa's educators design future-ready curricula that encourage critical thinking, creativity, and emotional intelligence, and that accelerate the acquisition of digital and STEM (science, technology, engineering, and mathematics) skills to match the way people will work and collaborate in the future.

A 2018 report on regional perspectives on the future of work argues that new technologies will play an increasingly important role in Africa's economic transformation in agriculture, manufacturing, modern services, local content, and infrastructure (AfDB et al. 2018). Currently, however, the region is ill-prepared, lacking adequately skilled workers to take advantage of the unique opportunities that will come with these disruptions. A 2018 International Monetary Fund paper combines history, economic modeling, empirical evidence, and scenario analysis to assess the challenges and opportunities of digital technologies within the context of population growth, climate change, and a changing trade environment (Abdychev et al. 2018). The paper argues for decisive policy actions in infrastructure investments, flexible education systems, smart urbanization, boosting trade integration, and expanding social safety nets. A 2019 study by the African Center for Economic Transformation uses field surveys to assess the awareness and preparedness of policy makers in Africa for new technologies and supporting technical and vocational educational training systems (ACET 2019). The study identifies reforms in education and training systems, support for enabling regulations and infrastructure, and public-private partnerships in technology upgrading and transfer as areas where policies and investments can help absorb millions of new entrants into the labor market each year.

Building on WDR 2019, this book takes a different approach by identifying several themes that are critical to the future of work in Sub-Saharan Africa. The book is structured around these themes. Chapter 1 surveys the current state and potential of digital skills, infrastructure, and technology in Sub-Saharan Africa; chapter 2 examines the human capital needs of a young and growing workforce; chapter 3 looks at the prevalence of informal workers and enterprises; and chapter 4 identifies social protection policies to mitigate and manage risks stemming from labor market disruptions. The book offers recommendations for policy action to turn the promise of digital technology adoption into reality. The book leverages findings from recently completed World Bank regional flagship studies and related work.[2] It highlights important unanswered policy questions where additional research, supplemented by new data, could yield learning with high policy payoffs. The book does not dwell on examining the various pathways for structural transformation for African countries, because these are treated elsewhere. Rather, it analyzes the opportunities and challenges of digital technologies and supportive policies to harness their potential. This overview summarizes the key messages and recommendations of the analysis, in general and then chapter by chapter. It also highlights some remaining policy questions for future study.

The book highlights three possible reasons that could lead less skilled workers in Sub-Saharan Africa to benefit more from the adoption of digital technology than in other regions.

- First, on the supply side, there appears to be a window of opportunity. Because manufacturing production and employment are low relative to other regions, skill-biased digital technologies that automate tasks specific to manufacturing sectors are not likely to displace many workers over the next years—though adoption in other countries could slow down or foreclose some local job opportunities. The manufacturing sector is small, accounting for 8 percent of employment on average, with most workers underemployed in the informal sector, in agriculture and services. And, because many low-educated workers are still relatively low-cost across most of Sub-Saharan Africa, it may not yet be cost-efficient for many businesses to invest in automation.

- Second, on the demand side, productivity improvements from digital technology adoption may increase the demand for many products. Such potential exists because there are still relatively low levels of domestic demand for many mass consumption products in Sub-Saharan Africa, such as processed food and tourism, retail, and hospitality services, in contrast to higher-income countries where demand for these products is more satiated and therefore less responsive to price reductions from further productivity improvements. This is good news for jobs—even based on the adoption of skill-biased digital technologies such as the internet—if production can competitively take place in Africa, because the cost and price reductions from improvements in productivity from the adoption of digital technologies can then generate increases in production that are sufficiently large to create more jobs for a wide range of workers.

- Third, on the endowments (skills) side, low levels of human capital provide ample scope to develop worker-enhancing digital technologies that can be adopted by businesses across Sub-Saharan Africa, in the formal and informal sectors. Many digital technologies accessible through the internet—digital financial services for low-income entrepreneurs and the unbanked, voice and video-based e-extension services for informal farms and firms, and Uber-like platforms that do not require reading and numeracy skills—are particularly well-suited for the types of less educated, less skilled workers who are more prevalent in Sub-Saharan Africa than in other, higher-income regions.

It is important to weigh these predicted benefits against the risks that countries may not be positioned to take advantage of these opportunities or, even worse, that they may result in a greater digital divide without further poverty reduction. To take advantage of these opportunities, a fundamental prerequisite is for public policies to ensure that digital infrastructure is available to and affordable for all. Existing evidence points to the importance of digital infrastructure regulation that promotes competition, and more effective subsidies to support universal access and integration to create bigger markets. Usable internet services also require complementary physical infrastructure such as electricity. To avoid the risks of a worsening digital divide, internet services must be affordably available in rural as well as urban areas, in secondary as well as primary cities, for women as well as men, and for older as well as younger people.

Public policies to boost productivity gains from the adoption of digital technology need to be complemented with measures that support entrepreneurs in creating local applications and enterprises and workers in adjusting. These measures include increased investment in skills training, procedures to facilitate productivity upgrading of informal firms, and effective social protection and labor policies that protect workers against those risks that affect Sub-Saharan Africa more than other regions, spur greater entrepreneurial and worker risk taking, and facilitate worker transitions between jobs. Additional policies will be needed to address the risks associated with consumer vulnerability to fraud, manipulation, and deception, and overindebtedness by less informed poor households, and to ensure data privacy and cybersecurity.

Many digital technologies come with the risk of excessive concentration of market power and anticompetitive conduct, such as dominant firms acquiring rivals instead of allowing new entrants to grow and eventually challenge them. There is also a risk that dominant firms will integrate horizontally and vertically across markets to prevent more robust competition. Public policies need to ensure that market structure and conduct across industries remain competitive enough to allow for the entry and expansion of entrepreneurs offering new goods and services, and to ensure that current and future prices remain as low as possible, that quality (including data protection) remains high, and that innovation is not stifled. If not, there is the risk that excessive economic power would allow dominant firms to prevent the adoption of policies in the economy-wide public interest.

Key Messages

Chapter 1: Enabling Inclusive Digital Technologies

WDR 2019 suggests that the future of work will be determined by the tension between automation in "old" sectors and innovation in "new" sectors. Sub-Saharan African countries, however, have the potential to create new jobs from technology adoption across all sectors and skill categories. This potential exists because the adoption of worker-enhancing digital technologies can boost the productivity and output of low-skilled workers across all sectors—including agriculture and services—and because manufacturing sectors, which have often been labeled "old" sectors in more advanced economies, remain small and largely unautomated. These factors create the potential for significant output expansion and jobs growth (figure O.1).[3]

Closing the gap in the availability of affordable digital infrastructure services could increase growth and reduce poverty in Sub-Saharan Africa (figure O.2). Evidence from the region shows that increased access to faster internet spurs the creation and adoption of digital technology–related local innovations that address market and coordination failures, boost productivity, and affect inclusion outcomes. Widespread adoption of mobile money accounts in some countries provides the starkest illustration of this to date.

The arrival of faster internet in Sub-Saharan Africa during the late 2000s and early 2010s increased the probability that an individual was employed by

Figure O.1 Impact of Technological Progress on Work Opportunities in Sub-Saharan Africa

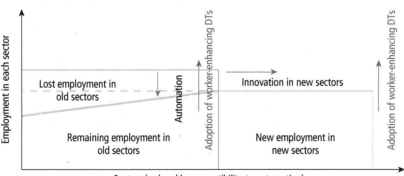

Source: Adapted from World Bank 2019.
Note: The red arrows illustrate the potential of the adoption of worker-enhancing digital technologies to boost the productivity of low-skilled workers across all sectors, lowering costs, expanding output, and increasing employment. The dotted line shows that lost employment in "old" sectors is expected to be smaller in Sub-Saharan Africa than in other regions. DT = digital technology.

Figure O.2 Correlation of Mobile Broadband with GDP per Capita and Poverty, Sub-Saharan Africa

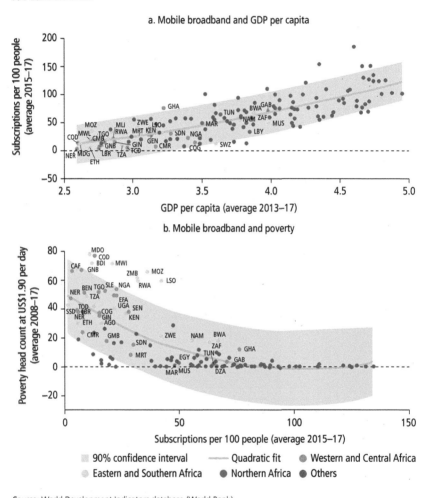

a. Mobile broadband and GDP per capita

b. Mobile broadband and poverty

■ 90% confidence interval   —— Quadratic fit   ● Western and Central Africa
● Eastern and Southern Africa   ● Northern Africa   ● Others

Source: World Development Indicators database (World Bank).
Note: The digital economy indicator is measured as mobile broadband subscriptions per 100 people averaged over 2015–17. Development variables are income (real gross domestic product [GDP] per capita in US dollars at constant prices, expressed in logs) and the poverty head count ratio. US$ = US dollar.

3.1 percent to 13.2 percent, depending on the mix of countries and surveys available, relative to areas unconnected to submarine cables (figure O.3). The impact on jobs for unskilled and less educated workers in the region was more positive than in higher-income countries. In terms of job categories, the probability that an individual held a skilled job increased by

Figure O.3 Impact of Faster Internet on Skilled Occupations and Jobs across Education Levels

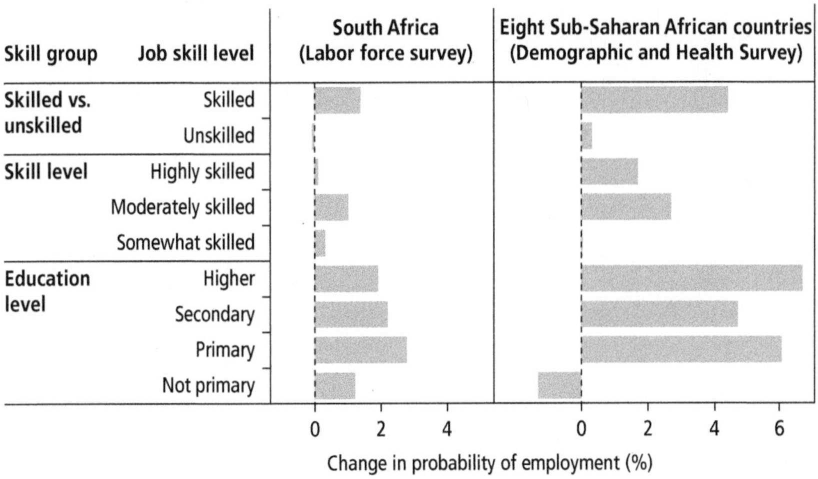

Skill group	Job skill level	South Africa (Labor force survey)	Eight Sub-Saharan African countries (Demographic and Health Survey)
Skilled vs. unskilled	Skilled		
	Unskilled		
Skill level	Highly skilled		
	Moderately skilled		
	Somewhat skilled		
Education level	Higher		
	Secondary		
	Primary		
	Not primary		

Change in probability of employment (%)

Source: Hjort and Poulsen 2019.

1.4 percent to 4.4 percent, whereas the probability of holding an unskilled job did not decrease (was not statistically different from zero). The increase in the employment rate was similar for those with primary, secondary, and tertiary schooling.

Sub-Saharan Africa is adjusting to the changing demand by businesses and firms for skills driven by technological advances. Among LinkedIn users in the region who are familiar with digital technologies, digital skills such as digital literacy and web development have been increasing, but large differences remain across skill types (figure O.4) and countries.

If they act quickly, countries in Sub-Saharan Africa may still have time to take advantage of globalization and follow the traditional industrialization-led growth path. Until now, assessments of the effects of digital technologies on the location of production bases have remained speculative, despite concern about re-shoring. To boost output and jobs in manufacturing sectors, countries in Sub-Saharan Africa should integrate further with global markets by participating in global value chains and attracting foreign direct investment. Such efforts should be supported by complementary improvements in the business environment, including public-private investments in electricity and transport and logistics infrastructure, and favorable trade policies.

Figure O.4 Growth of Digital Skills in Sub-Saharan Africa

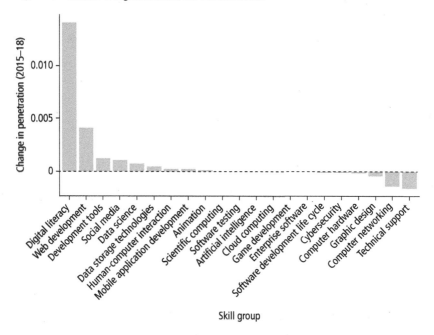

Source: World Bank elaboration based on LinkedIn data from 27 countries in Sub-Saharan Africa with at least 100,000 members.

Chapter 2: Building Human Capital

Building adequate human capital is more critical in Sub-Saharan Africa than anywhere else in the world (figure O.5). The region has not only the lowest level of human capital assets, but also the youngest and fastest-growing population. African countries should adhere to the broad recommendations of WDR 2019 and prioritize policies that build strong foundational and digital skills as a basis for lifelong learning.

Sub-Saharan Africa should leverage digital technologies to speed up acquisition of human capital and upgrading. Doing so will require increasing the availability of and access to higher-quality education offerings and the efficiency and productivity of the region's health care workers.

The region's large stock of low-skilled workers, often working in informal and low-productivity activities, sets it apart from the rest of the world and requires additional measures. African countries need to build and disseminate digital technologies to raise the productivity of their stock of low-skilled workers in their current occupations. The diffusion of basic digital skills would help workers take advantage of these new opportunities.

Figure O.5 Prerequisites and Selected Measures of Human Capital

a. Prerequisites for helping Sub-Saharan Africa reap
the benefits of digital technologies

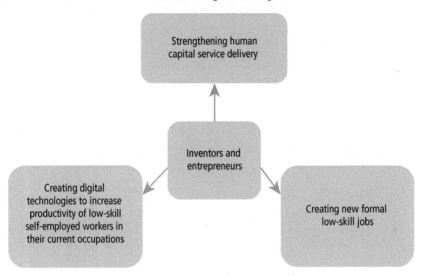

b. Share of population that has completed tertiary education,
Sub-Saharan Africa versus other regions

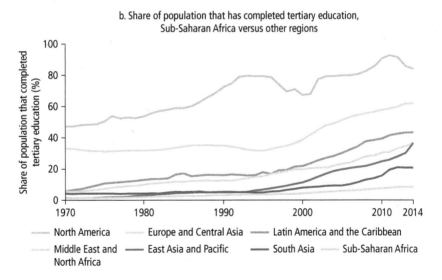

(continued next page)

Figure O.5 Prerequisites and Selected Measures of Human Capital (continued)

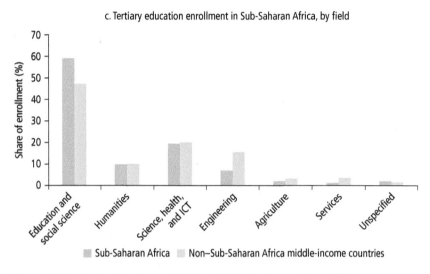

c. Tertiary education enrollment in Sub-Saharan Africa, by field

Sub-Saharan Africa   Non–Sub-Saharan Africa middle-income countries

Sources: World Bank elaboration; Roser and Ortiz-Ospina 2020; Arias, Evans, and Santos 2019.
Note: ICT = information and communication technology.

Digital technologies generate new tasks that provide new job opportunities for millions of low-skilled people. Adopting digital technologies that generate new demand for low-skilled workers will boost the creation of direct and indirect digital technology–enabled jobs, which will effectively leverage Africa's current labor force.

All digital technology–enabled opportunities for job creation and productivity gains require grassroots inventors and entrepreneurs that Sub-Saharan Africa currently does not produce or enable in sufficiently large numbers. In addition to investing in physical infrastructure expansion and improvements in the regulatory environment, as recommended by WDR 2019, the region must also act fast with targeted measures to build a critical mass of inventors and entrepreneurs to foster conditions that create formal, private sector jobs.

Chapter 3: Increasing Informal Sector Productivity
Of all world regions, Sub-Saharan Africa has the highest share of informal employment. Its informal sector differs from those in other developing regions in size—accounting for almost 90 percent of total employment (figure O.6)—and composition—including not only small but also large firms. Postreform formalization rates have been minimal despite the relatively high costs incurred by formalization programs.

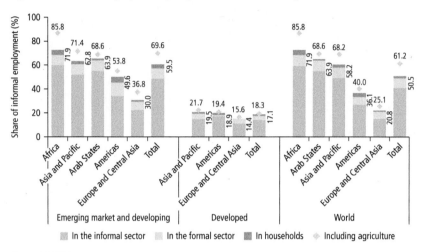

Figure O.6 **Informal Employment, by Region and Level of Development, 2016**

In the informal sector   *In the formal sector*   *In households*   *Including agriculture*

Source: ILO 2018.

Moving forward, short- to medium-term policies should focus more on increasing productivity and on interventions to upgrade skills for informal, small-scale firms and farms and unskilled workers. Formalization policies, as advocated in WDR 2019, should be more targeted in the short term toward large, informal firms that aggressively compete with formal firms. Leveraging digital technologies to boost productivity, job creation, access to credit, and financial inclusion in the informal sector should, in turn, make formalization easier over time.

Chapter 4: Extending Social Protection Coverage

Social protection and labor (SPL) programs have increased across Sub-Saharan Africa since the early 2000s, but coverage remains low because of fiscal and policy constraints (figure O.7). In addition to the risks posed by digital technologies, as identified in WDR 2019, SPL needs are created by other disruptions to labor markets that are particularly pronounced in Sub-Saharan Africa. Such disruptions include those arising from climate shocks, fragility, economic integration, and population transitions.

As noted in WDR 2019, governments in the region should focus SPL solutions on addressing the risks confronting the poorest and most vulnerable. Mitigating disruptions from digital technologies and trade adjustment costs will entail extending social insurance systems to cover informal workers. Adaptive social protection programs—integrated packages designed to help severely climate-stressed and very low-income countries, for example, in the Sahel—can be used to address vulnerabilities to climate change (map O.1) and conflict, by

Figure O.7 **Social Protection Coverage, by Region**

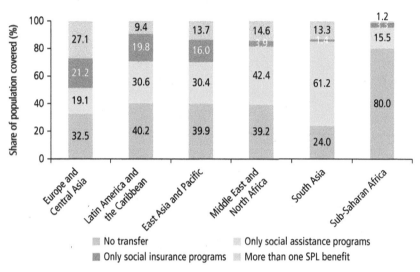

Source: World Bank Atlas of Social Protection Indicators of Resilience and Equity (ASPIRE) database, http://datatopics
.worldbank.org/aspire/region/sub-saharan-africa.
Note: SPL = social protection and labor.

Map O.1 **Effect of a 1°C Increase in Temperature on Real per Capita Output, Grid Level**

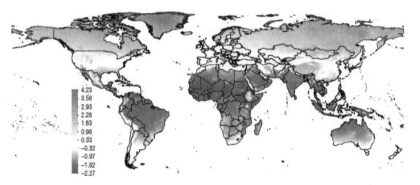

Source: IMF 2017. © International Monetary Fund. Reproduced with permission from the International Monetary
Fund; further permission required for reuse.
Note: C = Celsius.

increasing households' resilience to shocks and postcrisis response. To mitigate
the risks confronting populations in transition, short-term safety nets combined
with complementary active labor market interventions in urban areas can facilitate productive employment.

Expanding coverage of SPL programs for the poor and vulnerable will require
strengthening domestic revenue mobilization, as recommended in WDR
2019 (see performance of different tax types in figure O.8), and rebalancing

Figure O.8 **Performance of Different Tax Types, Sub-Saharan Africa**

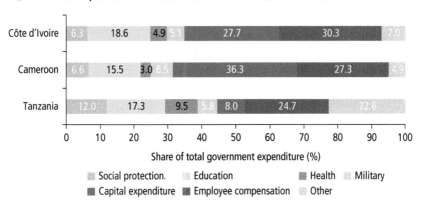

Tax revenue as share of GDP, five-year average (%)

- - - - - Personal income tax   - - - - - Corporate income tax   ——— Property tax   - - - - - Value added tax
——— Excises   ········· Trade taxes   ——— Other taxes

Sources: World Bank calculations based on internal data and United Nations University World Institute for Development Economics Research data.
Note: GDP = gross domestic product.

Figure O.9 **SPL Expenditures and Other Public Investments, Selected Countries**

Country	Social protection	Education	Health	Military	Capital expenditure	Employee compensation	Other
Côte d'Ivoire	6.3	18.6	4.9	5.1	27.7	30.3	7.0
Cameroon	6.6	15.5	3.0	6.5	36.3	27.3	4.9
Tanzania	12.0	17.3	9.5	5.8	8.0	24.7	22.6

Share of total government expenditure (%)

▨ Social protection.   ▨ Education   ■ Health ▨ Military
■ Capital expenditure ■ Employee compensation ▨ Other

Source: World Bank calculations based on public expenditure reviews.
Note: SPL = social protection and labor.

expenditures and instruments (figure O.9). Efforts to increase social safety nets for the poor often generate political resistance. To counter such resistance, governments should communicate more effectively the findings from public expenditure reviews on the need to rebalance resource allocation toward more vulnerable groups and to use instruments with more productive impacts.

Figure O.10 **Comparing OECD-DAC Bilateral Aid and Chinese Loans to Africa, 2016**

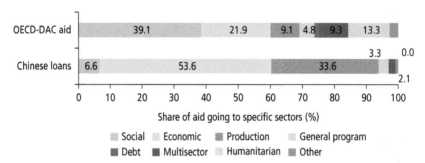

Share of aid going to specific sectors (%)

Social   Economic   Production   General program
Debt   Multisector   Humanitarian   Other

Source: World Bank calculations based on data from the Johns Hopkins University School of Advanced International Studies–China-Africa Research Initiative and the Organisation for Economic Co-operation and Development.
Note: Data from the Organisation for Economic Co-operation and Development's Development Assistance Committee (OECD-DAC) include data for bilateral donors and aid by European Union institutions. Social sectors include health, education, governance and civil society support, water, and population. Economic sectors include communications, energy, business, transport, and banking. Production sectors include agriculture, forestry, industry, mining, and trade.

SPL programs should also be part of broader national economic strategies on employment, poverty reduction, and economic transformation, rather than stand-alone initiatives. This incorporation can optimize finite resources and further tackle political resistance. Increasing public investment in productivity-increasing safety nets should be linked to a broader strategy to provide regional public goods in an era of increased integration.

The effective coordination of various stakeholders is crucial to expanding SPL coverage in Sub-Saharan Africa. At a transnational level, regional organizations should play a stronger coordination role on common taxation policies for revenue mobilization. Financial regulators at the regional and global levels should reduce the transfer costs for remittances. Development partners, including the Organisation for Economic Co-operation and Development's Development Assistance Committee (OECD-DAC) and new actors, should harmonize their development assistance for SPL on the basis of their comparative advantage and align it with recipient countries' economic strategies (see comparison of development assistance in figure O.10).

The Foundations of Economic Transformation through Digital Technologies

What Needs to Be Done: The Three Cs

The promise of digital technology adoption will not be realized without government support for essential analog complements (table O.1). This book refers

Table 0.1 Main Policy Recommendations Suggested by This Book

Outcome	Suggested policy actions
Enabling inclusive digital technologies[a]	• *Close the current gap* in digital infrastructure and enhance affordable broadband access with improved regulatory frameworks. Further regional harmonization, supported by increased regulatory capacity through regional hubs, should allow more effective subsidization to support universal access, and thereby boost poverty reduction, combined with more effective pro-competition regulation of digital infrastructure to create bigger markets. The positive interactions between subsidies (to boost demand) and lower costs (spurred by asset sharing and trading and greater economies of scale and scope) should allow larger markets to sustain more operators, with competition spurring innovation and access for all.
	• *Support the accumulation of digital skills.* Public-private partnership support could include education and worker training programs focused on digital literacy (for all users) and digital skills (for more specialized careers).
	• *Invest in analog complementary assets.* Doing so will require public-private investments in electricity and transport and logistics infrastructure. Favorable trade policies and broader business environment reforms remain crucial to enhance Sub-Saharan African firms' participation in global value chains and foreign direct investment attraction.
Building human capital	• *Use targeted measures to train a critical mass of inventors and entrepreneurs* to develop and scale digital technologies to boost the productivity of all workers, especially low-skilled workers in current and new occupations, and to strengthen the delivery of education and health services.
	• *Enable inventors and entrepreneurs* by fostering those ecosystems and mitigating appropriate risks that the private sector faces in funding them.
	• *Promote universal basic digital literacy* to enable broader participation of all segments of the population in the digital economy.
Increasing informal sector productivity	• *Focus on the promotion of productivity and the upgrading of skills* for small, informal farms and firms and unskilled workers. Leverage low-skill-biased digital technologies to access information and credit, broaden financial inclusion, build skills, and boost productivity, output, and jobs—thereby making formalization easier over time as more productive informal firms grow.
	• *Target traditional formalization policies toward larger informal firms* that aggressively compete with formal firms.
Extending social protection coverage	• *Create the enabling environment* to establish effective early warning systems, including insurance markets, to identify risks in time for effective mitigation.
	• *Increase public investments in social protection and labor systems* by improving revenue collection, using public expenditure reviews to justify the need for rebalancing government spending, and coordinating development assistance.
	• *Integrate social protection and labor policies into longer-term national and regional strategies* for economic transformation, employment, and poverty reduction.
	• *Coordinate regional organizations, financial regulators, and development partners* toward common objectives on tax policy, reducing remittances costs, and providing development assistance to enhance social protection coverage.

Source: World Bank.

a. The importance of increasing the availability of digital technologies is discussed in chapter 1. Because that chapter provides an overview of the availability of digital infrastructure and digital skills without exploring in detail specific policy actions, these policy actions are merely suggestive. They would benefit from additional research to explore the potential payoffs from more detailed implementation actions.

to them as the three Cs of Africa's digital transformation needs: competition, capital, and capacity.

1. Ensuring sufficient market competition is all about the rivalry between businesses that spurs and enables them to adopt and use the newest or most locally appropriate technologies and expand output at affordable prices. It is critical for improving the availability of digital technologies, by ensuring sufficient investment and deployment of digital infrastructure in response to consumer needs. And it is critical to stimulate adoption and use by all enterprises of cost-reducing and quality-enhancing digital technologies facilitated by access to broadband internet.

2. Ensuring sufficient capital is not just about the availability of sufficient financing to allow businesses to expand in existing markets and enter new markets. Businesses also need better entrepreneurial and worker human capital and better physical infrastructure capital—electricity and transport as well as digital infrastructure (also facilitated by more intense market competition). A key how-to message for boosting capital is to enable entrepreneurship. Policy makers must create business environments that let good ideas flourish no matter where they come from, so that local entrepreneurs also build apps that enable Africa's bulge of low-skilled, largely informal workers to improve their human capital as they work. A related key how-to message for addressing informality is that, rather than focusing policy largely on trying to formalize most informal enterprises, governments should put in place business environment conditions that boost the productivity of informal businesses and workers—so that they adopt and use technologies that can help them become more efficient.

3. Finally, governments need stronger capacity. To extend social protection coverage, countries need to improve revenue collection, rebalance government spending, and better coordinate development assistance. Doing so will help to support not only greater risk taking by entrepreneurs and workers but also worker transitions between jobs. The challenge of expansion of social protection is more daunting in Africa than elsewhere because of low initial coverage, huge needs, and limited fiscal resources.

How to Do It: The Three Es

As Africa sits on the precipice of digital transformation, governments will need to make some bold choices. Global risks emanating from climate shocks, fragility, economic integration, and population transitions are transforming the work landscape. The growing youth population makes it more urgent for Africa to invest in technologies that will create more and better jobs. The continuing high levels of poverty make it imperative to invest in ways that reduce rather than exacerbate the digital divide. Importantly, the commitment of the African

Union to promote digital technologies provides a window of opportunity to broaden the policy debate. Acting now should be a stimulus to facilitate all types of technology adoption—including many analog technologies complementary to digital ones—to generate the jobs and economic transformation that Africa needs.

How should African countries start on their path toward digital transformation? They need to prioritize the three Es. First, enable entrepreneurship: let good ideas flourish no matter where they come from—so that African entrepreneurs build technology solutions that enable Africa's workers to build their skills as they work. Second, enhance the productivity of the informal sector: create a business environment that helps boost the productivity of informal businesses and workers—rather than focusing only on trying to formalize them. Third, extend social protection coverage: improve revenue collection, rebalance government spending, and more effectively coordinate development assistance.

Additional research could yield learning with high policy payoffs in several areas (table O.2). The recently launched Digital Transformation for Africa research program by the Office of the Chief Economist of the World Bank's Sub-Saharan Africa region should help fill some of these knowledge gaps and answer some of the remaining questions about the promise of digital technologies for all Africans.

Table O.2 Important Unanswered Policy Questions

Outcome	Areas for additional research
Enabling inclusive digital technologies	• Better understand the economic case for moving to a harmonized and integrated regional approach to digital infrastructure regulation, supported by more competition and better spectrum design, together with the impact of innovative infrastructure solutions that could enhance access to and affordability of digital technologies for low-income people in rural locations (for example, lower-cost, low-earth-orbiting satellites).
	• Better understand the effects of different types of digital technologies—especially worker-enhancing (low-skill-biased, intelligence-assisting) digital technologies—on net job outcomes and the composition of skills.
	• Better understand the impacts of specific digital technologies on Sub-Saharan Africa's revealed comparative advantages—and build a broader understanding of the mechanisms that explain why the effects of digital technologies on low-educated and low-skilled workers could be different in Sub-Saharan African countries relative to higher-income countries.
	• Better use of big data supported by machine learning to inform policy discussions.
Building human capital	• Better understand how best to identify, train, and empower transformational inventors and entrepreneurs.
	• Along with using digital technologies to promote access to human capital services, explore the extent of the impact of digital technologies on the quality of human capital service delivery. Would digital technologies mainly complement already high-performing human capital workers to perform better, or can they improve the performance of low-performing workers? What is the extent of substitution and complementarity of digital technologies with prevailing lower-skill and higher-skill job tasks?
	• Develop better measures of worker, inventor, and entrepreneurial skills, especially soft skills and skills for adaptation.

(continued next page)

Table O.2 **Important Unanswered Policy Questions (continued)**

Outcome	Areas for additional research
Increasing informal sector productivity	• Better understand how various policies toward diffusion and adoption of digital technologies can influence the (mis)allocation of skills and resources across sectors, using a model of the channels through which the taste for digitization can shape occupational choices and entrepreneurship amid informality.
	• Assess the extent to which major development strategies for Africa, such as the 2030 Sustainable Development Goals and Agenda 2063, account for pervasive informality on the continent.
	• Identify and discuss the refinements warranted to improve the effective implementation of these strategies in achieving ambitious development goals.
	• Explore how digital business incubators and joint ventures can help firms to internationalize and boost their exports.
Extending social protection coverage	• Understand more precisely the implications of disruptive trends for labor dynamics within specific countries and subregions.
	• Assess rigorously the effectiveness of emerging social protection and labor interventions that aim to extend social protection to the informal sector and the "gig" economy.
	• Identify how to improve collaboration with the private sector to design and implement effective labor market policies to address urban poverty, youth unemployment, and population transitions.
	• Better leverage informal private transfers, including remittances and faith-based transfers, to serve a more effective risk-sharing and co-insurance function, especially in fragile settings.
Building a data agenda to support growth and inclusion outcomes of digital technologies	• Develop a forward-looking data agenda at the national, regional, and continental levels that highlights the kinds of data that should be collected and the types of analyses that are most important for policies to promote opportunities and mitigate risks associated with digital technology adoption for more productive and inclusive growth. Examples of risks include data collection by enterprises as a basis for consolidating and extending market power, data privacy and cybersecurity issues, and consumer protection issues related to fraud, manipulation, and deception.

Source: World Bank.

Notes

1. See also the Paga website, https://www.mypaga.com/.
2. The availability of these materials makes this companion report feasible and timely. The team undertook no new research, except for the analysis using LinkedIn data to understand the availability of digital skills in chapter 1 and the analysis on employment in the mining sector in chapter 4.
3. The dynamics underlying figure 1 in WDR 2019 are also relevant for Sub-Saharan Africa, because innovation creates jobs in "new" sectors by creating demand for new goods and services.

References

Abdychev, A., C. E. Alper, M. Perinet, A. Schimmelpfennig, D. Desruelle, S. Kothari, S. Rehman, and Y. Liu. 2018. "The Future of Work in Sub-Saharan Africa." Departmental Paper 18/18, International Monetary Fund, Washington, DC.

ACET (African Center for Economic Transformation). 2019. *The Future of Work in Africa: The Impact of the Fourth Industrial Revolution on Job Creation and Skill Development in Africa*. Accra: ACET.

AfDB, ADB, EBRD, and IADB (African Development Bank Group, Asian Development Bank, European Bank for Reconstruction and Development, and Inter-American Development Bank). 2018. *The Future of Work: Regional Perspectives*. Washington, DC: AfDB, ADB, EBRD, and IADB.

Arias, O., D. K. Evans, and I. Santos. 2019. *The Skills Balancing Act in Sub-Saharan Africa: Investing in Skills for Productivity, Inclusivity and Adaptability*. Africa Development Forum Series. Washington, DC: World Bank.

Hjort, J., and J. Poulsen. 2019. "The Arrival of Fast Internet and Employment in Africa." *American Economic Review* 109 (3): 1032–79.

ILO (International Labour Office). 2018. *Women and Men in the Informal Economy: A Statistical Picture*, 3rd ed. Geneva: International Labour Organization.

IMF (International Monetary Fund). 2017. "The Effects of Weather Shocks on Economic Activity: How Can Low Income Countries Cope?" In *Seeking Sustainable Growth: Short-Term Recovery, Long-Term Challenges*, World Economic Outlook October 2017, 117–83. Washington, DC: IMF.

Kordunsky, A. 2017. "In Africa, a Broadband Boom." *Ideas and Insights*, January 20, Columbia Business School, New York. https://www8.gsb.columbia.edu/articles/ideas -work/africa-broadband-boom.

Roser, M., and E. Ortiz-Ospina. 2020. "Tertiary Education." Our World in Data, Global Change Data Lab, University of Oxford. https://ourworldindata.org/tertiary-education.

WEF (World Economic Forum). 2017. "The Future of Jobs and Skills in Africa: Preparing the Region for the Fourth Industrial Revolution." Executive Briefing, WEF, Geneva.

World Bank. 2019. *World Development Report 2019: The Future of Work*. Washington, DC: World Bank Group.

Chapter 1

Enabling Inclusive Digital Technologies

Jieun Choi

Introduction

The 2019 *World Development Report* (WDR 2019) investigates the future of work at a time of growing concern that modern robots and a range of other worker-replacing automation technologies could take over millions of routine tasks, thereby reducing the need for less-skilled workers (World Bank 2019b). WDR 2019 explains that technological progress creates risks and opportunities for global production networks and for employment in developed and developing market economies.

This book addresses such concerns in the context of Sub-Saharan Africa, focusing on the unique characteristics of the region's economies, in particular their low levels of human capital, large informal sectors, and inadequate levels of social protection. This introductory chapter sets the stage by investigating the following:

- The extent to which digital technology infrastructure and digital skills are available in Sub-Saharan Africa and their likely effects on work-related outcomes
- Whether automation in advanced economies would prevent the traditional manufacturing-led growth path in Sub-Saharan Africa

The chapter argues for modifying the analytical framework of WDR 2019 to make it more relevant to the context of Sub-Saharan Africa. WDR 2019 focuses on the tension between process automation and product innovation as the key determinants of the future of work, predicting that automation will reduce the demand for low- and medium-skilled workers and that innovation will increase the demand for highly skilled workers. The future of work is likely to play out differently in Sub-Saharan Africa, given the region's low levels of human capital; its large, overwhelmingly informal and low-productivity agriculture and service sectors and small manufacturing sectors; and its large unmet demand for social protection. Unlike in other regions, enterprises' adoption of skill-biased digital technologies, such as the internet, has the potential in Sub-Saharan Africa to generate low-skill jobs as well, provided there are sufficiently large output expansion effects from the productivity benefits of these technologies. These effects may be more likely in Sub-Saharan Africa, given the still relatively low levels of domestic demand for many mass consumption products, for which demand is likely more elastic to productivity and price changes—provided production takes place in Africa. Thus, the situation in the region is in contrast with that in high-income countries, where demand is relatively more satiated and inelastic in its response to any further productivity and price changes (Bessen 2019).

In areas of Sub-Saharan Africa that have increased connections to faster internet, the demand for skilled workers has grown with no reduction in the demand for low-skilled workers; and the growth in jobs has been of comparable magnitude for individuals with primary, secondary, and tertiary education (Hjort and Poulsen 2019). Perhaps even more important for inclusion outcomes, the adoption of low-skill-biased, worker-enhancing digital technologies accessible through the internet has the potential to boost the productivity of the large number of low-skilled agricultural workers. This process has largely been completed in developed economies, as well as across all manufacturing and services sectors. The uptake of such digital technologies is likely to be facilitated by internet that is accessible to and affordable by all.

Finally, those manufacturing sectors typically considered "old" in more developed economies represent only a small share of employment in Sub-Saharan Africa. To date, automation of these sectors has been limited in the region—likely because enterprises have not yet found it cost-efficient to invest intensively in the machines required for such automation. Given the relatively low levels of adoption of newer process and product technologies across all sectors in the region, it is not appropriate to view the region's economies as populated by "old" and "new" sectors. Rather, Sub-Saharan Africa has the potential to catch up and learn from the mistakes of more developed economies—with businesses adopting new, worker-enhancing digital technologies, lowering production costs, and boosting demand and jobs across all economic sectors.

The chapter finds that, if they quickly close the gaps in digital infrastructure and digital skills, Sub-Saharan African countries have the potential for positive net job effects from digital technology adoption. Widespread automation of specific processes across the agriculture and manufacturing sectors as well as economy-wide adoption of other digital technologies have not yet taken place, partly because of the limited access to and affordability of digital internet infrastructure services. Contributing factors also include other key defining attributes of Sub-Saharan Africa—including low levels of human capital, high levels of informality, and inadequate social protection measures. The chapter reports that the availability of broadband, rather than just mobile voice, has positive correlations with diverse work-related outcomes, including increased income and inclusion. Furthermore, the adoption of basic digital technologies—such as access to mobile phone devices—has spurred additional local digital technology innovations like mobile payment systems. These digital financial services, in turn, have begun to address widespread market and coordination failures, thus boosting productivity, increasing income and employment opportunities, and reducing vulnerability.

Sub-Saharan Africa is adjusting to the changing demand for skills driven by technological development. The chapter shows that, among LinkedIn users who are more familiar with digital technologies, digital skills are increasing rapidly, although from a low base. Importantly, large heterogeneity exists across skill types and country income levels: for instance, Kenya, Nigeria, and South Africa have more diversified digital skills than other countries in the region. Meanwhile, the level of digital infrastructure, particularly broadband, is highly correlated with the induced demand for and availability of digital skills across countries. Complementary analog assets, such as electricity and human capital, are important determinants for expanding digital infrastructure and digital skills.

Despite rising concern that automation in developed countries may limit the traditional growth path through industrialization for developing countries, Sub-Saharan African countries still have time—if they act quickly—to take advantage of globalization to boost productivity and jobs in manufacturing sectors. Assessments of the effects of new technology adoption on the location of production bases remain speculative. Thus far, worldwide evidence is limited that digital technologies such as big data analytics, additive manufacturing, 3-D printing, and advanced robotics have a significant impact on the location of production bases and foreign direct investment (FDI). Globally, there has been little evidence of reshoring to date, and thus negligible effects of reshoring are expected to affect Sub-Saharan Africa for the time being. Moreover, the risk of displacement is low because of the limited presence of offshoring firms in the region. A more important question is how to increase the current low level of integration of Sub-Saharan African firms into global markets through participation in global value chains (GVCs) and by attracting FDI, both of which facilitate technology transfer. A related question is whether countries in the region can keep the unit cost of labor in line with and from exceeding growing productivity levels, because this cost will determine whether firms choose to automate production or move elsewhere. At present, traditional determinants of competitiveness, such as favorable trade policies

and a supportive business environment, remain crucial to growth; such policies are expected to be supported by digital connectivity and consequent
stronger manufacturing-service links.

WDR 2019 Analytical Framework and Predicted Effects for Sub-Saharan Africa

WDR 2019 highlights how new technologies are affecting the changing nature
of work. It posits that the future of work will be determined by the tension
between automation in "old" sectors that destroys some jobs and innovation
in "new" sectors that creates other jobs producing new goods and services
(figure 1.1). Newer digital technologies, such as advanced robotics, big data,
3-D printing, the Internet of Things, cloud computing, blockchain, and emerging platforms, are transforming industries, firms, and jobs. WDR 2019 predicts
that automation will reduce the demand for low- and medium-skilled workers
in routine jobs in old sectors and that innovation will increase the demand for
highly skilled workers in new sectors, as well as for technical skills that necessitate adaptability through lifelong learning about new technologies.

Within the set of available new technologies, this book focuses on digital
technologies because their widespread adoption, including the adoption of
low-skill-biased digital technologies that allow low-skilled workers to learn and
upgrade their skills as they work, offers the possibility of particularly strong
productivity and jobs growth benefits.[1] The following section provides available

Figure 1.1 Impact of Technological Progress on Work Opportunities

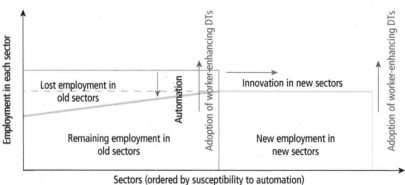

Source: Adapted from World Bank 2019b.
Note: The dotted line shows that lost employment in old sectors is likely to be significantly smaller in Sub-Saharan Africa than in other regions. DTs = digital technologies.

evidence on how the generation and adoption of digital technologies have boosted growth and inclusion outcomes in Sub-Saharan Africa to date.

The dynamics underlying figure 1.1 have relevance for Sub-Saharan Africa because innovation creates jobs in new sectors by creating demand for new goods and services. For instance, in the financial services sector, rapid adoption of mobile payments in Kenya led to the closing of bank branches (39 bank branches closed in Kenya between 2016 and 2018 [*Bloomberg Markets* 2018]) and consequent job losses. The Bank of Kenya reports that 6,020 bank staff jobs were lost between 2014 and 2017. Concurrently, however, the number of mobile financial services agents increased by 69,342 during the period (Ndung'u 2018), demonstrating a large, positive net effect on jobs driven by technology.

At the same time, the trends illustrated in figure 1.1 manifest themselves differently in Sub-Saharan Africa, because the production and employment composition across sectors, the likely responsiveness of demand to productivity improvements, and the appropriate skill bias of technologies differ significantly from other regions. For several reasons, the predicted inclusive jobs effects of digital technology adoption on low-skilled or less educated workers may be different and more favorable for low-income Sub-Saharan African countries than for higher-income developing and developed countries. Three possible reasons examined here relate to (1) supply-side effects of the sectoral composition of production and employment coupled with the relatively low cost of less-skilled labor (so that skill-biased, worker-replacing automation technologies are not yet likely to be cost-effective and, even if adopted, are not likely to displace many workers), (2) demand-side effects of the elasticity of demand to productivity improvements (so that the output expansion effect of skill-biased digital technology adoption is likely to be particularly large), and (3) the likely greater relevance of generating and adopting low-skill-biased digital technologies appropriate to worker needs in the region.[2]

First, on the sectoral composition of production and employment in Sub-Saharan Africa, the share of employment in agriculture is still very high (31 percent versus 18 percent for developing countries in other regions and 2 percent for developed economies in 2017), whereas the share of employment in manufacturing is exceptionally low (8 percent).[3] Despite a similar share of employment in services sectors (34 percent) compared with other regions (35 percent for other developing countries and 42 percent among developed economies), Sub-Saharan Africa's services sectors are distinct because they are largely informal (World Bank 2020). The rapid automation of manufacturing sectors considered old in more advanced countries has not yet taken place, partly because of the limited availability of foundational digital infrastructure.[4] The low share of manufacturing employment in Sub-Saharan Africa means that skill-biased, low-skill-worker-replacing automation digital technologies will not likely displace many workers yet, even if adopted (see the newly added dotted line in figure 1.1, which shows that lost employment in old sectors is likely to be significantly smaller in Sub-Saharan Africa than in other regions)—provided that automation in other countries does not slow down or foreclose local job opportunities. And the relatively low cost of less educated, low-skill workers across most of the region means that businesses may not yet find it cost-efficient to invest in worker-replacing digital technologies, even if higher-income countries increasingly use such technologies for the automation of more repetitive tasks.

Second, the predicted effects of businesses' adoption of skill-biased digital technologies on less-skilled workers depend on the responsiveness of demand to the price decreases that follow from the cost savings enabled by such technologies. Sufficient competition in product markets (so that prices fall more than they would in monopolized markets) and sufficiently elastic demand will result in a significant output expansion effect. As long as the output expansion effect is large enough to outweigh the substitution of less-skilled workers for technology at initial output levels, the number of jobs will increase not only for high-skilled workers but also for low-skilled workers.[5] The still relatively low levels of domestic demand for many mass consumption products in Sub-Saharan Africa mean that demand is likely to be more elastic to productivity and price changes—in contrast to high-income countries where demand is relatively more satiated for these products and therefore more inelastic in its response to any further productivity changes.[6]

Third, given the low levels of human capital and high levels of informality in low-income Sub-Saharan African countries relative to higher-income countries, businesses in Sub-Saharan Africa likely have more scope for developing and adopting low-skill-biased, worker-enhancing digital technologies. The adoption of such technologies that are accessible through the internet has the potential to boost the productivity of the region's many low-skilled workers in agriculture, a process largely completed in developed economies, as well as across all manufacturing and services sectors. These digital technologies, such as apps to allow workers to boost their numeracy skills and learn how to apply better farming practices and sell their products more effectively through markets, can help upskill workers with low literacy and numeracy skills and provide productivity-boosting information to low-income informal farmers and retail street sellers. These types of less educated, low-skilled workers are less prevalent in higher-income countries. Looking at these predicted channels from digital technology adoption to more-productive jobs for less educated, low-skilled workers, it is therefore less relevant to view Sub-Saharan African economies as populated by old and new sectors. Rather, the adoption of worker-enhancing digital technologies, skill-biased and low-skill-biased, has the potential to boost the productivity, output, and jobs for low-skilled workers across all sectors of the economy, as illustrated by the red process innovation arrows in figure 1.1.

The predicted effects of the adoption of digital technologies suggest pro-inclusion opportunities for Sub-Saharan African countries if sufficiently large output expansion effects result and if entrepreneurs can invest profitably in low-skill-biased digital technologies that help boost the skills of low-educated workers. But the effects will materialize only in an appropriate business environment with pro-competition government regulation and appropriately targeted subsidies to ensure that the internet is available to and affordable for all. Available and usable internet services also require complementary physical infrastructure, such as electricity and transport and logistics. To avoid the risks of a further digital divide, internet services must be affordably and equally available in urban and rural areas, in secondary and primary cities, for women and men, and for older and younger people. In addition, the predicted effects are average effects. The reallocation of physical capital and workers in response to productivity increases by some firms and not by others is not without frictions, and thus the benefits of increased competition and efficiency will not be equally distributed. Poorer workers will gain from lower prices of products in their consumption basket; however, some of those workers may lose if employed in enterprises that do not adopt new digital technologies and that are forced into decline by those enterprises that do. Negative individual effects will likely result at the regional and industry levels, particularly for specific low-skilled workers, despite potentially large overall benefits. Policies to boost productivity gains from digital technology adoption thus need to be complemented with measures to help enterprises and workers adjust. Such policies include increased investment in skills training, as discussed in chapter 2; measures to facilitate the productivity upgrading of informal enterprises, as discussed in chapter 3; and targeted social protection and labor policies, as discussed in chapter 4, including job search support.

Their adoption of digital technologies also changes enterprises' demand for skills—particularly for digital skills. The skill composition demanded by enterprises has changed across all occupations. To illustrate the increasing importance of information technology (IT) literacy over the past 20 years, WDR 2019 cites the changing job requirements of a Hilton Hotel management trainee (figure 1.2). Because of the region's low levels of human capital, however, Sub-Saharan Africa may experience the change in demand for skills differently than other regions have. This chapter reviews the availability of high-demand digital skills in the subpopulation of workers who use LinkedIn, the online platform that provides intermediary services for workers and enterprises. It finds that Sub-Saharan African economies appear to be gradually adjusting to the changing demand for skills: digital skills are growing, although from a low starting point and with large heterogeneity across skill types and countries. The availability of digital skills is highly correlated with the availability of broadband infrastructure, but not with mobile voice infrastructure.

Figure 1.2 Example of Changing Skill Composition Demand, 1986 versus 2018

Job requirements of Hilton Hotel management trainee in Shanghai, China

1986	2018
• Excellent character, willingness to learn • Ages 20–26 • Bachelor's degree or associate degree • Proficient in English • Good health • Live close to the hotel location	• Positive attitude and good communication skills • Ability to work independently and as part of a team • Competent level of IT proficiency • Four-year university degree with at least two years of experience

Sources: 1986: *Wenhui News*, August 17, 1986, http://www.sohu.com/a/194532378_99909679; 2018: http//www.hosco.com/en/job/waldorf-astoria-shanghai-on-the-bund/management-trainee-front-office.
Note: IT = information technology.

WDR 2019 also raises the concern that technological progress will facilitate automation in developed countries driven by reshoring, which in turn would mean that African countries never experience a traditional industrialization-led growth path. Automation occurs more quickly in locations with high labor costs, assuming the incentive to reduce labor costs exceeds other profit-related differences between locations. Figure 1.3, which appears also in WDR 2019, illustrates how automation and globalization affect manufacturing employment worldwide. Adapting this figure to Sub-Saharan Africa would likely make the pictured curves much flatter, because formal sector and manufacturing employment across most countries in the region is at much lower levels. This situation will continue because workers shifting out of agriculture are most likely to move to services sectors.

This chapter examines whether the adoption of new worker-saving digital technologies in developed countries could challenge the traditional manufacturing-led growth model in Sub-Saharan Africa, as the region's comparative advantage in labor costs becomes less salient. It finds that the potential effects of new digital technologies on global production networks and employment remain speculative for now. The demise of offshoring appears vastly exaggerated, at least for the foreseeable future. Until now, robotization in developed countries is concentrated in a few technology-intensive sectors, such as the automotive, rubber and plastics, metals, and electronics sectors. It is limited in labor-intensive sectors such as textiles. And increased automation in richer countries can enhance productivity and income, thus further increasing demand for intermediate inputs and other goods from developed countries. Although new digital technologies, such as 3-D printing, could provide new opportunities for Sub-Saharan Africa by facilitating the growth of regional value chains and enhanced manufacturing-service links, a bigger concern for

Figure 1.3 Automation, Globalization, and Manufacturing Employment

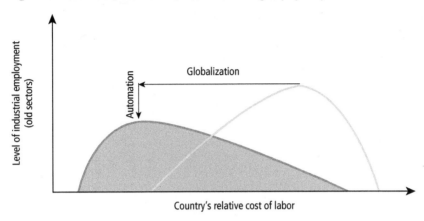

Source: Glaeser 2018.
Note: The curves are inverse U-shaped to reflect the empirical regularity that manufacturing employment constitutes a larger share of employment in middle-income countries; higher-income countries tend to specialize in services; and low-income countries have a relatively higher share of employment in agriculture.

the region is the current low level of integration with global markets through GVCs and FDI, commonly understood to be channels by which technology is transferred from more advanced foreign firms.

As noted previously, the future of work is likely to play out differently in Sub-Saharan Africa than in other regions. Sub-Saharan Africa's unique specificities—including continuing low levels of human capital in most countries, the region's particularly large informal sector, its insufficient and inefficient social protection systems, and shortcomings in the adoption and availability of broadband and related digital technologies and digital skills—provide the context for a more detailed examination of these issues in the following chapters.

Sub-Saharan African countries have a large stock of ill-equipped workers and low levels of human capital. This situation is likely to persist despite growing efforts by countries to enhance human capital. On the upside, digital technologies can improve the availability and quality of education and health services, boosting human capital upgrading. Digital technologies can enable ill-equipped workers to learn and perform more sophisticated tasks in their existing occupations, while also generating new occupations. Chapter 2 discusses the links between digital technologies, human capital, and the future of work.

Sub-Saharan Africa's informal sector, which typically has the lowest levels of productivity, accounts for a sizable proportion of employment (almost 90 percent of total employment). It will likely remain large over the coming years, because efforts to formalize farms and firms have had limited success.

Appropriately designed digital technologies can offer opportunities to enhance the productivity of informal firms and farms by enabling informal entrepreneurs and workers not only to learn but also to access credit and insurance products, thereby making formalization more likely over time for those informal firms that grow and start benefiting from more formal services. Chapter 3 discusses the links between digital technologies, informality, and the future of work.

Other factors beyond technologies—such as increased economic integration, climate change, fragility, and demographic transitions—will disrupt labor markets in Sub-Saharan Africa. All these factors create not only opportunities but also risks for enterprises and workers, increasing the need for risk-sharing social protection policies. Currently, however, the coverage of social protection remains low in Sub-Saharan Africa, given governments' fiscal constraints, inefficient public spending, and competing policy priorities for limited public investments. Chapter 4 discusses how Sub-Saharan African countries can improve their social protection policies to prepare for the future of work, supported by more effective and efficient domestic and international resource mobilization.

Availability of Digital Technologies and Their Effects to Date

Automation and innovation today are largely driven by the availability of digital technologies, with most digital technologies facilitated by the internet and mobile telecommunications. Globally, it is widely documented that digital technologies reduce the economic costs associated with search, replication, transportation, tracking, and verification (Goldfarb and Tucker 2019), thereby supporting inclusion (expanding market access to individuals and firms), efficiency (boosting the productivity of the different inputs), and innovation (through the creation of new business models, among other things) (Deichmann, Goyal, and Mishra 2016; World Bank 2016). This section investigates to what extent these digital technologies are available in Sub-Saharan Africa and their known effects to date in the region.

Availability of Digital Infrastructure

Mobile voice users and networks are rapidly expanding in Sub-Saharan Africa.[7] Mobile voice subscriptions were 15 times greater in 2015–17 than in 2010–12. After rapid expansion since 2010, almost 86 percent of the region's population is covered by mobile networks, although this share is still lower than for emerging market economies in other regions, such as East Asia, which reached universal access to mobile voice networks by the end of 2017. Quality in mobile cellular services is poor relative to other regions. The rates of unsuccessful calls (2.2 percent) and dropped calls (1.1 percent) in Sub-Saharan Africa were larger than those of lower-middle-income countries (1.5 percent and 0.8 percent, respectively, in 2015–17). Moreover, the affordability of mobile cellular services is a concern. Connection charges and the fee for a one-minute call have decreased significantly in Sub-Saharan Africa but are still high relative to income levels. Figure 1.4, panel a, plots mobile narrowband (analog voice and short message service) subscribers (per 100 people), using quarterly data from the first quarter of 2010 through the third quarter of 2018. In developed economies, the number of mobile voice subscriptions was 1,348 per 1,000 people. In Sub-Saharan Africa, mobile subscribers amounted to 806 per 1,000 people in 2017, up from 226 in 2007.

Despite the increase in mobile voice availability, Sub-Saharan Africa continues to have limited access to broadband networks that provide internet and data services. Overall, access to internet service remains unattainable for most people on the continent. Africa's continent-wide level of international internet bandwidth used in 2017 (7,314 billion bits per second) represented only 1 percent of the world's total, one-third the level of the Middle East, and about equal to the level of Chile or Romania (TeleGeography 2018). Of the 20 least wirelessly connected countries in 2017, 18 are in Sub-Saharan Africa (GSMA 2018).

Figure 1.4 Unique Mobile Broadband Penetration, by Region, 2010–18

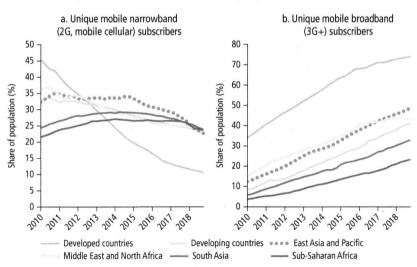

(continued next page)

Figure 1.4 Unique Mobile Broadband Penetration, by Region, 2010–18 (continued)

c. Large heterogeneities in broadband and narrowband penetration across countries in Sub-Saharan Africa

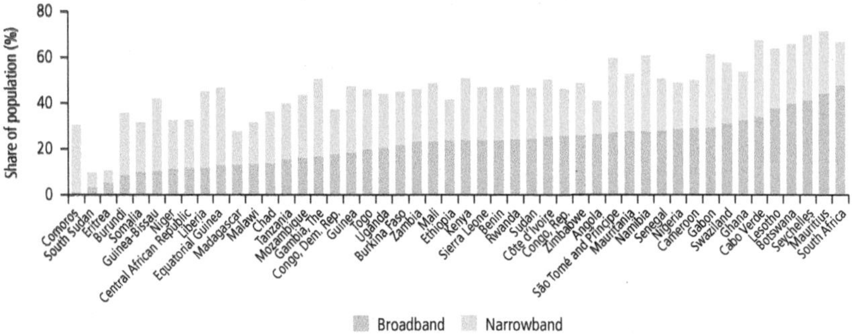

Broadband   Narrowband

Source: GSMA.
Note: In panel a, the regional figures depicted are medians across countries for each corresponding year. Unique subscribers imply total unique users who have subscribed to mobile services at the end of the period, excluding machine-to-machine services. In panel b, mobile internet unique subscribers imply total unique users who have used internet services on their mobile device(s) at the end of the period. Mobile internet services are defined as any activity that consumes mobile data (excluding Short Message Service, Multimedia Messaging Service, and cellular voice calls). 2G = second-generation; 3G+ = third-generation and later. The name Swaziland was officially changed to Eswatini in April 2018.

Fixed broadband access is extremely low, with less than 0.6 percent of the Sub-Saharan African population having fixed broadband subscriptions in 2015–17. Although fixed broadband provides stable connectivity and is suitable for large-scale data needs, it is less cost-effective than mobile broadband: deploying it requires a significant amount of installation work. It is on average three times more expensive than mobile broadband—on average mobile broadband costs $40 in purchasing power parity dollars (PPP$) versus PPP$134 for fixed broadband for 1 gigabyte of data across less developed countries.[8]

The share of mobile broadband subscriptions in Sub-Saharan Africa is somewhat higher, at 30 percent (24 percent for unique users, counting only one user for those with multiple connections). This share is significantly lower than in other regions (68 percent in Asia and the Pacific and 90 percent in Europe) at the end of 2018 (GSMA 2018). The rapid expansion of mobile voice networks and ongoing upgrades of telecommunication networks by mobile operators in Sub-Saharan Africa give opportunities to expand mobile broadband in the future (Mahler, Montes, and Newhouse 2019). Although most operators in the region still provide second- or third-generation networks with limited data services, 11 of the 48 Sub-Saharan African countries are now covered by a fourth-generation network (TeleGeography 2018).

Panels a and b of figure 1.4 present the expansion of mobile narrowband and mobile broadband unique subscriptions across different regions. It shows a large gap in mobile broadband infrastructure in Sub-Saharan Africa—which has not yet replaced mobile narrowband—in contrast to developed economies where mobile broadband has been replacing mobile narrowband. Figure 1.4, panel c, shows unique mobile broadband penetration relative to total subscribers across Sub-Saharan African countries and the high heterogeneity in mobile broadband penetration across these countries.

Digital Technologies' Effect on Growth and Inclusion Outcomes

Digital technologies can generate significant poverty reduction and inclusion outcomes, if supported by appropriate public policies. Those policies include measures to mitigate the risks of widening digital divides—associated with challenges of affordable access and use of internet by all (including women, old people, and people in rural areas and secondary cities, supported by sufficient relevant local content) and low skills (particularly prevalent in Sub-Saharan Africa's large informal sector), among others. Inclusion outcomes are generated to the extent that digital technology adoption results in more jobs and higher incomes for less skilled workers, higher returns to low-income entrepreneurs, more efficient income transfers and other government services for poor people, and lower-priced goods and services consumed by poor people, including health and education services.

Digital technologies influence development outcomes in Sub-Saharan Africa through diverse channels. Despite scarce evidence at the aggregate level, evidence is emerging at the enterprise and individual levels from different countries. At the aggregate level, digital technologies can lead to growth and poverty reduction. Whereas a large amount of literature exists on growth and productivity in developed economies,[9] the empirical evidence of the effect of digital technologies across countries and industries is rare in Sub-Saharan Africa. A recent study, however, finds that mobile voice and broadband infrastructures have positive and significant impacts on real gross domestic product (GDP) growth per capita and on poverty reduction. Reaching the African Union's "Digital Transformation for Africa" digital infrastructure goal of universal and affordable internet network coverage with universal penetration of mobile cellular phones would raise real GDP growth per capita by 2 percentage points per year and would reduce the poverty head count by 1 percentage point per year across Sub-Saharan African countries. With appropriate human capital investments, the effects could more than double: real GDP growth per capita would increase by roughly 5.0 percentage points per year and the poverty head count would fall by roughly 2.5 percentage points per year (for the methodology underlying these results, see World Bank [2019a], section 3.4 and annex 3B).

The usage of digital technologies has positive correlations with economic outcomes across countries of different income levels. Although causality is difficult to establish, these patterns suggest that the availability of digital technology infrastructure complements growth and inclusion. Specifically, the greater the percentage of the population using mobile broadband (internet) and mobile cellular (voice), the higher the levels of per capita income and human capital and the reliability of the electricity supply (figure 1.5).

Interestingly, those economic outcome indicators have a linear relationship with mobile broadband but a nonlinear relationship with mobile voice service, which may reflect almost universal cell phone subscriptions above a certain income level. Most Sub-Saharan African countries, however, are below this "universal access" income level. Additionally, mobile broadband and mobile voice subscriptions are negatively associated with poverty. Although use of mobile broadband is negatively associated with income inequality (as proxied by the Gini index), use of mobile voice services does not show a clear pattern with the inequality level for Sub-Saharan African countries. All panels show a great deal of heterogeneity in income inequality across countries.

At the enterprise and individual levels, more evidence, including emerging evidence from randomized experiments, is becoming available on the effects of digital technologies on productivity growth and inclusion outcomes. Importantly, new empirical findings from Sub-Saharan Africa suggest that digital technology adoption may not necessarily reduce the demand for low- and medium-skilled workers. As explained in greater detail in box 1.1, the arrival of faster internet across Sub-Saharan Africa has provided a natural experiment for assessing the impact of internet adoption (and presumably related digital technologies that rely on faster internet) on individuals and businesses. The study finds that the predictions explored in the previous section, namely that the adoption of skill-biased digital technologies like the internet can lead to more favorable pro-inclusion outcomes in Sub-Saharan Africa than in higher-income countries, are supported by available data. The demand for skilled workers increased sizably, with no reduction in the demand for low-skilled workers in the region in areas where the connection to faster internet increased; and job growth has been of comparable magnitude for those with different levels of education (Hjort and Poulsen 2019). Earlier empirical work by Dutz, Almeida, and Packard (2018) shows that low-skilled workers also benefit from significant job expansion from the adoption of internet and related skill-biased digital technologies. As explained in box 1.2, the increased demand and consequent output expansion from technology adoption represent an important empirical

Figure 1.5 Correlation between Availability of Mobile Broadband or Mobile Voice and Income and Inclusion Indicators

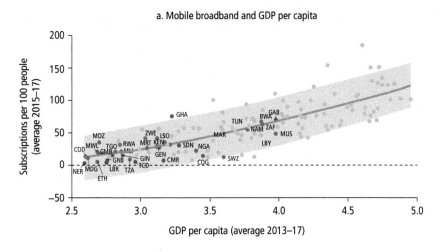

a. Mobile broadband and GDP per capita

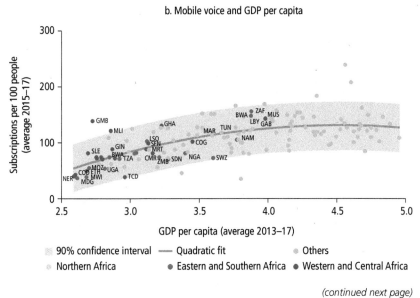

b. Mobile voice and GDP per capita

(continued next page)

Figure 1.5 Correlation between Availability of Mobile Broadband or Mobile Voice and Income and Inclusion Indicators (continued)

c. Mobile broadband and the Human Capital Index

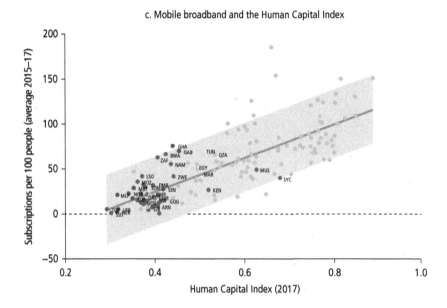

d. Mobile voice subscriptions and the Human Capital Index

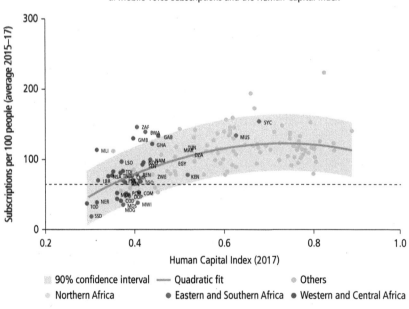

90% confidence interval — *Quadratic fit* • *Others*
• *Northern Africa* • *Eastern and Southern Africa* • *Western and Central Africa*

(continued next page)

Figure 1.5 **Correlation between Availability of Mobile Broadband or Mobile Voice and Income and Inclusion Indicators (continued)**

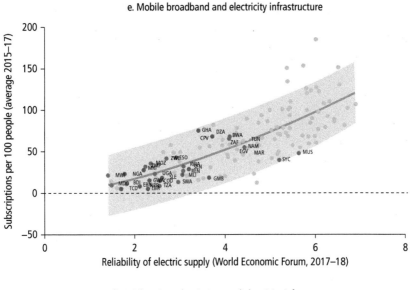

e. Mobile broadband and electricity infrastructure

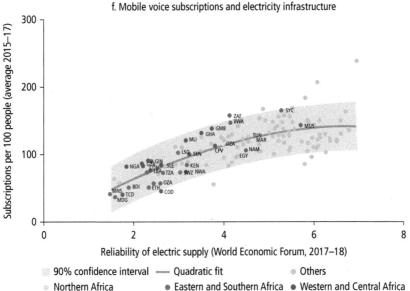

f. Mobile voice subscriptions and electricity infrastructure

(continued next page)

Figure 1.5 Correlation between Availability of Mobile Broadband or Mobile Voice and Income and Inclusion Indicators (continued)

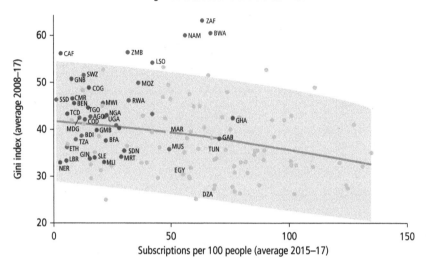

g. Mobile broadband and the Gini index

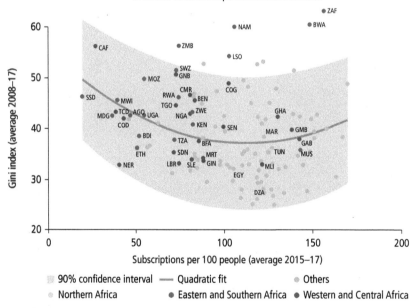

h. Mobile voice subscriptions and the Gini index

(continued next page)

Figure 1.5 Correlation between Availability of Mobile Broadband or Mobile Voice and Income and Inclusion Indicators (continued)

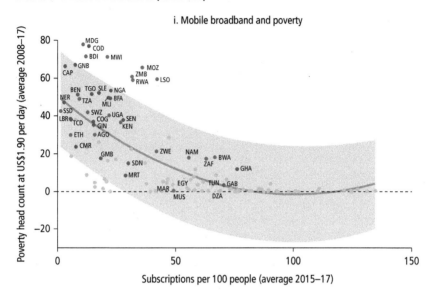

i. Mobile broadband and poverty

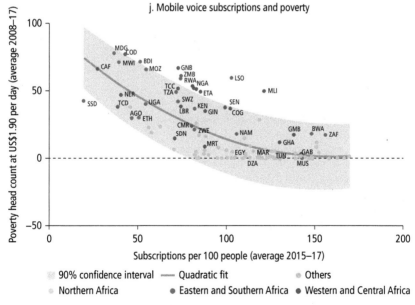

j. Mobile voice subscriptions and poverty

Source: World Development Indicators database (World Bank).
Note: The digital economy indicator is measured as mobile broadband subscriptions per 100 people and cell phone subscriptions per 100 people, averaged over 2015–17. Development variables are income (real gross domestic product [GDP] per capita in US dollars at constant prices, expressed in logs), complementary assets (the World Bank's Human Capital Index and the World Economic Forum's indicator of the reliability of the electricity supply), the Gini index of inequality, and the poverty head count ratio. US$ = US dollar.

Impact of Faster Internet Adoption on Jobs, by Skill and Education Levels

When faster internet became available in Sub-Saharan Africa, the probability that an individual is employed increased by 6.9 and 13.2 percent, respectively, for countries in different samples (Demographic and Health Surveys [DHS] across eight Sub-Saharan African countries and Afrobarometer across nine Sub-Saharan African countries), and by 3.1 percent in South Africa, relative to areas unconnected to submarine cables.[a] Importantly, the increase in employment in these areas was not due to displacement of jobs in unconnected areas. These impacts attributable to faster internet are net positive job increases and sizable in magnitude (Hjort and Poulsen 2019).[b]

These aggregate findings can be broken down by skilled and unskilled employment categories to examine their impact on job inclusion outcomes. In South Africa and DHS countries, the probability that an individual holds a skilled job increases by 1.4 and 4.4 percent, respectively, when faster internet becomes available, as shown in the upper part of figure B1.1.1. The probability of holding an unskilled job does not decrease (the change is statistically insignificant), so those individuals are not negatively affected on average. These findings imply that faster internet adoption is skill-biased in Sub-Saharan Africa—that is, it complements more skilled jobs, as has been shown in high-income countries. Importantly, a relatively large estimated increase occurs in the probability of moderately skilled employment when the skilled category is broken into its subcategories, as shown in the middle part of the figure. Moderately skilled employment contributes most of the overall increase in skilled employment when faster internet becomes available.[c]

Most important, an examination of the impact of faster internet arrival on workers by educational attainment rather than by job categories highlights that the estimated increase in the employment rate is of comparable magnitude for those with primary school, secondary school, and tertiary education in all samples studied.[d] In the Afrobarometer countries (not shown here), the estimates suggest that faster internet also increases the employment rate for those who did not complete primary school. And, importantly, a proxy for incomes rises as a result: analysis of data on nighttime lights from satellite images shows that fast internet causes increased average incomes in the areas that benefited from jobs growth.

These findings of net positive effects on jobs and incomes, also for less educated worker groups, are important because they are based on the identification of causal impacts. Causal effects are identified by comparing individuals and firms in locations in Sub-Saharan Africa that are on the terrestrial network of internet cables with those that are not, during the gradual arrival of 10 submarine cables from Europe in the late 2000s and early 2010s that greatly increased speed and capacity on the terrestrial network.

What are the mechanisms through which faster internet increases jobs, including for less educated workers? Hjort and Poulsen (2019) report that part of the increase in jobs may be explained by net firm entry (about 23 percent when fast internet arrived in

(continued next page)

Figure B1.1.1 Impact of Faster Internet on Skilled Occupations and Jobs across Education Levels

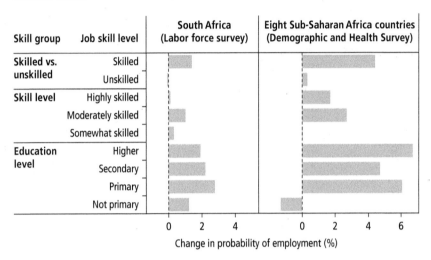

Source: Hjort and Poulsen 2019.

South Africa), including a large increase in firm entry and a decrease in firm exit of similar magnitude. Another part of the jobs increase appears to be due to increased productivity in existing manufacturing firms (in Ethiopia). Hjort and Poulsen (2019) also show that firms in Ghana, Kenya, Mauritania, Nigeria, Senegal, and Tanzania export more, communicate with clients more, and train employees more, according to World Bank Enterprise Survey data.[e] They suggest that the productivity of less educated workers may have benefited from provision by employers of targeted on-the-job training.

a. The DHS sample covers Benin, the Democratic Republic of Congo, Ghana, Kenya, Namibia, Nigeria, Tanzania, and Togo. The Afrobarometer sample covers Benin, Ghana, Kenya, Madagascar, Mozambique, Nigeria, Senegal, South Africa, and Tanzania. The South Africa Quarterly Labor Force survey is a nationally representative cross-section carried out every quarter. The three data sets together cover 12 countries in Sub-Saharan Africa with a combined population of roughly half a billion people.
b. Additional robustness checks by Hjort and Poulsen (2019) include sensitivity analysis on the definition of "connectivity" by altering the radius from the backbone network, measuring the impact of other infrastructure, and labor displacement effects arising from commuting, all resulting in indiscernible changes in the reported outcomes. The authors also note that the response in employment did not appear to arise from formalization of "pre-existing informal jobs," nor did they find evidence of employment rising in connected areas prior to the arrival of submarine cables.
c. Data on the "somewhat skilled" job category are not available for the DHS sample.
d. The changes for workers who did not complete primary school are not significant in these samples, and the difference in estimated job gains for those with primary relative to secondary school is also not statistically significant.
e. In earlier related work based on a sample of 26,000 manufacturing firms including 15 African countries from World Bank Enterprise Survey data, Dutz et al. (2012) find that firms innovate more in products and processes and show greater employment growth if they use the internet.

BOX 1.2

Impact of Digital Technology Adoption on Low-Skill Jobs through the Output Expansion Effect

A key mechanism that likely underlies the inclusive jobs outcome of skill-biased digital technology adoption found by Hjort and Poulsen (2019) is the output expansion effect highlighted by Dutz, Almeida, and Packard (2018) in Latin American countries. Those authors (see their appendix A) take advantage of firm-level data from national enterprise surveys where the causal effects of firm investments in information and communication technology (ICT) capital and firm-level use of fast internet on high- versus low-skilled-worker jobs are identified by the gradual rollout of internet across these countries.[a] In separate complementary studies on Argentina, Brazil, Chile, Colombia, and Mexico, they show that low-skilled workers also benefit from the more intensive use of the internet as firm productivity increases. The inclusive jobs outcomes arise when the effects of increased productivity, lower prices, and expanding output overcome the substitution of low-skilled workers for technology at initial output levels. Although the substitution effect replaces some low-skilled workers with new technology and more highly skilled labor (as shown by the movement from A to B in figure B1.2.1, holding output constant), the output effect can lead to an increase in the total number of jobs for less-skilled workers (as shown by the movement from B to C). Critically, output can rise sufficiently to increase jobs across all tasks and skill types within adopting firms, including jobs for low-skilled workers (as shown in the low-skill jobs column of table B1.2.1). This effect holds as long as low-skill task content remains complementary to new technologies and related occupations are not completely automated and replaced by machines.

Figure B1.2.1 Impact of Skill-Biased Digital Technology Adoption and Output Expansion on High- and Low-Skill Jobs

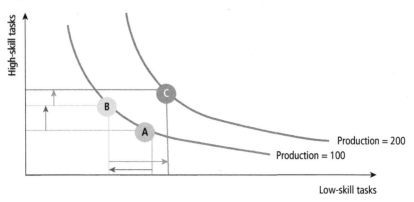

Source: Dutz, Almeida, and Packard 2018.

(continued next page)

Table B1.2.1 Impact of Digital Technology Adoption and Output Expansion on Jobs and Productivity in Latin American Countries

Country	Years	Sectors	Variable	Jobs				Productivity
				Total	High-skill	Low-skill	Gap	
Argentina	2010–12	Manufacturing	Investment in ICT capital	+	+	+	+	+
Brazil	2000–14	Tradables	Percent internet availability	+	+	0	—	+
Chile	2007–13	Economy-wide	Complex software use	+	0	+	–	—
Colombia	2008–14	Manufacturing	High-speed internet use	+	+	+	—	+
Mexico	2008–13	Manufacturing	Internet use	+	+	+	+	+
		Services	Internet use	+	+	+	0	+
		Commerce	Internet use	+	+	+	0	+

Source: Dutz, Almeida, and Packard 2018.
Note: ICT = information and communication technology; — = not available.
a. The studies exploit plausible exogenous changes in the availability of ICT access or its quality over time and space. The Mexico study, for instance, interacts average ICT intensity in the United States with the average elevation of municipalities to reflect the geographical challenges of internet availability in more difficult-to-access areas.

mechanism that likely underlies the inclusive outcomes found in Sub-Saharan African countries.

Subsequent chapters present evidence of how digital technologies can improve human capital, can improve the impact of digital technologies on farms and firms in the informal sector, and can improve the provision of social protection services in Sub-Saharan Africa. This subsection provides a summary of some of the available evidence of the effects of mobile money, an area where some of the most significant effects have appeared to date.

Mobile money, which allows people to deposit, withdraw, and send money using their mobile phones, has widespread adoption in Sub-Saharan Africa, where traditional financial accounts are not widely available. More than one in five adults in the region has a mobile money account, and more than half of all mobile money services in the world are in Sub-Saharan Africa (Demirgüç-Kunt et al. 2018; GSMA 2018). Kenya's M-Pesa, one of the most successful mobile money services, has been adopted by at least one individual in 96 percent of households outside Nairobi since its launch in 2007, and over half the population uses the system at least once a month (Suri and Jack 2016). As a result, the number of Kenyans included in the formal financial system has grown by 50 percent, and financial exclusion has more than halved—down to 17.4 percent as of 2016. M-Pesa reported annual service revenue of US$2.4 billion for the financial year to the end of March 2019.[10]

Evidence shows that access to mobile money has increased productivity through individual economic outcomes and occupational choices and different financial behavior. Increases in productivity in turn typically lead to an expansion in output and thus to increases in employment. Inclusion effects can be generated through a variety of related channels. Access to M-Pesa facilitated occupational choice in Kenya and increased the efficiency of the allocation of labor, particularly for female-headed households, and it induced women to move out of agriculture and change their main occupation to business or retail (Suri and Jack 2016). More detailed information about the effect of mobile money on occupational choice is provided in box 1.3.

Ongoing policy experiments are investigating the effects of mobile money accounts on enterprises and workers in Sub-Saharan Africa, and these experiments will soon provide additional insights. For instance, Gautam et al. (2018) examine a policy intervention that promotes access to mobile savings among female microentrepreneurs in Tanzania, and those authors suggest the importance of complementary financial literacy training to help individuals benefit from access to mobile accounts. To understand the impact of redistributive

---

BOX 1.3

Impact of Access to M-Pesa on Users' Occupational Choices over Time

Suri and Jack (2016) investigate the causal effects of M-Pesa on the economic outcomes of Kenyan households over time. Using five rounds of a household panel survey over 2008–14, they estimate the changes in access to mobile money at the household level, measured by the geographic proximity of households to M-Pesa agents, and explore their effects on economic outcomes of the households and the factors that influence these effects.

They find that the usage of M-Pesa increased per capita consumption levels and lifted an estimated 2 percent of Kenyan households (194,000 households) out of poverty. The impacts appear to be larger for female-headed households, partially because of changes in labor market outcomes: access to M-Pesa enabled 185,000 women to move out of subsistence farming and into business or sales occupations.

Figure B1.3.1 shows that individuals with increased access to M-Pesa agents were more likely to be working in business or sales, and less likely to be working in farming. Access to M-Pesa reduced women's reliance on multiple part-time jobs (or secondary occupations) and led to a reduction in the average household size.

(continued next page)

Box 1.3 (continued)

Figure B1.3.1 **The Influence of Access to M-Pesa on Individuals' Occupational Choices**

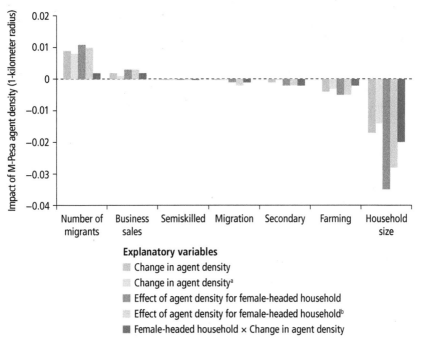

Source: Suri and Jack 2016.
a. Shows the effect when broken down by gender of household head, as opposed to the initial overall effect. The regression controls for the effect of agent density for female-headed household shown in the dark green bars and the interactive effect reported in the last dark blue bar.
b. Shows the overall effect of gender from a separate regression when controlling for interactions with education of the household head, wealth, and bank account.

pressure on workers' labor supply and earnings in Côte d'Ivoire, Carranza et al. (2018) look at the effects of a direct-deposit account that cannot be accessed by others. Buehren et al. (2018) investigate the impacts in Ghana of mobile savings accounts with different commitments for salaried workers and customers (for more detailed information on these experimental designs, see World Bank [2019a]).

Meanwhile, the more direct effects of mobile money accounts are changes in financial behaviors, driven by the reduced cost of transfers and payments and resulting in enhanced saving, consumption-smoothing, and risk-sharing mechanisms. In countries or areas with an increased network of M-Pesa–affiliated agents, total financial savings have increased, especially among female-headed households. Registered users of M-Pesa are more likely to save than those who are not registered (Demombynes and Thegeya 2012). Recent evidence from Burkina Faso shows that mobile money users—especially women, less educated individuals, and rural populations—are more likely to save for health emergencies (Ky, Rugemintwari, and Sauviat 2018). Mobile money provides a safe method for individuals to deposit savings and make changes in the composition of household assets (Aker and Wilson 2013; Ky, Rugemintwari, and Sauviat 2018). In response to income shocks, the consumption of M-Pesa users remained invariant, because these users were more likely to receive remittances, whereas the consumption of nonusers declined. Increased savings can help microentrepreneurs increase their ability to cope with unexpected shocks and finance lumpy investments. Greater risk-sharing ability than the previous costly self-insurance mechanisms and informal risk-sharing networks was followed by increased saving, higher consumption, and positive occupational changes for user households (Jack and Suri 2014). Similarly, usage of mobile money is associated with an increase in investment of small formal firms among those Sub-Saharan African countries for which World Bank Enterprise Survey data are available (Islam, Muzi, and Rodriguez Meza 2018).

Mobile money accounts enhance inclusion by supporting access to financial services and loans to the unbanked, particularly women and rural populations, who cannot meet the collateral requirements of traditional financial institutions (Mbiti and Weil 2016). For instance, female entrepreneurs are less likely to have collateral because of inequality in the ownership of fixed assets (for example, land or a house). Mobile loan providers use telecommunications data to develop alternative credit scores, thus facilitating the extension of loans to users without collateral or traditional scores calculated by a credit bureau. Digital-based credit scores may grant financial inclusion to individuals without credit scores in environments that lack verifiable financial history or have nonexistent or ineffective credit bureaus (Jack and Suri 2014). As an alternative to traditional collateral for Ethiopia's female entrepreneurs, Alibhai et al. (2018) tested psychometric technology that predicts the likelihood that an entrepreneur will be able to repay a loan. Customers scoring at a high threshold on the psychometric test were seven times more likely than low-performing customers to repay their loans. Changes in access to mobile money services have also raised the probability of using a bank account. This effect may reflect the fact that banking institutions started to collaborate or compete with M-Pesa. Mobile accounts can enhance the efficiency of public transfer programs and payments, which if provided to women will likely affect resource allocation within households (Aker et al. 2013; Duflo and Udry 2004). Access to M-Pesa has led to an increase in consumption per capita among households living in areas with increased access to mobile money agents—and this effect was twice as large for female-headed households, with

2 percent of households (mostly female headed) pulled out of extreme poverty over 2008–14 (Suri and Jack 2016).

Availability of Digital Skills and Their Determinants

Despite the gradual increase in basic education and literacy rates in recent decades, Sub-Saharan Africa still lacks basic skills. The starting level was very low, and recent gains in enrollment and completion do not necessarily translate into improvements in the quality of education. High repetition rates, teacher shortages, and underperformance on test scores all contribute to the poor quality of education in the region (UNESCO 2016). Sub-Saharan Africa has the lowest literacy rates among all world regions. On average, only about 33 percent of the population older than age 15 is able to read and write, well below the global average of 86 percent (UNESCO 2016). The level of basic skills varies significantly across countries: higher-income Sub-Saharan African countries tend to have higher literacy rates than poorer countries (90 percent of adults in the Seychelles are literate, compared with 19 percent in Mali). The level of basic skills also varies within countries by income level: for example, in Tanzania and Uganda, the pass rate for basic literacy and numeracy skills falls by nearly 50 percent from nonpoor to ultrapoor populations (Evans, Arias, and Santos 2019). Chapter 2 provides more detailed information on the human capital landscape in Sub-Saharan African countries.

This section provides a closer look at the availability of high-demand digital skills in the subpopulation of workers who use LinkedIn. The section reviews specific growing and declining skills across selected Sub-Saharan African countries and explores the determinants of those skills.

Availability of Digital Skills

This section uses data from self-reported information by LinkedIn users and therefore reflects a relatively narrow, nonrandom subset of the working-age population. This subset consists primarily of tech-savvy, white-collar professionals employed in knowledge-intensive sectors, such as information and communication technology (ICT) and professional services. Additionally, these user-generated data have large heterogeneity across users in their willingness to report their specific skills and in the interpretation of different skills across cultures and countries, influencing the interpretation of cross-country skill comparisons. Nonetheless, the LinkedIn data offer value, specifically for the skill composition of the labor force, where other sources of data are limited.

In Sub-Saharan Africa, the LinkedIn data capture information for 27 countries, each with at least 100,000 LinkedIn members, and for certain countries, such as South Africa, with more than 1 million members. The share of LinkedIn members as a proportion of each country's labor force (population ages 15–65) is presented in figures, as appropriate. A more detailed discussion of the benefits and caveats of using LinkedIn data for cross-country comparisons can be found in annex 1A.

Although all members of the LinkedIn platform have at least some basic digital skills as a prerequisite, this section narrowly focuses on business-related digital skills.[11] This definition differs from other available definitions of digital skills, such as that used by the United Nations Educational, Scientific, and Cultural Organization (UNESCO), which broadly refers to the abilities needed to access and understand information from digital devices,[12] and by the Organisation for Economic Co-operation and Development (OECD), which provides a less precise definition but notes that digital skills differ from exclusively ICT skills.[13]

The LinkedIn data suggest that Sub-Saharan African workers have a lower level of digital skills than workers in other regions, even among the small portion of the labor force that uses LinkedIn, which constitutes, on average, 4 percent of the labor force among the 27 Sub-Saharan African countries for which LinkedIn data are available. In North America, by contrast, 70 percent of the labor force uses the platform (figure 1.6). The availability of digital skills varies significantly across Sub-Saharan African workforces. In South Africa, 17 percent of the labor force are LinkedIn members, and they report digital

Figure 1.6 Digital Skills in Sub-Saharan Africa Relative to Other Regions

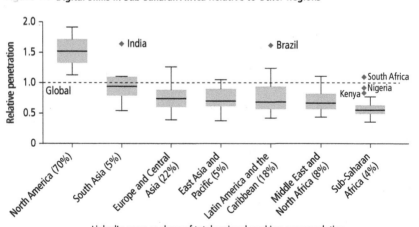

LinkedIn users as share of total regional working-age population

Source: World Bank calculations using LinkedIn data.
Note: Parentheses show the share of LinkedIn users in the total working-age population of each World Bank region.

skills equivalent to the global average. Although Kenya and Nigeria have relatively high digital skills, these countries have only a small population of LinkedIn users relative to the total labor force. Despite these differences, Kenya, Nigeria, and South Africa are often referred to as the Sub-Saharan African countries with greater relative demand for technical skills and established tech hubs and communities (Kelly and Firestone 2016). Most Sub-Saharan African countries, in contrast, have digital skills at roughly 50 percent the average global adoption level (denoted by 1.0 in figure 1.6), with the lower tail falling below 30 percent, and have relatively small numbers of LinkedIn users relative to the labor force (figure 1.7).

For certain digital skills, availability varies even more across Sub-Saharan African countries, suggesting that some countries will need to catch up more than others in developing the needed level of specific digital skills. For one-third of the specific skills, fewer than one-half of the Sub-Saharan African countries have a penetration rate greater than zero (figure 1.8, gray areas). Moreover, the countries with higher overall digital skill penetration are also the ones with the most diversified digital skills. Exceptions include digital literacy, development tools, web development, and, to a lesser degree, mobile application development, where penetration rates are more equally distributed across countries. This information on specific digital skill gaps across Sub-Saharan African countries could inform the design of technology and digital skills training programs in the region.

To improve cross-country comparability, figure 1.9 shows the comparison of specific digital skills among selected countries in Sub-Saharan Africa and Europe with similar ratios of LinkedIn users to the labor force, listed by relative penetration of the most advanced skills: Germany, Poland, South Africa, Kenya, Nigeria, Namibia, Mauritius, and Botswana. Certain selected Sub-Saharan African countries—Kenya, Mauritius, Nigeria, and South Africa—reflect increasing reliance on digital technologies, particularly mobile cellular and internet. The relatively high levels of skills, such as digital literacy, web development, and mobile application development, in these countries are consistent with the findings reported in Etzo and Collender (2010). Despite high levels in certain skills, however, these countries lag in other advanced skills (for example, artificial intelligence, scientific computing, and human-computer interaction).

From 2015 through 2018, Sub-Saharan African countries have shown higher growth in more transferable digital skills, such as digital literacy, web development, development tools, and data science, than in more traditional digital skills, such as technical support and computer networking, which are declining (figure 1.10). This tendency is in line with global trends and the increased availability of digital infrastructure in Sub-Saharan Africa for the same period.

Figure 1.7 Large Heterogeneity in Relative Penetration of Digital Skills across Countries in Sub-Saharan Africa

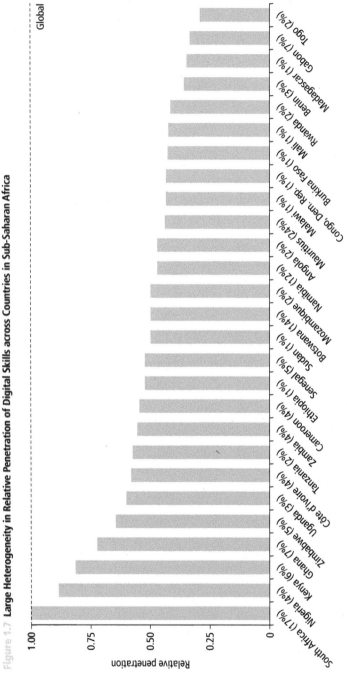

Source: World Bank calculations using LinkedIn data.
Note: Parentheses show the share of LinkedIn users in the total working-age population of each country. Relative penetration of digital skills is measured as the sum of the penetration of each digital skill across occupations in a given country, divided by the average global penetration of digital skills across the same occupations. Skill group penetration is defined as the percentage of the top-50 individual skills that belong to a given skill group (that is, if 5 of the top-50 skills for data scientists in South Africa fall into the artificial intelligence skill group, artificial intelligence has a 10 percent penetration for data scientists in South Africa).

Figure 1.8 **Relative Penetration of Various Digital Skills in Sub-Saharan African Countries**

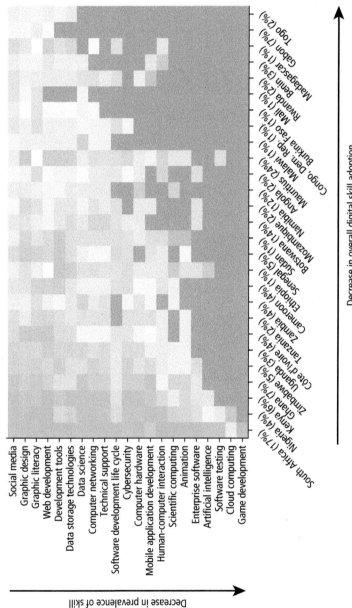

Source: World Bank calculations using LinkedIn data.
Note: Parentheses show the share of LinkedIn users in the total working-age population of each country. Relative penetration scaled by row for comparison across countries. The different shades of green and the white correspond to the degree of relative penetration. The darker the color, the higher the relative penetration of that specific skill in that country compared with others. Gray boxes indicate a relative skill penetration of zero.

Figure 1.9 Adoption of Various Digital Skills in Selected Sub-Saharan African Countries and Benchmark Countries in Europe

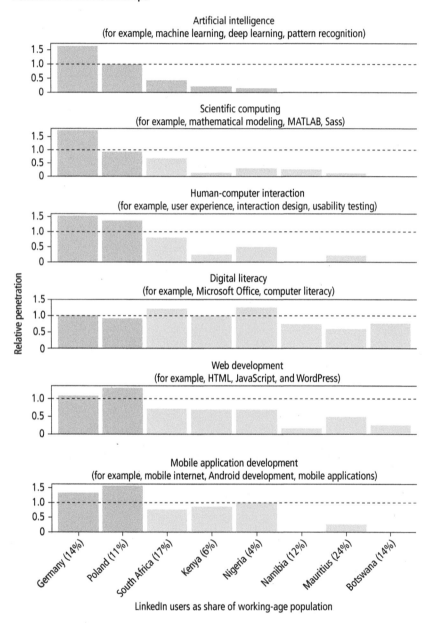

Source: World Bank calculations using LinkedIn data.
Note: On the relative penetration axis, 1 represents the global average adoption of a skill. Benchmark countries were chosen on the basis of similar shares of LinkedIn members in their working-age population to the shares in selected Sub-Saharan African countries. Parentheses show the share of LinkedIn users in the total working-age population of each country.

Figure 1.10 **Growth of Digital Skills in Sub-Saharan Africa**

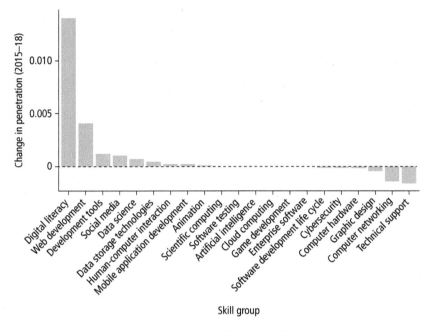

Skill group

Source: World Bank calculations using LinkedIn data for 27 Sub-Saharan African countries with at least 100,000 LinkedIn members.
Note: Penetration means the percentage of the top-30 specific skills belonging to digital skills to highlight the types of skills that are growing or declining in Sub-Saharan Africa. A 0.010 increase in penetration in digital literacy between 2015 and 2018 means that the penetration of digital literacy has increased approximately three times faster than the second-fastest growing digital skill, web development. Specifically, in Sub-Saharan Africa digital literacy increased by ~0.014 (0.068–0.054) compared with an increase in Europe and Central Asia of ~0.019 (0.052–0.032).

Determinants of Digital Skills

This section sets out correlations between digital skills and the availability of infrastructure, such as the internet, mobile voice telephony, and electricity. The correlations indicate that digital skills move in tandem with access to the internet and electricity, but the relationship is less clear with mobile cellular subscriptions. Figure 1.11 shows the relationship between digital skills and complementary assets across countries, yielding positive correlations greater than 0.30 at the 99 percent confidence interval for internet access indicators and access to electricity.[14] Mobile cellular (voice) subscriptions yield weaker correlation.

Internet access and electricity have the closest correlations with digital skills, whereas mobile voice subscriptions do not have a strong correlation with digital skills. These results may shed light on the impetus for robust integration of digital technologies in Sub-Saharan African economies. As emphasized by WDR 2019, broadband access is a prerequisite for business in

Figure 1.11 Correlation between Digital Skill Adoption and Complementary Factors

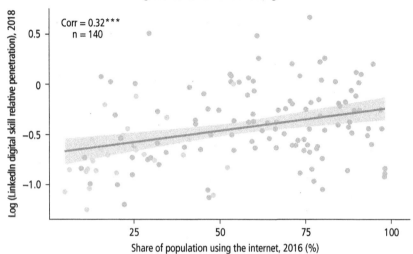

a. Digital skills versus individuals using the internet

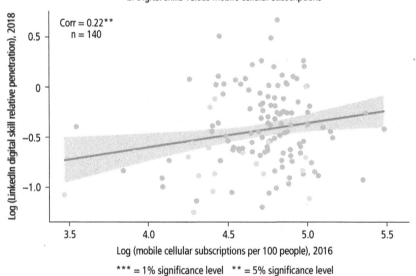

b. Digital skills versus mobile cellular subscriptions

*** = 1% significance level   ** = 5% significance level

(continued next page)

Figure 1.11 **Correlation between Digital Skill Adoption and Complementary Factors (continued)**

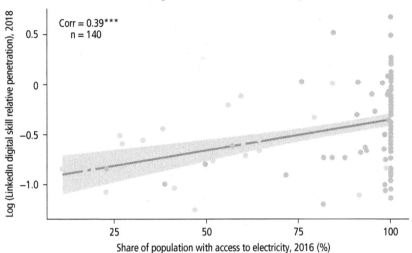

c. Digital skills versus access to electricity

Corr = 0.39***
n = 140

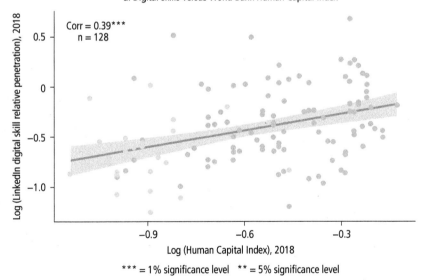

d. Digital skills versus World Bank Human Capital Index

Corr = 0.39***
n = 128

*** = 1% significance level   ** = 5% significance level

Source: World Bank calculations using data from LinkedIn and the World Development Indicators database.
Note: Yellow dots denote Sub-Saharan African countries. Share of population using the internet, mobile cellular subscriptions per 100 people, share of population with access to electricity, and level of Human Capital Index are from the 2016 World Development Indicators. Digital skill is the average adoption (relative penetration) of digital skills in each country. n = number of observations.

the digital era: "mobile phone access is not enough; broadband technologies push down transaction costs further" (World Bank 2019b, 41). This finding is consistent with the recent paper by Hjort and Poulsen (2019) showing that demand for high-skilled workers has increased in Sub-Saharan Africa in areas with access to undersea high-speed internet cables from Europe. This work challenges countries in the region to implement digital infrastructure to move beyond the initial, smaller benefits of slower internet connectivity and mobile phone subscriptions.

Digital skills show a positive and statistically significant correlation with the World Bank's Human Capital Index, a broader indicator of human capital across 128 countries (figure 1.11). The index measures what a child can expect to achieve in terms of full health (defined as no stunting and survival up to at least age 60) and completion of his or her educational potential (defined as 14 years of high-quality school by age 18), relative to other countries. Chapter 2 discusses the way forward on the human capital landscape and areas of prioritization to position the continent to take fuller advantage of the wide-ranging opportunities of digitization.

Technology and the Global Production Base

WDR 2019 raises the concern that automation in developed countries may mean that many African countries will not experience a "traditional" industrialization-led growth path. As noted previously, automation occurs more quickly in locations with high labor costs, assuming the incentive to reduce labor costs exceeds other profit-related differences between locations.

This section examines whether the development of new labor-replacing technologies and their widespread adoption in developed countries and emerging market Asian countries could challenge the traditional manufacturing-led growth model in Sub-Saharan Africa as the region's comparative advantage in labor costs becomes less salient. The section reviews the recent literature on the effects of new technologies on the location of production networks globally and assesses the empirical evidence for reshoring, the relocation of manufacturing to developed economies. It also reviews trends in Africa's FDI and trade flows over the past decade, with a focus on the ability of countries in the region to attract market- and efficiency-seeking FDI and grow exports in manufactured goods and services.

Is Reshoring Happening?

It is widely assumed that automation will lead to a reshoring of industry back to Europe, Japan, and North America, and that the increasing complexity of production will exclude developing countries from new GVCs. The 2014 African

Economic Outlook argues that "3D printing and smart robotics bear the potential of reducing this cost advantage far enough to kick off a shift toward reshoring of production activities towards the high wage headquarter economies" (AfDB, OECD, and UNDP 2014). A report by Citigroup and Oxford Martin School (2016) finds that 70 percent of Citigroup's institutional clients surveyed believe automation and developments in 3-D printing will encourage companies to move manufacturing closer to home, with North America seen as having the most to gain from this trend and China, the Association of Southeast Asian Nations, and Latin America having the most to lose. A well-known example is that of an Adidas shoe factory that has brought production from East Asia back to Germany. The company reports that it produces more quickly and at lower cost in its automated German factory featuring 3-D printers, permitting it to adapt better to changing market and design demands (*Economist* 2017).

Theoretical rationales for reshoring include (1) the changing cost structure (notably, rising labor costs) in many developing and emerging market economies; (2) firms' underestimation of the full costs of offshoring; (3) enabling the colocation of research and development, innovation, and production in a single jurisdiction; (4) reducing threats to intellectual property from offshoring; (5) balancing cost savings and risk dispersion; (6) potentially, closer proximity to markets, enabling greater flexibility; and (7) supply risks posed by the length and complexity of contemporary GVCs (De Backer et al. 2016). Box 1.4 discusses the possible impact of automation and reshoring for Sub-Saharan African countries.

Little empirical evidence of reshoring exists, however, and the risk of reshoring out of Sub-Saharan Africa is particularly low because the region's participation in GVCs has thus far been limited. Drawing on data from the Reshoring Initiative, Banga and te Velde (2018) identify 7 foreign companies in Africa that have reshored over 2010–16 (most are in South Africa) compared with more than 1,100 firms returning production from Asia back to OECD countries.[15] Moreover, the effect of reshoring is not yet significant. For instance, De Backer et al. (2016) show that about 4 percent of sampled firms in 11 European countries have moved production activities back home, a much lower share than the 17 percent of firms that offshored activities in the preceding decade.

At the same time, evidence is mixed on the impact of new technologies on the location of production bases. Some technologies, such as robots, have been in widespread use in industry since the 1980s, although the pace of progress and the reliability and relevance for modern production have been growing rapidly. Each of the technologies has different implications and influences the nature of production differently, depending on the respective sector.

Digital technologies such as the internet and artificial intelligence reduce the costs of (1) matching buyers and sellers across countries, allowing firms in developing countries to access global markets; and (2) trade and coordination

BOX 1.4

Impact of Automation in Sub-Saharan African Countries

The impact of automation on labor markets may differ across countries with different comparative advantages and specializations. For instance, recent studies find heterogeneous impacts from automation between manufacturing and agriculture, although the impact of automation depends significantly on how exposure to automation is defined and measured (see Frey and Osborne 2013).

For developing countries, Hallward-Driemeier and Nayyar (2017) find that automation threatens between 2 percent and 8 percent of today's jobs. They group industries into clusters on the basis of intensity of robots and the level of export concentration. Industries affected by high levels of export concentration and automation, such as transport equipment, pharmaceuticals, or electronics, are likely to become increasingly infeasible as entry points for less developed countries. On the opposite end of the spectrum, industries such as wood, paper, and chemical products as well as basic metals are likely to see more limited impacts. As such, industries where the increased service content of output and new labor-saving technologies reduce the relevance of comparative advantage in labor costs may witness less viable production in developing countries, including in Sub-Saharan Africa. In this context, the authors advise focusing on policies to promote competitiveness, capabilities, and connectedness. Most Sub-Saharan African countries rank near the bottom in all three categories and will need to invest to withstand pressures, to maintain their current export baskets and diversify into new products. Moreover, manufacturing is expected to have a less adverse impact in Sub-Saharan Africa than in some of East Asia's newly industrialized economies.

In this context, services hold a promise to drive productivity gains and development. For example, the wholesale and retail sector accounted for almost 50 percent of employment expansion in India between 1993–94 and 2004–05 (Nayyar 2011). But increasing evidence suggests that elementary services occupations are among those with the lowest returns, with more productivity-enhancing sectors likely to be skill-biased. This evidence informs the upcoming World Bank Group report "Services-Led Development: Myth or Reality" (World Bank, forthcoming [b]), which focuses on whether services can support productivity growth and large-scale job creation and addresses what is needed for a productivity-enhancing and inclusive services-led development strategy.

among fragmented trade partners globally. These digital technologies reduce the impact of physical distance and provide opportunities for geographically disadvantaged countries (such as landlocked and small island nations) and rural businesses in all countries to integrate into global markets. One example is the recent introduction of English and Spanish machine translation on eBay, which contributed to a significant increase in users' exports to Latin America (Brynjolfsson, Hui, and Liu 2018). Large multinational and online firms rely increasingly on big data and machine learning to investigate consumer behavior and manage their supply chains.

Robotics and, more broadly, automation have thus far had an ambiguous impact on production location. Earlier models predicted that industrial robotics would reinforce agglomeration because it requires large-scale complementary expenditures on safety barriers, sensors, and system implementation. About 75 percent of industrial robots are in five countries—China, Germany, Japan, the Republic of Korea, and the United States. Robots primarily benefit a few industries, such as motor vehicles, transportation equipment, electronics, and machinery, that historically have been susceptible to fragmented production along GVCs. The complexity of these industries limits the ability of developing countries to participate in such GVCs (Citigroup and Oxford Martin School 2016). Banga and te Velde (2018) use data from the furniture manufacturing industry to estimate when robots will become more cost-competitive than workers in the production of furniture. They find the inflection point to be 2034 for Kenya, 11 years later than for the United States, on the basis of Kenya's low labor costs and higher operational costs for robots.

Meanwhile, growing evidence suggests that automation in developed countries is associated with their larger imports of intermediate inputs from developing countries. Artuc, Bastos, and Rijkers (2018) show that robotization is concentrated in a few high-income countries and a few capital-intensive sectors, such as automotive, rubber and plastics, metals, and electronics, but is limited in traditionally labor-intensive sectors such as textiles.[16] This finding implies that low-income countries still may have time to follow the traditional export-led industrialization path in these sectors.

Additive manufacturing technologies, such as 3-D printing, could potentially have a profound impact on production location. Rehnberg and Ponte (2018) examine whether 3-D printing functions as a complement to or substitute for traditional manufacturing technologies. They conclude that 3-D printing reduces the number and cost of GVC processes and allows new players to access GVCs more easily. It reduces the importance of economies of scale and can lead to more dispersed economic activity, that is, to a "micromanufacturing" model. Laplume, Petersen, and Pearce (2016) conclude that diffusion of 3D printing technology in specific industries is associated with GVCs that are shorter and more dispersed. De Backer et al. (2016) argue that new technologies may just lead to regionalization of GVCs rather than full reshoring, because demographic factors and the growth of the middle class in many developing countries make them attractive consumer markets.

Dispersed GVCs (or regional value chains) driven by 3-D printing technologies may present opportunities for many Sub-Saharan African countries that have small domestic markets and cannot compete globally, by enabling them to produce manufactured goods for regional trade. Several regional trade agreements already exist in Sub-Saharan Africa, such as several tripartite agreements between parties to the Common Market for Eastern and Southern Africa, the East African Community, and the Southern African Development Community, and the now-ratified African Continental Free Trade Area (AfCFTA) agreement. Intraregional trade has been below its potential in Sub-Saharan Africa, however, for several reasons: the large cost differences between the most efficient members in the region and external producers, product complementarities between members of a regional trade agreement, and continuing high nontariff barriers in the region.

In addition, 3-D printing can have a substantial impact on trade in services. Service agreements have become more important because services now supplement or even replace intermediary goods and goods-related activities: 3D printers build physical objects from 3-D computer-aided design data and replace certain transportation of goods by transmission of data. At the level of the General Agreement on Trade in Services, debates may result about what constitutes a good and a service in World Trade Organization (WTO) legislation; and, in turn, some WTO rules may need to be revisited. Moreover, 3-D printing can substitute trade in services (through the payment of license fees and royalties for designs) for the goods trade and can provide opportunities for countries with restrictive policies toward trade in services (Sweden 2016; Lodefalk 2015; World Bank, forthcoming [b]). Service trade regulations in Sub-Saharan Africa are no more restrictive than in other regions, as measured by the World Bank's Service Trade Restrictiveness Index; but existing de jure restrictions are often compounded by many additional de facto barriers or the nonimplementation of existing agreements (Heuser and Mattoo 2017). Although some Sub-Saharan African regional economic communities have agreed to liberalize services, negotiations in this area have moved at a glacial pace, and the AfCFTA framework does not currently include services.

In summary, the potential effects of new technologies on global production networks and employment remain speculative; for now, the available information provides ambiguous results. Although it is widely assumed that new technologies will lead to reshoring of industries back to Europe, Japan, and North America, the evidence reveals an apparently exaggerated demise of offshoring for now and the foreseeable future. So far, robotization in developed countries is concentrated in a few technology-intensive sectors, and it has been limited in labor-intensive sectors. Further, increased automation in richer countries can enhance productivity and income; thus, it can raise demand from developed countries for exports of intermediate inputs and other goods from developing countries. At the same time, new digital technologies such as 3-D printing could provide opportunities for Sub-Saharan Africa by developing regional value chains and enhancing manufacturing-service links. The upcoming World Bank Industrializing for Jobs report will provide in-depth discussion about structural transformation and trade integration issues for Sub-Saharan

African economies (World Bank, forthcoming [a]). To inform policy discussions, the following section provides a short review of the current position of Sub-Saharan Africa in GVC integration and as an FDI destination, two important indicators for showing the competitiveness of African economies.

GVC Integration and Non-Resource-Seeking FDI

GVCs have become the building blocks of an increasingly integrated global economy. They allow countries to trade know-how and to make things together, with each step in the process adding value to the final product. GVCs can create jobs through two main channels: (1) catalyzing the structural transformation of the economy, which increases firm productivity; and (2) spillovers from backward and forward links within the chains. A recent paper shows that, among Ethiopian manufacturing firms, firms participating in GVCs tend to be more productive, and in turn provide higher wages and employ more workers than other firms (Choi, Fukase, and Zeufack 2019).

Sub-Saharan African countries, however, have limited GVC participation. Most exports are in raw materials, with the region lagging all others in high-technology exports. Currently, Sub-Saharan African countries account for 12 percent of the world's population, but for less than 3 percent of its trade and GDP (see figure 1.12). In key GVC sectors like apparel and automobiles, this share is even lower (2.5 percent of final and 0.5 percent of intermediate apparel and footwear exports; 1.3 percent of final and 1.0 percent of

Figure 1.12 Exports of Raw Materials and Technology-Intensive Products from Sub-Saharan Africa

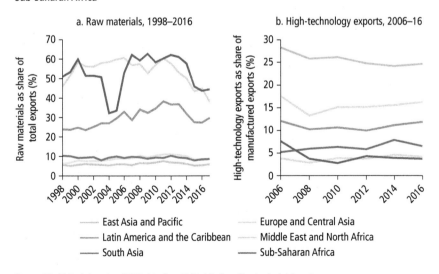

Source: World Bank based on 2019 data from United Nations Comtrade database.

intermediate vehicles). Among low-income Sub-Saharan African countries, development through engagement in GVCs is primarily limited to individual sectors such as textiles and apparel in Ethiopia and Lesotho, and agribusiness and horticulture in several Southern and Eastern African countries.[17]

Developing countries that have managed substantial growth gains through GVCs note that a key determinant of their success is not low wages but rather low unit labor costs, the ratio of average wages to per capita GDP (Ahmad and Primi 2017; Golub et al. 2018; Golub and Hayat 2015; Malikane 2015) (figure 1.13). This distinction presents a challenge for low- and lower-middle-income countries in Sub-Saharan Africa that lack a comparative advantage in labor-intensive and capital-intensive tradables, relative to developing countries

Figure 1.13 Unit Labor Costs and Wages in Developing Countries That Are Significantly Involved in Global Value Chains

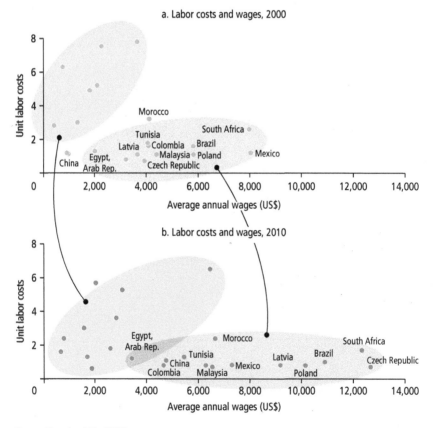

Source: Ahmad and Primi 2017.
Note: US$ = US dollar.

in other regions. For instance, some Sub-Saharan African countries have not only higher labor costs but also a higher cost of capital than some Asian countries, with capital costs in Kenya more than nine times those in Bangladesh (Gelb et al. 2017). At the same time, among countries that show job growth in manufacturing sectors, the direction of change of labor costs has been mixed: manufacturing sector wages and value added per worker have increased in Ethiopia, but they have declined in Côte d'Ivoire (Abreha et al. 2019). These findings suggest that changes in unit labor costs should be further investigated.

Empirical evidence highlights the importance of complementary factors and policies in facilitating GVC participation in such areas as standards, internet and physical connectivity, education, and skills (Farole and Winkler 2014; Kummritz, Taglioni, and Winkler 2017). Policies must be designed with consideration given to (1) policy sequencing over time, (2) coordination between different levels of government and across regions (so that, for example, policies are not set and undone at different levels and competition between regions does not erode the fiscal base), and (3) minimization of implementation uncertainties that can erode good incentives by exposing firms to unnecessary risks.

As another channel for technology transfer, FDI can boost economic growth, reduce poverty, and help countries integrate into GVCs (Agrawal 2015; Alfaro et al. 2004; Lall 2000). FDI has positive effects on the labor market in that it increases wages and employment (Blalock and Gertler 2008). Ndikumana and Verick (2008) find that, in Sub-Saharan Africa, FDI crowds in domestic investment and benefits countries that improve their investment climate. Most FDI in Sub-Saharan Africa is, however, in low-technology sectors, with limited effects on technology transfer and employment. Among African regions, only East Africa saw a rise in FDI between 2005–08 and 2015–18. This exception could be partially explained by the recent increase in Chinese offshoring production in Ethiopia and other East African destinations. China has increased its FDI in Sub-Saharan Africa since 2010 and become one of the largest investors in the region.[18] FDI in Sub-Saharan Africa is primarily market seeking, followed by natural resources–related FDI and by a negligible amount related to tourism. In particular, resource-seeking FDI, which is more prevalent in Sub-Saharan Africa, has a lower impact on job creation (Abate and Engel, forthcoming).

A large body of FDI literature documents that the business environment is an important determinant of FDI flows in developing countries, including those in Sub-Saharan Africa. For example, Walsh and Yu (2010) analyze the impacts of macroeconomic and institutional determinants of FDI flows in emerging markets. They find that the exchange rate, financial depth, school enrollment, and institutional factors such as judicial independence and labor market flexibility affect FDI flows in secondary and tertiary sectors (but not in primary sectors). Using firm-level data covering 709 cities in 128 countries, Reyes, Roberts, and Xu (2017) examine the role of the business environment at the subnational level, using indicators such as basic protection, access to finance, infrastructure, the existence of a strong agglomeration environment, human capital, labor regulations, taxes, and land access. Kariuki (2015) finds that infrastructure, trade openness, and stock market developments have a significantly positive impact on FDI flows, whereas factors such as high economic risk, political risk, and financial risk had negative impacts across 35 African economies during 1985–2010. Abate and Engel (forthcoming) find that corruption, taxes, and access to finance were important determinants of FDI flows to cities in 15 Southern African countries over 2010–16.

Perhaps most important in creating an appropriate business environment for Sub-Saharan African workers to reap the benefits of digital technology adoption and to take full advantage of greater participation in GVCs and FDI is boosting the low levels of human capital across the region. The next chapter therefore focuses on human capital. It argues that Sub-Saharan Africa needs to focus on training the innovators—building a critical mass of highly skilled inventors and entrepreneurs who will help position countries to take advantage of the opportunities provided by digital technologies and greater economic integration. With digital technologies adapted to local capabilities and needs, Sub-Saharan Africa's low-skill workers will be able to upgrade their skills as they use them.

In summary, although concern about reshoring may be exaggerated, a bigger concern for Sub-Saharan Africa is the current low level of integration with global markets through GVCs and FDI, which are commonly understood to be channels by which technology is transferred from more advanced foreign firms. GVCs have had only a limited impact on employment in Sub-Saharan Africa. To enhance GVC participation and attract FDI, countries in the region need to upgrade their productivity and improve the analog components of complementary factors and the business environment.

Policy Implications and Future Research Agenda

The following is a series of policy recommendations for moving toward a less zero-sum view of the emergent paradigm of industrial development in an age of digitization and globalized production networks.

- *Close the current gap in digital infrastructure, and enhance affordable broadband access with improved regulatory frameworks.* Further regional harmonization, supported by increased regulatory capacity through regional hubs, should allow (1) more effective subsidization to support universal access and thereby boost poverty reduction, and (2) more effective pro-competition regulation of digital infrastructure to create bigger markets. The positive interactions between subsidies (to boost demand) and lower costs (spurred by asset sharing and trading, and greater economies of scale and scope) should allow larger markets to sustain more operators.

- *Add complementary support for digital skills.* To enhance digital skill flows, policy support could include improving the quality of education through educational content focused on socioemotional and entrepreneurial skills. To improve the digital skill stock, policy support could focus on measures to increase labor productivity by enabling workers to benefit from worker-enhancing technologies, through (1) retraining workers to adjust their skills to meet the changing demands of business, such as digital literacy and digital skills; (2) supporting youth and enterprises working in technology-intensive sectors, including the development of locally relevant digital content and supporting the scaling up of homegrown innovation; (3) improving the overall ecosystem for businesses and start-ups; and (4) facilitating low-skilled workers' adoption of worker-enhancing technologies.

- *Enhance analog complementary assets and the business environment.* Complementary components, such as electricity, infrastructure, and human capital, are important determinants for expanding digital infrastructure and digital skills. The impact of the adoption of skill-biased digital technologies such as the internet is likely to boost the jobs of low-skilled workers only if such adoption is accompanied by sufficiently large output expansion effects, which in turn are facilitated by greater product market competition, more investments in transport and logistics, regional integration, lower trade costs, and greater exports. The key is strengthening an environment that is conducive to diversification, innovation, and productivity in the era of digital innovation, working toward keeping the unit cost of labor low for labor-intensive and capital-intensive tradable products.

- *Facilitate regional integration.* Together with the business environment, trade and investment policies also play roles in supporting Sub-Saharan African firms' integration into GVCs and attracting market-seeking FDI and efficiency-seeking FDI, both of which have a higher employment multiplier than resource-seeking FDI. Given the relatively small market size of many Sub-Saharan African countries, regional integration (and especially the AfCFTA) can be an important tool for boosting trade and FDI. At the same time, technological innovation could help Sub-Saharan Africa benefit more from regional trade and manufacturing-services links.

Evidence-based solutions will be needed to support firms and individuals, so they benefit from digital technologies.

- Knowledge is limited in the areas of (1) newer and innovative technologies that could enhance access to and affordability of digital technologies (for example, lower cost low-Earth-orbiting satellites); (2) rigorous evaluations of the effects of digital technologies on net job outcomes and the composition of skills in low-income economies; (3) effective ways to support less-skilled workers with technology adoption and development and diffusion of low-skill-biased digital technologies; (4) the effects of specific digital technologies on Sub-Saharan Africa's revealed comparative advantages; (5) how much time it would take for newer digital technologies to have larger growth and inclusion effects in Sub-Saharan Africa; and (6) better use of nontraditional sources of data, such as big data supported by machine learning, to inform policy discussions in Sub-Saharan Africa.

- The upcoming *Digital Africa: Building the Infrastructure Foundations and Facilitating the Adoption of Technologies for Jobs* flagship report (Begazo-Gomez, Blimpo, and Dutz, forthcoming) and the associated longer-term research could fill some of these knowledge gaps, including (1) key barriers to the availability and adoption of digital technologies in Africa; (2) better measures of the impact of adoption of digital technologies on productivity growth, output, and aggregate jobs outcomes; (3) better measures of the impact of adoption of digital technologies on poverty reduction and inclusion outcomes; (4) the benefits of regional digital infrastructure and spectrum regulation, and policy suggestions to make such initiatives feasible; and (5) a forward-looking digital data agenda at the national, regional, and continental levels.

Annex 1A. Opportunities and Caveats of Using LinkedIn Data

LinkedIn data, provided by the World Bank Group–LinkedIn collaboration, offer unique insights into the labor markets of some of the most dynamic global industries. The data are derived from a web-based, nonrandom sample of labor market participants across more than 100 countries, offered in the structure of a single taxonomy optimized for cross-country/industry benchmarking and comparisons. These unconventional data capture real-time labor market sentiment through tracking employment and skill trends based on the self-reported information of LinkedIn users. The use of web-based labor market data sets for economic analysis has seen rising interest, driven by the ability to construct new indicators for answering questions not covered in traditional data sources (Hammer, Kostroch, and Quiros 2017). In recent years many applications of such data can be seen throughout the relevant literature (Antenucci et al. 2014; Askitas and Zimmermann 2009, 2015; Chancellor and Counts 2018; Gandomi and Haider 2015; Guerrero and Lopez 2017).

Using big data information is particularly useful in Sub-Saharan Africa where limited data exist to offer knowledge about new types of skills, such as digital skills. For instance, the World Bank's skill surveys have been conducted for 17 countries globally, but for only two Sub-Saharan African countries—Ghana (Household Survey) and Kenya (Enterprise Survey) in 2013 and 2017, respectively. Although web-based data have been used for labor market analysis in other countries, mainly the United States but also recently India (Nomura et al. 2017), no published papers appear to exist that use such data for skill analysis in Sub-Saharan Africa. Applications of big data in Sub-Saharan Africa are limited to data-sharing initiatives that use telecom company data and mobile money data (M-Pesa) to measure the impact of their use on personal finance (Mbiti and Weil 2016).

The usage of LinkedIn data, and other web-based big data, requires understanding their limitations and caveats. In addition to the fact that LinkedIn data represent mostly white-collar, digitally savvy workers who are mainly employed in knowledge sector industries, several caveats arise in regional and cross-country comparisons. For example, differences in sample size and occupational distribution across countries are a concern. The metrics available in the data sets take steps to control for these differences; however, these potential sources of bias should be considered in the interpretation. When necessary, the analysis presented here highlights differences in member composition between comparison countries and regions. Detailed discussion of metrics and data representativeness is outlined in the World Bank–LinkedIn collaboration methodology paper (Zhu, Fritzler, and Orlowski 2018).

For a better understanding of how well the LinkedIn member base represents the workforce in Sub-Saharan Africa, this book compares LinkedIn member data in Sub-Saharan Africa with International Labour Organization labor force data.[19] On the one hand, the comparison shows that LinkedIn members in Sub-Saharan Africa have a solid presence in ICT, financial and insurance activities, and professional scientific and technical activities. On the other hand, sectors such as agriculture, wholesale, and manufacturing have relatively poor coverage. In addition to validation exercises reported in the World Bank–LinkedIn collaboration report, this book finds that LinkedIn migration outflows from Sub-Saharan Africa are positively and significantly correlated with OECD (2016) migration outflow data.

Notes

1. Digital technologies are all based to a greater or lesser extent on combinations of the digits 0 and 1, enabling immense amounts of information to be compressed, preserved, and transmitted. Digital technologies reduce economic costs associated with search, replication, transportation, tracking, and verification and result in significant economies of scale and scope (through the production of multiple related products), network effects (where additional users enhance the value of the product to others), and feedback loops (Goldfarb and Tucker 2019).

2. More empirical work is needed to understand the relative importance of these and other mechanisms that could help explain whether the adoption of digital technologies is more pro-inclusion in low-income Sub-Saharan African countries relative to higher-income countries.

3. Data from the World Bank's 2019 World Development Indicators.

4. For instance, Sub-Saharan African countries' export products are less vulnerable to automation (IMF 2018, using Index of Countries' Export Vulnerability to Automation, suggested by Brynjolfsson, Mitchell, and Rock [2018]) and the demographic composition of these countries contrasts with that of developed economies, where aging leads to greater (industrial) automation (Acemoglu and Restrepo 2018).

5. Box 3.1 in Dutz, Almeida, and Packard (2018) summarizes the predictions of a model developed by Brambilla (2018), which extends Acemoglu and Autor's (2011) task-based model of digital technology adoption by realistically allowing firms to differ in their efficiency of production and allowing workers' wages to vary across firms. It is summarized later in this chapter in box 1.2.

6. Bessen (2019) analyzes the productivity and jobs growth dynamics in the cotton cloth, steel, and motor vehicles industries in the United States, highlighting how, when demand was elastic and not yet relatively satiated for these products, large increases in productivity were accompanied by even larger increases in employment, followed by declines in employment in more recent stages of maturity. He interprets this pattern through a model of heterogeneous final demand that changes over time: price declines in the initial stages of productivity growth make formerly prohibitively expensive products affordable for mass consumption, yielding a large positive demand response. Once large unmet needs become saturated and demand becomes less elastic, further productivity gains in these industries may bring reduced employment.

7. The data in this paragraph come from World Bank (2019a), based on data from GSMA (2018) and from the International Telecommunication Union's 2018 World Telecommunications/ICT Indicators Database.

8. Data from the International Telecommunications Union's 2018 World Telecommunications/ICT Indicators Database.

9. For example, some of the literature explains digital technology investment and usage as major drivers of productivity and income growth in the United States relative to the European Union (see Bloom et al. 2010; Pilat and Lee 2001).

10. Information from the Safaricom website, https://www.safaricom.co.ke/.

11. As defined by LinkedIn, the digital skills considered are animation, artificial intelligence, cloud computing, computer hardware, computer networking, cybersecurity, data science, data storage technologies, development tools, digital literacy, enterprise software, game development, graphic design, human-computer interaction, mobile application development, scientific computing, social media, software development life cycle, software testing, technical support, and web development.

12. UNESCO defines digital literacy as the ability to access, manage, understand, integrate, communicate, evaluate, and create information safely and appropriately through digital devices and networked technologies for participation in economic and social life. It includes competencies that are variously referred to as computer literacy, ICT literacy, information literacy, and media literacy.

13. The OECD's digital literacy definition states that, to thrive in the digital economy, individuals will need more than ICT skills and that other complementary skills will be needed, ranging from good literacy and numeracy skills through the right socioemotional skills to work collaboratively and flexibly.

14. Data on access to internet, mobile cellular, and electricity come from the World Bank's World Development Indicators.

15. For more information on the Reshoring Initiative, see http://www.reshorenow.org/.

16. They find that a 10 percent increase in robot density in developed economies' industries not only increases their exports to developing countries by 11.8 percent but also induces a 6.1 percent increase in their imports from developing countries. They explain that robotization in developed countries lowers their production costs relative to foreign ones, and thus makes them more competitive. As a result, developed countries expand their production and increase their imports of intermediate inputs from developing countries. Moreover, the authors measure robotization as the ratio between the average stock of robots and the number of working hours between 1993 and 2015, using data from the International Federation of Robotics.

17. Data from the World Bank's World Development Indicators.

18. Data from the *Financial Times*' fDi Markets database.

19. LinkedIn member data by industry (2017) are compared with International Labour Organization industry-level employment data for 2015–17 (ILO 2018) and for Côte d'Ivoire, Ethiopia, Ghana, Madagascar, Mali, Mauritius, Mozambique, Namibia, Rwanda, Senegal, Tanzania, and Zimbabwe. This report also explores the potential of comparing LinkedIn skills data in Kenya with the World Bank's STEPS Skills Measurement Program in Kenya (2016–17). Differing definitions of occupations and measurement methods for skills prevent a fair comparison.

References

Abate, G., and J. Engel. Forthcoming. "FDI in the SADC Region: Stylized Facts, Determinants and Impacts." World Bank, Washington, DC.

Abreha, K., P. Jones, E. Lartey, T. Mengistae, and A. Zeufack. 2019. "Manufacturing Job Growth in Africa: What Is Driving It and What Will Sustain It? The Cases of Côte d'Ivoire and Ethiopia." Unpublished, World Bank, Washington, DC.

Acemoglu, D., and D. Autor. 2011. "Skills, Tasks and Technologies: Implications for Employment and Earnings." In *Handbook of Labor Economics*, vol. 4, edited by O. Ashenfelter and D. Card, 1043–171. San Diego: North Holland.

Acemoglu, D., and P. Restrepo. 2018. "Demographics and Automation." Working Paper 24421, National Bureau of Economic Research, Cambridge, MA.

AfDB, OECD, and UNDP (African Development Bank, Organisation for Economic Co-operation and Development, and United Nations Development Programme). 2014. *African Economic Outlook 2014: Global Value Chains and Africa's Industrialisation*. Paris: AfDB, OECD, and UNDP.

Agrawal, G. 2015. "Foreign Direct Investment and Economic Growth in BRICS Economies: A Panel Data Analysis." *Journal of Economics, Business and Management* 3 (4): 421–24.

Ahmad, N., and A. Primi. 2017. "From Domestic to Regional to Global: Factory Africa and Factory Latin America?" In *Global Value Chain Development Report 2017: Measuring and Analyzing the Impact of GVCs on Economic Development*, Chapter 3. Geneva: World Trade Organization.

Aker, J., R. Boumnijel, A. McClelland, and N. Tierney. 2013. "How Do Electronic Transfers Compare? Evidence from a Mobile Money Cash Transfer Experiment in Niger." Tufts University, Medford, MA.

Aker, J., and K. Wilson. 2013. "Can Mobile Money Be Used to Promote Savings? Evidence from Northern Ghana." Working Paper 2012-003, SWIFT Institute, London.

Alfaro, L., A. Chanda, S. Kalemli-Ozcan, and S. Sayek. 2004. "FDI and Economic Growth: The Role of Local Financial Markets." *Journal of International Economics* 64 (1): 89–112.

Alibhai, S., N. Buehren, R. Coleman, M. Goldstein, and F. Strobbe. 2018. "Disruptive Finance: Using Psychometrics to Overcome Collateral Constraints in Ethiopia." Working Paper, World Bank, Washington, DC.

Antenucci, D., M. Cafarella, M. Levenstein, C. Ré, and M. D. Shapiro. 2014. "Using Social Media to Measure Labor Market Flows." Working Paper 20010, National Bureau of Economic Research, Cambridge, MA.

Artuc, E., P. Bastos, and B. Rijkers. 2018. "Robots, Tasks and Trade." Policy Research Working Paper 8674, World Bank, Washington, DC.

Askitas, N., and K. F. Zimmermann. 2009. "Google Econometrics and Unemployment Forecasting." *Applied Economics Quarterly* 55 (2): 107–20.

———. 2015. "The Internet as a Data Source for Advancement in Social Sciences." *International Journal of Manpower* 36 (1): 2–12.

Banga, K., and D. W. te Velde. 2018. "Digitalisation and the Future of Manufacturing in Africa." Supporting Economic Transformation, Overseas Development Institute, London.

Begazo-Gomez, T., M. P. Blimpo, and M. A. Dutz. Forthcoming. *Digital Africa: Building the Infrastructure Foundations and Facilitating the Adoption of Technologies for Jobs.* Washington, DC: World Bank.

Bessen, J. 2019. "Artificial Intelligence and Jobs: The Role of Demand." In *The Economics of Artificial Intelligence: An Agenda*, edited by A. Agrawal, J. Gans, and A. Goldfarb, 291–307. Cambridge, MA: National Bureau of Economic Research.

Blalock, G., and P. Gertler. 2008. "Welfare Gains from Foreign Direct Investment through Technology Transfer to Local Suppliers." *Journal of International Economics* 74 (2): 402–21.

Bloom, N., M. Draca, T. Kretschmer, R. Sadun, H. Overman, and M. Schankerman. 2010. "The Economic Impact of ICT." SMART N. 2007/0020, Centre for Economic Performance, London School of Economics.

Bloomberg Markets (D. Herbling). 2018. "National Bank Kenya Considering Branch Closures to Cut Costs." March 6. www.bloomberg.com/news/articles/2018-03-06/national-bank-kenya-considering-branch-closures-to-cut-costs.

Brambilla, I. 2018. "Digital Technology Adoption and Jobs: A Model of Firm Heterogeneity." Policy Research Working Paper 8326, World Bank, Washington, DC.

Brynjolfsson, E., X. Hui, and M. Liu. 2018. "Does Machine Translation Affect International Trade? Evidence from a Large Digital Platform." Working Paper 24917, National Bureau of Economic Research, Cambridge, MA.

Brynjolfsson, E., T. Mitchell, and D. Rock. 2018. "What Can Machines Learn, and What Does It Mean for Occupations and the Economy?" *AEA Papers and Proceedings* 108 (May): 43–47.

Buehren, N., V. Ceretti, E. Dervisevic, M. Goldstein, L. Klapper, T. Koroknay-Palicz, and S. Schaner. 2018. "Salary Delays and Overdrafts in Rural Ghana." *AEA Papers and Proceedings* 108 (May): 449–52.

Carranza, E., A. Donald, F. Grosset, and S. Kaur. 2018. "Working under Pressure: Improving Labor Productivity through Financial Innovation." Policy Brief Issue 31, Gender Innovation Lab, World Bank, Washington, DC.

Chancellor, S., and S. Counts. 2018. "Measuring Employment Demand Using Internet Search Data." *Proceedings of the 2018 CHI Conference on Human Factors in Computing Systems*, 1–14. Association for Computing Machinery, Montreal.

Choi, J., E. Fukase, and A. Zeufack. 2019. "Global Value Chains, Competition and Markups: Firm-Level Evidence from Ethiopia." Unpublished, World Bank, Washington, DC.

Citigroup and Oxford Martin School. 2016. "Technology at Work v2.0: The Future Is Not What It Used to Be." *Citi GPS: Global Perspectives and Solutions*, January, Citigroup.

De Backer, K., C. Menon, I. Desnoyers-James, and L. Moussiegtet. 2016. "Reshoring: Myth or Reality?" Science, Technology and Industry Policy Paper 27, OECD Publishing, Paris.

Deichmann, U., A. Goyal, and D. Mishra. 2016. "Will Digital Technologies Transform Agriculture in Developing Countries?" Policy Research Working Paper 7669, World Bank, Washington, DC.

Demirgüç-Kunt, A., L. Klapper, D. Singer, S. Ansar, and J. Hess. 2018. *The Global Findex Database 2017: Measuring Inclusion and the Fintech Revolution*. Washington, DC: World Bank.

Demombynes, G., and A. Thegeya. 2012. "Kenya's Mobile Revolution and the Promise of Mobile Savings." Policy Research Working Paper 5988, World Bank, Washington, DC.

Duflo, E., and C. Udry. 2004. "Intrahousehold Resource Allocation in Côte d'Ivoire: Social Norms, Separate Accounts and Consumption Choices." Working Paper 10498, National Bureau of Economic Research, Cambridge, MA.

Dutz, M. A., R. K. Almeida, and T. G. Packard. 2018. *The Jobs of Tomorrow: Technology, Productivity and Prosperity in Latin America and the Caribbean*. Directions in Development. Washington, DC: World Bank.

Dutz, M. A., I. Kessides, S. O'Connell, and R. Willig. 2012. "Competition and Innovation-Driven Inclusive Growth." In *Promoting Inclusive Growth: Challenges and Policies*, edited by L. de Mello and M. A. Dutz, Chapter 7. Paris: OECD Publishing.

Economist. 2017. "Adidas's High-Tech Factory Brings Production Back to Germany." January 14.

Etzo, S., and G. Collender. 2010. "The Mobile Phone 'Revolution' in Africa: Rhetoric or Reality?" *African Affairs* 109 (437): 659–68.

Evans, D., O. Arias, and I. Santos. 2019. *The Skills Balancing Act in Sub-Saharan Africa: Investing in Skills for Productivity, Inclusivity, and Adaptability*. Washington, DC: World Bank.

Farole, T., and D. Winkler, eds.. 2014. *Making Foreign Direct Investment Work for Sub-Saharan Africa: Local Spillovers and Competitiveness in Global Value Chains*. Directions in Development. Washington, DC: World Bank.

Frey, C. B., and M. A. Osborne. 2013. "The Future of Employment: How Susceptible Are Jobs to Computerisation?" Working Paper, Oxford Martin Programme on Technology and Employment, University of Oxford.

Gandomi, A., and M. Haider. 2015. "Beyond the Hype: Big Data Concepts, Methods, and Analytics." *International Journal of Information Management* 35 (2): 137–44.

Gautam, B., I. Bianchi, M. Goldstein, and J. Montalvao. 2018. "Short-Term Impacts of Improved Access to Mobile Savings, with and without Business Training: Experimental Evidence from Tanzania." Working Paper 478, Center for Global Development, Washington, DC.

Gelb, A., C. Meyer, V. Ramachandran, and D. Wadhwa. 2017. "Can Africa Be a Manufacturing Destination? Labor Costs in Comparative Perspective." Working Paper 466, Center for Global Development, Washington, DC.

Glaeser, E. L. 2018. "Framework for the Changing Nature of Work." Working paper for *World Development Report 2019: The Changing Nature of Work*, Harvard University, Cambridge, MA.

Goldfarb, A., and C. Tucker. 2019. "Digital Economics." *Journal of Economic Literature* 57 (1): 3–43.

Golub, S. S., J. Ceglowski, A. A. Mbaye, and V. Prasad. 2018. "Can Africa Compete with China in Manufacturing? The Role of Relative Unit Labour Costs." *World Economy* 41 (6): 1508–28.

Golub, S., and F. Hayat. 2015. "Employment, Unemployment and Underemployment in Africa." In *The Oxford Handbook of Africa and Economics: Volume 1: Context and Concepts*, edited by C. Monga and J. Y. Lin, 136–53. Oxford: Oxford University Press.

GSMA. 2018. "The Mobile Economy Sub-Saharan Africa 2018." GSMA, London.

Guerrero, O. A., and E. Lopez. 2017. "Understanding Unemployment in the Era of Big Data: Policy Informed by Data-Driven Theory." *Policy & Internet* 9 (1): 28–54.

Hallward-Driemeier, M., and G. Nayyar. 2017. *Trouble in the Making? The Future of Manufacturing-Led Development*. Washington, DC: World Bank.

Hammer, C., D. C. Kostroch, and G. Quiros. 2017. *Big Data: Potential, Challenges and Statistical Implications*. Washington, DC: International Monetary Fund.

Heuser, C., and A. Mattoo. 2017. "Services Trade and Global Value Chains." Policy Research Working Paper 8126, World Bank, Washington, DC.

Hjort, J., and J. Poulsen. 2019. "The Arrival of Fast Internet and Employment in Africa." *American Economic Review* 109 (3): 1032–79.

ILO (International Labour Organization). 2018. *World Employment and Social Outlook—Trends 2018*. Geneva: ILO.

IMF (International Monetary Fund). 2018. "The Future of Work in Sub-Saharan Africa." In *Regional Economic Outlook: Sub-Saharan Africa—Capital Flows and the Future of Work*, Chapter 3. Washington, DC: IMF.

Islam, A., S. Muzi, and J. L. Rodriguez Meza. 2018. "Does Mobile Money Use Increase Firms' Investment? Evidence from Enterprise Surveys in Kenya, Uganda, and Tanzania." *Small Business Economics* 51: 687–708.

Jack, W., and T. Suri. 2014. "Risk Sharing and Transactions Costs: Evidence from Kenya's Mobile Money Revolution." *American Economic Review* 104 (1): 183–223.

Kariuki, C. 2015. "The Determinants of Foreign Direct Investment in the African Union." *Journal of Economics, Business and Management* 3 (3): 346–51.

Kelly, T., and R. Firestone. 2016. "How Tech Hubs Are Helping to Drive Economic Growth in Africa." Background Paper for *World Development Report 2016: Digital Divide*. World Bank, Washington, DC.

Kummritz, V., D. Taglioni, and D. Winkler. 2017. "Economic Upgrading through Global Value Chain Participation: Which Policies Increase the Value-Added Gains?" Policy Research Working Paper 8007, World Bank, Washington, DC.

Ky, S., C. Rugemintwari, and A. Sauviat. 2018. "Does Mobile Money Affect Saving Behaviour? Evidence from a Developing Country." *Journal of African Economies* 27 (3): 285–320.

Lall, S. 2000. "FDI and Development: Policy and Research Issues in the Emerging Context." Working Paper 43, Oxford Department of International Development, University of Oxford, UK.

Laplume, A. O., B. Petersen, and J. M. Pearce. 2016. "Global Value Chains from a 3D Printing Perspective." *Journal of International Business Studies* 47: 595–609.

Lodefalk, M. 2015. "Servicification of Manufacturing Firms Makes Divides in Trade Policymaking Antiquated." Working Paper 1/2015, Örebro University School of Business, Örebro, Sweden.

Mahler, D. G., J. Montes, and D. L. Newhouse. 2019. "Internet Access in Sub-Saharan Africa." Poverty & Equity Note 13, World Bank Group, Washington, DC.

Malikane, C. 2015. "The Theory of the Firm in the African Context." In *The Oxford Handbook of Africa and Economies: Volume 1: Context and Concepts*, edited by C. Monga and J. Y. Lin, 86–103. Oxford: Oxford University Press.

Mbiti, I., and D. N. Weil. 2016. "Mobile Banking: The Impact of M-Pesa in Kenya." In *African Successes, Volume III: Modernization and Development*, edited by S. Johnson, 247–93. University of Chicago Press.

Nayyar, G. 2011. "The Quality of Employment in India's Services Sector: Exploring the Heterogeneity." *Applied Economics* 44 (36): 4701–19.

Ndikumana, L., and S. Verick. 2008. "The Linkages between FDI and Domestic Investment: Unravelling the Developmental Impact of Foreign Investment in Sub-Saharan Africa." *Development Policy Review* 26 (6): 713–26.

Ndung'u, N. 2018. "Next Steps for the Digital Revolution in Africa: Inclusive Growth and Job Creation Lessons from Kenya." Africa Growth Initiative, Brookings Institution, Washington, DC.

Nomura, S., S. Imaizumi, A. C. Areias, and Y. Futoshi. 2017. "Toward Labor Market Policy 2.0: The Potential for Using Online Job-Portal Big Data to Inform Labor Market Policies in India." Policy Research Working Paper 7966, World Bank, Washington, DC.

OECD (Organisation for Economic Co-operation and Development). 2016. "Skills for a Digital World." Policy Brief on The Future of Work, OECD Publishing, Paris.

Pilat, D., and F. Lee. 2001. "Productivity Growth in ICT-Producing and ICT-Using Industries: A Source of Growth Differentials in the OECD?" Science, Technology and Industry Working Paper 2001/4, OECD Publishing, Paris.

Rehnberg, M., and S. Ponte. 2018. "From Smiling to Smirking? 3D Printing, Upgrading and the Restructuring of Global Value Chains." *Global Networks* 18 (1): 57–80.

Reyes, J.-D., M. Roberts, and L. C. Xu. 2017. "The Heterogeneous Growth Effects of the Business Environment: Firm-Level Evidence for a Global Sample of Cities." Policy Research Working Paper 8114, World Bank, Washington, DC.

Suri, T., and W. Jack. 2016. "The Long-Run Poverty and Gender Impacts of Mobile Money." *Science* 354 (6317): 1288–92.

Sweden, National Board of Trade. 2016. "Trade Regulation in a 3D Printed World— A Primer." National Board of Trade, Stockholm.

TeleGeography. 2018. *TeleGeography Report.* Carlsbad, CA: PriMetrica, Inc.

UNESCO (United Nations Educational, Scientific and Cultural Organization). 2016. *Global Education Monitoring Report 2016—Education for People and Planet: Creating Sustainable Futures for All.* Paris: UNESCO.

Walsh, P. J., and J. Yu. 2010. "Determinants of Foreign Direct Investment: A Sectoral and Institutional Approach." Working Paper 10/187, International Monetary Fund, Washington, DC.

World Bank. 2016. *World Development Report 2016: Digital Dividends.* Washington, DC: World Bank.

———. 2019a. *Africa's Pulse: An Analysis of Issues Shaping Africa's Economic Future,* vol. 19. Washington DC: World Bank.

———. 2019b. *World Development Report 2019: The Changing Nature of Work.* Washington, DC: World Bank.

———. 2020. *Boosting Productivity in Sub-Saharan Africa.* Washington, DC: World Bank.

———. Forthcoming (a). *Industrializing for Jobs in Africa?* Washington, DC: World Bank.

———. Forthcoming (b). *Services-Led Development: Myth or Reality?* Washington, DC: World Bank.

Zhu, T. J., A. Fritzler, and J. A. K. Orlowski. 2018. "World Bank Group–LinkedIn Data Insights: Jobs, Skills and Migration Trends Methodology and Validation Results." World Bank Group, Washington, DC.

Chapter 2

Human Capital

Moussa P. Blimpo and Solomon Owusu

Introduction

The era of digital technologies offers an opportunity to leverage human capital to create faster jobs growth and better inclusion outcomes. Technology is changing the nature of jobs and affecting the labor market prospects of workers across different sets of skills. Labor's role as an indispensable factor of production is expected to change progressively in the face of continuous technological change, with labor becoming a more skilled and complementary partner of machines. Digital technologies create newer opportunities but at the same time make certain skills obsolete more quickly, as old economy jobs give way to newer jobs (World Bank 2016). The level, quality, and composition of human capital will play a more pivotal role in the future of work. Specific types of skills, such as soft skills, will gain in importance, as will the high-end skills needed to generate and maintain a momentum of innovation. To this end, the 2019 *World Development Report* (WDR 2019) proposes several areas where policy should focus to manage the disruptions of digital technologies in the labor market and to leverage digital technology opportunities so that their benefits are widely shared (World Bank 2019). The unique nature of the skills, labor force, jobs, and production structure of Sub-Saharan African countries calls for additional analyses and recommendations to leverage digital technology opportunities.

WDR 2019 recommends a focus on creating stable, formal, private sector jobs for workers in the unproductive informal sector. Currently, the formal sector of most Sub-Saharan African economies offers limited employment opportunities. For most workers in the region, the informal sector seems the only pathway to generate income. The informal sector still functions as a key part of the structure of the region's economies, and the sector's unique attributes make it very resilient and slow to change. In addition, the potentially large skills mismatch with the requisites of the formal sector may be difficult to address in the short to medium term. Chapter 3 examines in greater detail issues pertaining to informality.

WDR 2019 recommends that policies focus on investing in human capital broadly—namely, in early childhood development, tertiary education, lifelong learning programs, advanced cognitive skills, and socio-behavioral and adaptability skills, in addition to foundational literacy and numeracy skills. Sub-Saharan Africa has long lagged in building foundational skills, with the result being continued bottlenecks for building and developing more advanced skills (see box 2.1). Therefore, while adhering to the recommendation of WDR 2019 to build adequate human capital along these broad lines in its long-term strategy, the region should prioritize addressing the challenge of building strong foundational skills as well as basic digital literacy. This prioritization is in line

BOX 2.1

Lack of Investment in Early Childhood Development in Sub-Saharan Africa

Sub-Saharan Africa already lags in building foundational skills, which creates bottlenecks for building and developing future advanced skills for a growing population of children. Nearly 130 million children under age six live in the region. Every year, 27 million children are born, and 4.7 million children under age five in the region die every year. About 17.5 million (65 percent) of the 27 million children born every year will experience poverty, 20 percent may never attend primary and lower-secondary school, and 24 percent of those children who enroll will likely drop out despite a continuous increase in primary and lower-secondary school completion rates. Only 12 percent of these children will enjoy pre–primary school education, a figure that— although perhaps not surprising—is far below the developing country average of 36 percent and global average of 50 percent (Arias, Evans, and Santos 2019; Bashir et al. 2018; Garcia, Pence, and Evans 2008). Despite efforts to increase total education expenditures since 2010, the share of the region's education budget allocated to pre–primary school was a paltry 0.3 percent in 2012, compared with 8.8 percent spent by North America and Western Europe in 2012 (World Bank 2019).

The quality of education at the primary and lower-secondary education levels is abysmally low. Countries in the region on average perform lower than other countries in all internationally comparable assessments on lower-secondary mathematics and science knowledge skills (Bashir et al. 2018). Additionally, results from four international assessment programs show that upper-primary (grades 4 to 6) students in the region remain challenged by foundational literacy and numeracy tasks. The figures are sometimes staggering. In 6 of 10 countries in the region, nearly 40 percent of the students, by the time they reach grade 4, cannot read a single letter, 70 percent cannot read a paragraph, a staggering 90 percent cannot read a complete paragraph, and only 5 percent can solve a mathematical word problem. And poor people in the region are further disadvantaged, recording the lowest performance among an already low-performing sample.

(continued next page)

Box 2.1 (continued)

Teachers overall teach too little at the foundational level; even when they do teach, they lack the pedagogical knowledge and skills to teach effectively. According to a survey of teachers in primary schools in seven countries in the region (representing 40 percent of the region's population), on average, about 6 percent of teachers possess 80 percent of the knowledge equivalent to a fourth-grader and only 7 percent possess the minimum requisite knowledge for teaching (Bold et al. 2017). Only 11 percent of the teachers surveyed could interpret data in a graph, and only 15 percent could solve a difficult math story problem. Additionally, only 31 percent of the teachers surveyed understand Venn diagrams, and only 35 percent can solve algebra problems. Although gross enrollment in primary education is rapidly expanding, the primary education sector, largely managed by the public sector, is weakly governed and so its quality remains poor (Bold et al. 2017).

The region's inability to build strong foundational skills has affected the skills of working adults. The average reading proficiency levels of urban working adults ages 25–64 in Ghana and Kenya are lower than equivalent counterparts in other regions' low- and middle-income countries. Of working-age adults surveyed in the study, 82 percent in Ghana, and 65 percent in Kenya performed at level 1 or below on the STEP reading proficiency test, meaning they possess only basic reading skills.[a]

a. Data from the World Bank's STEP Skills Measurement Program—see https://microdata.worldbank.org /index.php/catalog/step/about.

with an earlier WDR recommendation for emerging digital economies where the foundational skills base remains weak (World Bank 2016).

A more pressing and achievable challenge in the short to medium term is that the region has not adequately invested in tertiary education, particularly in fields related to STEM (science, technology, engineering, and mathematics). Because it also has failed to incorporate entrepreneurship in its mainstream educational curriculum, it cannot train and create the critical mass of inventors and entrepreneurs who are desperately needed across the region. The region must correct this course in order to keep up with the pace of innovation, be globally competitive in the fast-changing world, and leverage digital technologies to create newer, stable, formal private sector jobs for its masses and its growing unskilled and unemployed labor force. To that end, this chapter argues that additional strategies must be prioritized to take fuller advantage of digital technology opportunities. Because individuals need basic foundational skills, such as literacy and numeracy, as well as digital skills to use digital technologies, the region should prioritize speeding up human capital acquisition and upgrading. Technology can play a role in this process. Digital technologies also have the potential to reinforce learning and learning outcomes when those technologies enable better interactions between learners and teachers (World Bank 2018), increase access to education, and offer access to high-quality material where teachers do not have the needed skills. And, in terms of health, digital technologies have the potential to make up for the shortage of health care workers in the region through increased efficiency and productivity of existing health care staff.

Additionally, with more than one-quarter of its population currently using the internet, the region is growing more connected than before and digital development in the region is accelerating. This means that the region can leverage the opportunities of digital technologies to increase the productivity of workers in their existing occupations. But the region also needs to create more new, formal private sector jobs adapted to the current stock of skills in the region. Doing so will gradually shift employment toward higher-productivity occupations across sectors. Because more than 60 percent of the labor force is made up of ill-equipped adults who need jobs (see box 2.2), enabling these workers to access and use digital technologies will allow them to benefit from newer job creation opportunities in the formal sector (box 2.3). For this part of the labor force, the use of context-adapted digital technologies and apps could compensate for lower skills and make it easier to do low-skill production and service jobs. Designing and creating these context-adapted digital technologies, however, will require inventors and entrepreneurs, leading to the creation of new, formal private sector jobs or the conditions for their creation.

Achieving such goals will, in turn, require smart and targeted investments and greater regional collaboration among universities, businesses, and

BOX 2.2

Adult Illiteracy in Sub-Saharan Africa

Because of its low-quality education, Sub-Saharan Africa has a large stock of illiterate adults and a continuing large flow into adult illiteracy. This stock will persist for several years. In addition to using digital technologies to increase the productivity of this group's workers in their current occupations, building their skills to access and use digital technologies will help them adjust and adapt to the changing nature of work. It will open them up as a new market that can benefit from newer and more productive job creation opportunities made possible by digital technologies. But doing so will require digital skills training and efficient lifelong learning programs to build their skills.

Globally, about 2.1 billion working-age adults (ages 15–64) have low reading proficiency, and 16 percent are illiterate (Soares, Rocha, and Ponczek 2011; World Bank 2019). In most countries in the region, a significant share of the adult population is illiterate (figure B2.2.1). About 61 percent of working-age adults are not proficient in reading, and 19.5 percent of adults ages 15 and older can neither read nor write (UIL 2017). Adult learning and education (ALE) programs are important in equipping illiterate adults with basic education and basic skills. Given the positive impact of lifelong learning programs in promoting labor productivity, employability, social cohesion, citizen engagement, and sustainable economic growth, ALE programs remain a major priority of most countries in the region—26 countries have laws, regulations, or other public policy initiatives that primarily focus on supporting adult literacy (UIL 2013), and 18 countries have enacted new ALE policies since 2009 (UIL 2016).

(continued next page)

Figure B2.2.1 Adult Illiteracy in Sub-Saharan Africa

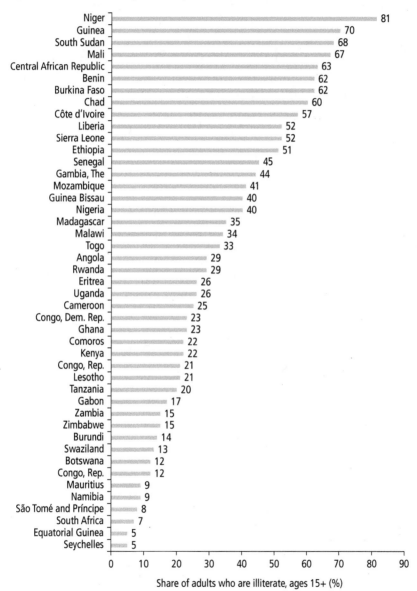

Source: World Bank elaboration based on data from UIL 2017.
Note: The name Swaziland was officially changed to Eswatini in April 2018.

Leveraging Digital Opportunities: Investing in the Skills Needed in the Modern Economy

A recent World Bank report establishes that managing the disruptions and opportunities that digital technologies may create in the labor market requires the adoption of policies that build strong foundational cognitive and socioemotional skills and promote basic digital skills and lifelong learning (World Bank 2016). Sub-Saharan Africa will have to do so through strategic investment in the right skills needed at the right stages of life of its population (see figure B2.3.1), given the region's fundamental skills base and digital development needs (Arias, Evans, and Santos 2019).

In order to address the skills gap problem and produce a versatile, productive, inclusive, and adaptable workforce better prepared for the future of work, the region must make essential investments in foundational cognitive and socioemotional skills at the early childhood development (ECD) stage. An evaluation of a preschool program in Mozambique reports the importance of preschool in building strong foundational and sociobehavioral and socioemotional skills at the ECD stage. Participants of the program reported having stronger skills than nonparticipants for interacting with others. Additionally, participants of the program became better at managing their emotions, were better at dealing with stress, and could follow instructions (World Bank 2019). For children and youth, the recommended strategy arising from this evaluation is to invest in building these skills. In addition, children need to build information and communication technology skills, higher-order skills (complex problem-solving skills such as critical thinking and the ability to comprehend concepts requiring higher-order abstraction), and technical skills. For young and older adults, the evaluation's recommended strategy is to invest in all these skills, with additional investments in

Figure B2.3.1 Life-Cycle Skills Development in Sub-Saharan Africa for the Future of Work

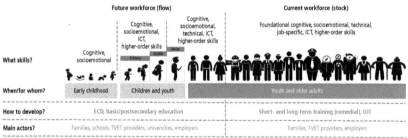

Source: Arias, Evans, and Santos 2019.
Note: ECD = early childhood development; ICT = information and communication technology; OJT = on-the-job training; TVET = technical and vocational education and training.

(continued next page)

technical (technical and vocational education and training, and apprenticeship programs), job-specific skills (on-the-job training, e-entrepreneurship, and business training programs), and digital literacy training.

For the stock of the adult population who have no education at all because they lacked access, for early dropouts, or for those adults who received a poor-quality education and subsequently ended up with little or no foundational skills, the evaluation recommends giving them a second chance to build their foundational and basic digital skills. Because of the special nature of these groups, this second chance must be provided with due diligence, particularly in building adults' skills to adjust, adapt, and fit into the changing nature of work. Beyond providing education that builds foundational skills, special educational programs offered should include customized pedagogies that consider the specific constraints these adults face and that link learning to employment opportunities. Such programs could thereby improve and increase individuals' chances of making it in the labor market. Governments must lead and coordinate the activities of all stakeholders involved in this process to ensure effective and efficient execution of any such strategies, to realize optimal returns for the targeted population and the region.

international best-practice partners to create a critical mass of highly skilled inventors and entrepreneurs in science, technology, and business. Other measures include investment in scholarship schemes that provide students with incentives to return home after completing their studies, and getting the diaspora more involved by tapping into its skills pool, especially for those trained in entrepreneurship and STEM-related fields. Finally, the region will have to address critical constraints, such as by funding start-ups in their early stage, and ensure sufficient investment in complementary assets (including available, reliable, and affordable electricity and broadband connectivity).

Human Capital and the Future of Work: What Is Different in Sub-Saharan Africa?

The Promise of Human Capital for the Future of Work in Sub-Saharan Africa

The quality and composition of human capital will play a more pivotal role in the future of work. Specific types of skills, such as soft skills, will gain in importance, as will the high-end skills needed to maintain a momentum of innovation. In addition to these imperatives, the region has a low level of human capital, making it even more important to make the best use of the current stock of skills and build stronger skills foundations going forward.

Relative to other regions, Sub-Saharan Africa has the fastest-growing labor force yet the lowest levels of human capital (figure 2.1) and the largest stock of

Figure 2.1 Sub-Saharan Africa's Poor Performance on the World Bank's Human Capital Index

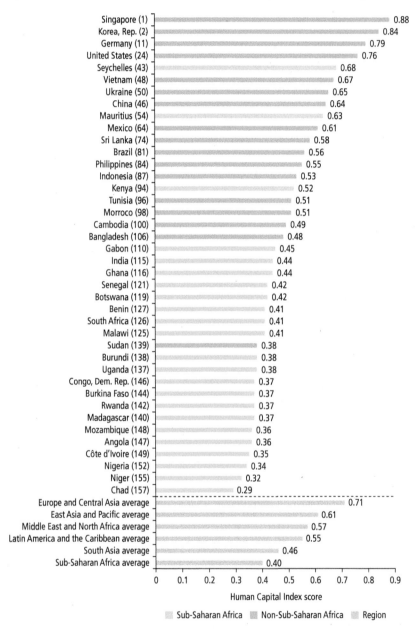

Source: Adapted from World Bank 2019.
Note: Numbers in parentheses signify Human Capital Index rankings.

ill-equipped adults. Between 2017 and 2030, the labor supply in the region will increase by an estimated 198 million, with 11 million young women and men expected to enter the labor market each year for the next decade. In the wake of rapid growth in the working-age population, the number of unemployed people increased by more than 1 million between 2017 and 2018 (ILO 2018). The region has fared most poorly on the World Bank's Human Capital Index, especially with respect to access to quality education, stunting, and maternal and child mortality (World Bank 2019)—all made worse by high fertility, which prevents sufficient income growth per person to escape poverty. This situation has partially contributed to an increase in the number of poor people, from 276 million in the 1990s to 413 million in 2015. The region's education system is in crisis, with 50 million children out of school, students learning very little in the early grades (figure 2.2), low secondary school completion rates, and weak learning outcomes: large proportions of second-grade pupils cannot read a single word of connected text (Arias, Evans, and Santos 2019). One in three children is stunted,[1] more than three times the rate in Latin America and the Caribbean. And maternal and under-five mortality rates in the region, although declining, are still the highest in the world.

Investment in human capital in the region remains a key priority for better preparing the labor force for the opportunities made possible by digital technologies. The growing potential of digital technologies as learning and health delivery tools means that many jobs, especially low-skill production and health service delivery jobs, may not necessarily require more advanced cognitive

Figure 2.2 Poor Learning Outcomes for Students in Many Sub-Saharan African Countries

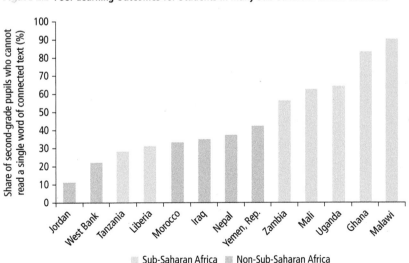

Source: Arias, Evans, and Santos 2019.

skills at the entry level. Rather, digital technologies (together with analog complements) can compensate for lower skills. Similarly, digital technologies may enable a more equitable and effective deployment of high-skilled workers and high-end services in health and education within countries, especially in countries experiencing acute shortages of personnel in the human capital sector.

Focus on Formal Jobs: Sub-Saharan Africa Cannot Afford to Ignore the Low-Skill Informal Sector

WDR 2019 recommends a focus on stable and formal jobs. In Sub-Saharan Africa, however, the informal sector remains large and persistent (figure 2.3). That sector consists of a large stock of people whose skills are often inadequate for modern formal jobs (figures 2.4 and 2.5). Most economies in the region have limited employment opportunities in the formal sector; for most of the labor force, working in the informal sector is the only pathway to generate

Figure 2.3 Wage-Earning Employment in Sub-Saharan Africa

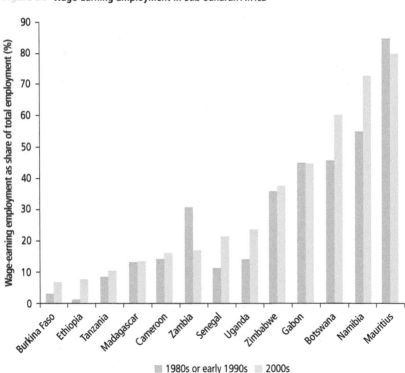

Source: Adams, Johansson de Silva, and Razmara 2013.

Figure 2.4 Self-Employment in Sub-Saharan Africa

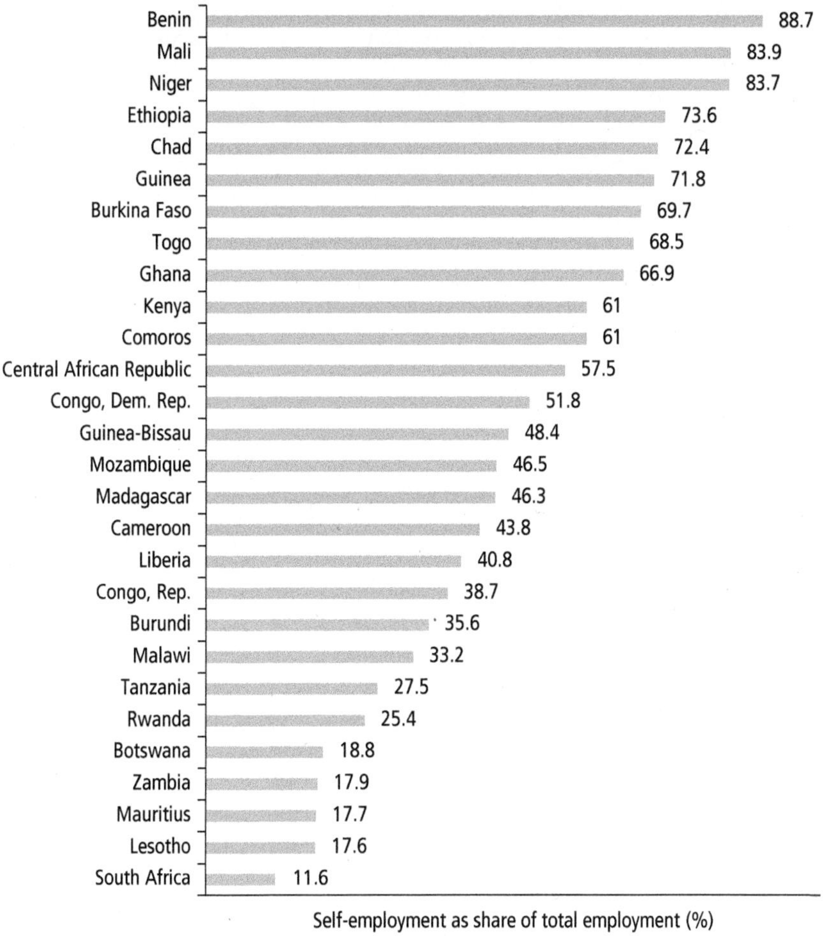

Country	Self-employment (%)
Benin	88.7
Mali	83.9
Niger	83.7
Ethiopia	73.6
Chad	72.4
Guinea	71.8
Burkina Faso	69.7
Togo	68.5
Ghana	66.9
Kenya	61
Comoros	61
Central African Republic	57.5
Congo, Dem. Rep.	51.8
Guinea-Bissau	48.4
Mozambique	46.5
Madagascar	46.3
Cameroon	43.8
Liberia	40.8
Congo, Rep.	38.7
Burundi	35.6
Malawi	33.2
Tanzania	27.5
Rwanda	25.4
Botswana	18.8
Zambia	17.9
Mauritius	17.7
Lesotho	17.6
South Africa	11.6

Self-employment as share of total employment (%)

Source: World Bank elaboration based on data from Adams, Johansson de Silva, and Razmara 2013.
Note: In this figure, self-employment excludes farm employment.

income, in the absence of opportunities for wage employment—as discussed in greater detail in chapter 3. Wage employment accounts for less than 20 percent of total employment in countries such as Burkina Faso, Cameroon, Ethiopia, Madagascar, Tanzania, and Zambia (Adams, Johansson de Silva, and Razmara 2013; Benjamin and Mbaye 2012; Böhme and Thiele 2012; Cassim et al. 2016; McKenzie and Sakho 2010).

Figure 2.5 Impact on Productivity of High Jobs Growth in Certain Sectors, Sub-Saharan Africa, 1960s–2015

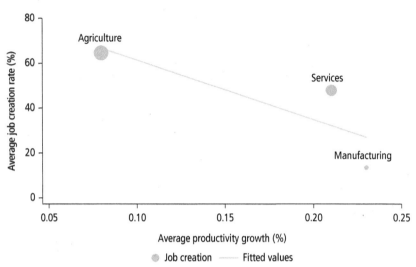

Source: World Bank calculations based on data from Mensah et al. 2018.
Note: Sectoral average job creation rate (1960s–2015) is plotted against sectoral productivity growth weighted by sectoral employment shares (as of 2015), indicated by the size of the circle.

Despite a steady increase in wage and salaried employment in the region (figure 2.3), the scope and size of self-employment will persist (figure 2.4). A short-term strategy to improve welfare in the sector must recognize this persistence and focus on skill formation strategies and policies using digital technologies to boost productivity.

Conditions are increasingly difficult for the creation of formal jobs in high-productivity sectors such as manufacturing and tradable services. Nontradable services often associated with high levels of informality, low-paid jobs, and low-skilled and low-productivity tasks have grown relatively rapidly, absorbing surplus labor released from the agriculture sector, at the expense of tradable services and manufacturing. This trend will persist.[2] Using digital technologies to improve the productivity of the massive workforce absorbed in these sectors should be given priority (box 2.4).

The highest annual job creation in the region is in agriculture and non-tradable services, which are mostly informal with low productivity growth. Although currently declining, nearly one-half of annual job creation in the region continues to take place in agriculture, the sector with the lowest productivity growth since the 1960s. In the services sector, the lowest average annual job creation rate is in business services (made up of financial, insurance, real

Pathways to Developing Skills in the Informal Sector

In Sub-Saharan Africa, the skills level in the informal sector remains low (figure B2.4.1), and the most frequent form of skills training in the informal sector is traditional apprenticeships (figure B2.4.2), concentrated in Western and Central Africa. An estimated 70 percent of urban informal sector workers have been trained through the traditional apprenticeship system. In Tanzania, 45 percent of informal sector workers acquired skills through informal apprenticeship training. In this setup, the master craftsperson commits to the parents or youth and provides training for a specified period in exchange for small fees or the apprentice's labor. Informal apprenticeship training is usually flexible and affordable and has lower entry standards—few participants have passed beyond lower-secondary education, and most have not completed primary education. In addition to these factors, the training's direct connection with future employment makes it an attractive source of skills (Adams, Johansson de Silva, and Razmara 2013).

Figure B2.4.1 **Skill Levels in Selected Sub-Saharan African Countries, by Workforce Sector**

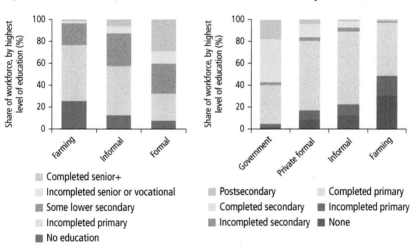

■ Completed senior+
  Incompleted senior or vocational   ■ Postsecondary   Completed primary
■ Some lower secondary   Completed secondary   ■ Incompleted primary
  Incompleted primary   ■ Incompleted secondary   ■ None
■ No education

Sources: Adams, Johansson de Silva, and Razmara 2013.

(continued next page)

Box 2.4 (continued)

Figure B2.4.2 **Sources of Skills Training in Tanzania's Informal Sector, 2006**

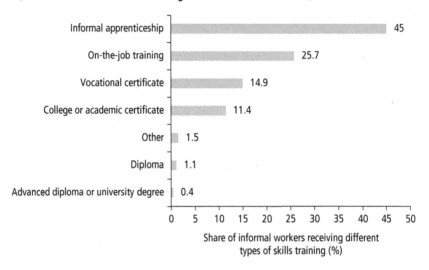

Source: World Bank elaboration based on data from Adams, Johansson de Silva, and Razmara 2013.

estate, and other business services) rather than in the more informal trade (wholesale and retail) services. The skilled labor– and capital-intensive nature of business services makes it difficult for the sector to absorb labor released from other sectors. Annual average employment creation in the manufacturing sector remains relatively small compared with the other two sectors, despite its relatively higher productivity growth (figure 2.5) (Mensah et al. 2018).

Further to this point and more generally, the literature seems to agree that the industrialization-led growth model faces more problems today than it did in the past. Starting from 1990, the manufacturing sector, previously very important for growth at early stages of development, has become a more difficult road to growth. Technological demands of the sector today have made it more capital and skill intensive, which has reduced the sector's scope of labor absorption and therefore means that "late industrializers and countries at the intermediate level of development may no longer benefit from manufacturing the same way as early industrializers did" (Szirmai and Verspagen 2015, 58; see also Fagerberg and Verspagen 2002). And, although the hike in labor costs in China could open offshoring opportunities for economies in Sub-Saharan Africa, the region could still miss out—on the one hand, because it lacks complementary foundational infrastructure, a good working environment, and efficient institutions, and, on

the other hand, because of the success of other emerging Southeast Asian economies as alternative investment destinations (Cadot et al. 2016; Gelb, Meyer,
and Ramachandran 2013; Rodrik 2016).

Tertiary Education: The Engine of Future Inventors and Entrepreneurs

To be competitive in a fast-changing world, countries must keep up with the
pace of innovation. For other regions of the world, tertiary education is the
driver of innovation, but Sub-Saharan Africa has not sufficiently invested in
tertiary education. No long-term sustainable innovation is possible without
correcting this course. At a time when other parts of the world are rethinking
their tertiary education systems, Sub-Saharan Africa must move away from its
earliest institutions of higher education, which focused disproportionately on
teaching and much less on research and entrepreneurship.

Sub-Saharan Africa has very low enrollment in tertiary education. Although
enrollment has grown in recent years, the pace of growth is not enough to catch
up with the rest of the world, given that the region has historically lagged global
experience (figure 2.6). The average gross enrollment rate in tertiary education
in the region is 10.0 percent—10.4 percent for men and 8.8 percent for women.
For more than one-third of the countries in the region, however, the average
gross enrollment rate in tertiary education is only 5.0 percent. In countries

Figure 2.6 Share of Population with Completed Tertiary Education, Sub-Saharan Africa versus Other Regions

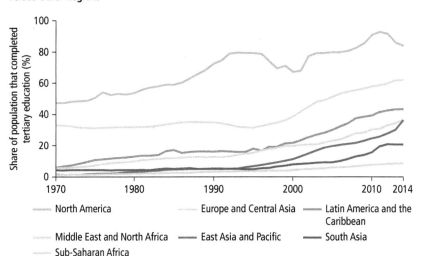

Source: Roser and Ortiz-Ospina 2020.

such as Malawi and Niger, average gross enrollment in tertiary education is 2.0 percent, in contrast to an average of 30.0 percent and higher in Botswana and Mauritius (Arias, Evans, and Santos 2019).

In addition to low gross enrollment in tertiary education, Sub-Saharan Africa has even lower enrollment of students in STEM fields. On average, about 19 percent of students in tertiary education are enrolled in STEM-related programs (figure 2.7). The share of tertiary students enrolled in STEM-related programs is only about 16 percent in Benin, 21 percent in Mali, 23 percent in The Gambia and Niger, and below 25 percent in Ghana despite that country's years of effort to increase enrollment in STEM-related programs. Currently in low supply, STEM skills are a critical part of the region's pursuit of innovation and knowledge production to exploit opportunities offered by digitization for creating conditions for job creation and expansion.

Technology creates jobs, but to do so it requires quality education, particularly in STEM fields. And it requires investment in specialized high-end skilled inventors to design technologies that create conditions for jobs. At the moment, the region has neither. With the exception of South Africa, currently the region's technological hub and home to world-class academic and research institutions that attract young talent from across the region, all other countries rank low in terms of the quality of university education, innovation performance, and knowledge production. South Africa consistently has 6 of

Figure 2.7 Tertiary Education Enrollment in Sub-Saharan Africa, by Field

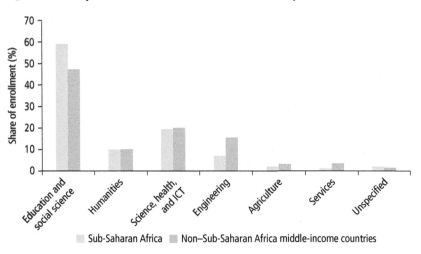

Source: Arias, Evans, and Santos 2019.
Note: ICT = information and communication technology.

the region's top-10 universities, according to the Times Higher Education and QS rankings.[3] In addition, in 2017, South Africa ranked as the most innovative country in Africa, in the 57th position globally (Cornell University, INSEAD, and WIPO 2017). Of the total number of patents granted to countries in the region (133,534) between 1990 and 2017, South Africa recorded the highest number (124,581) and share (93.3 percent).[4] Most countries in the region spend on average less than 1 percent of their gross domestic product on research and development (R&D); despite spending less than 1 percent, South Africa still spends more on R&D than any other country in the region.

In order to increase the production of quality STEM graduates and professionals over the medium and long term, the region will have to build poles of excellence to promote regional collaboration among universities and international best-practice partners (box 2.5). The World Bank in collaboration with West and Central African countries in 2014 launched the African Center of

BOX 2.5

Canadian Networks of Centres of Excellence: Success and Lessons for Sub-Saharan Africa

Canada has one of the world's most successful and long-standing experiences with centers of excellence. Prior to the 1989 launch of Canada's Networks of Centres of Excellence (NCEs) model, the nature of most academic research in the country was curiosity-driven basic research. Researchers had no requirement to demonstrate the social or economic benefits of their research for Canada before securing research grants. And there was little consideration for the creation of centers of critical mass. Canada realized that, despite its science and technology policy and its strategic research grants policy to promote knowledge production, the "vast majority of academic research groups in Canada were relatively small, without critical mass and formal structures for knowledge translation and technology transfer" (Halliwell 2012, 10). Creating a critical mass of experts in areas of importance to Canada became a national goal, namely, to enhance and support a few large-scale research initiatives that would put Canada on the world research map. This goal led the country to come up with the new NCE initiative.

NCEs are large-scale, academically led virtual research networks. They bring together partners from academia, industry, government, and not-for-profit organizations distributed across the country. Their goal is to collaborate on common research problems to generate research outcomes that socially and economically benefit the country, according to the priorities laid down in the country's science and technology policy that frames the operations of the NCEs. Funded NCEs are selected through a competitive process according to five criteria—the excellence of the research program, the development of highly qualified personnel, networking and partnerships,

(continued next page)

knowledge and technology exchange, and exploitation, governance, and management of the network. The NCEs are monitored and evaluated annually. Since 2007, NCEs receive funding for a five-year period, with the possibility of renewing for up to two further cycles of five years.

Evaluations of the program's impact on the country's research system in 2002, 2007, and 2008 reveal that the program has been transformative. It has enabled institutions in the country to attract and retain world-class researchers who have contributed significantly to the country's research excellence. NCE researchers have published each year an average of over 4,000 articles in peer-reviewed journals each year. The program has also helped create groups of critical mass in areas of strategic importance to Canada—such as in prion science and others. By helping build partnerships between academia and industry, the program has yielded tangible outcomes such as patents and spin-off companies. NCEs have applied for or been granted a reported 100 to 130 patents. Between 2003 and 2011, NCE-related research led to the formation of 50 spin-off companies, creating new jobs and other market opportunities for the country. The program has helped foster strong international collaborations and partnerships: on average about 400 non-Canadian organizational entities participate each year in the NCEs.

Excellence (ACE) initiative. Through an open, rigorous, transparent, and merit-based assessment procedure, the ACE initiative selects and invests in "Centers of Excellence" at selected well-performing universities, in disciplines related to STEM, agriculture, and health. The ACE initiative seeks to increase the quality and quantity of STEM graduates by establishing high-quality specialized, well-resourced centers in selected universities to train students in STEM-related fields—such as applied mathematics in Benin, information and communication technology (ICT) in Cameroon, statistics in Côte d'Ivoire, and mathematics, informatics, and ICT in Senegal—in order to increase knowledge production that will create knowledge-based competitive advantages. By 2018, about 8,100 students had been enrolled under the ACE project; of those students, 2,025 were female, 6,500 were master's students, and 1,600 were PhD students. The Association of African Universities has been very effective in coordinating and checking the quality of the various ACEs.

Another initiative launched in the region to increase the production of qualified professionals in STEM-related programs is the Partnership for Skills in Applied Sciences, Engineering and Technology (PASET). Launched in 2013 with the World Bank, and currently led by five countries in the region (Ethiopia, Kenya, Côte d'Ivoire, Rwanda, and Senegal), PASET recognizes that the region does not produce enough skilled individuals in STEM fields. The region currently contributes 1.1 percent of the global share of scientific researchers. By bringing together governments, universities offering science, engineering, and technology disciplines, the private sector, donors, and other partners and sharing best practices from Brazil, China, India, the Republic of Korea, and Japan through faculty and student exchanges, PASET seeks to strengthen the region's scientific and technological capacity. It does so by building skills in research, innovation, and technology to create a critical mass of highly skilled science and technology professionals who can exploit the opportunities of technology to create conditions for job creation that will boost growth and development. About 26 countries in the region have participated in PASET activities so far, and it is hoped that more countries will join in the coming years.[5]

From Digital Technologies to Jobs through Adequate Human Capital

In light of the diagnostics in this chapter's earlier section "Human Capital and the Future of Work: What Is Different in Africa," human capital will play a prominent role going forward in determining the options available to many countries in Sub-Saharan Africa. Digital technologies can be leveraged to increase the productivity of the region's stock of low-skilled labor in their current jobs and to create new and more-productive jobs adapted to the current stock of skills. Additionally, digital technologies can offer opportunities to speed up the human capital acquisition process across health and education services. The overarching human capital prerequisites for all these options are high-skilled inventors (to create the various appropriate digital technologies needed) and entrepreneurs (to commercialize the innovations and thereby create many more jobs) (figure 2.8). Training and enabling these inventors and entrepreneurs must thus be a first-order priority for all countries in the region.

Digital Technologies, Human Capital, and the Productivity of the Low-Skill Labor Force

Adequate digital technologies can increase the productivity of low-skill adults in their current occupations. Some of these workers may require complementary training (for example, adult and digital literacy), which could also be delivered better through digital technologies (box 2.6). Coming up with adequate, context-specific solutions is paramount.

In Ghana and other countries in the region, companies like Farmerline leverage digital technologies to boost the productivity of farmers. Established in 2013, Farmerline transforms farmers into successful entrepreneurs by increasing their productivity through improved access to information, inputs, and resources. It provides an online platform that connects and communicates with small-scale farmers in their native languages through innovative mobile technology. About 200,000 farmers across 11 countries have spent more than 300,000 minutes on

Figure 2.8 Prerequisites for Helping Sub-Saharan Africa Reap the Benefits of Digital Technologies

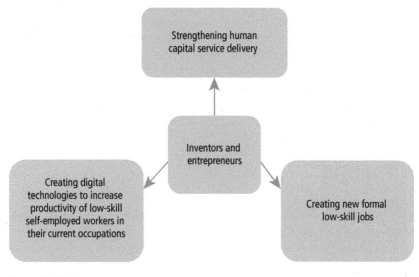

Source: World Bank.

BOX 2.6

Adult Literacy Programs, Skills, and Employment: What the Evidence Shows

Adult learning and education (ALE) programs have until now been used as a route to fill the adult skills gap in many developing countries and to boost the productivity and employability of unskilled adults. About 61 percent of working-age adults in Sub-Saharan Africa are low skilled, which has a negative impact on career prospects, job quality, and productivity growth. Adult workers with low skills tend to have fewer job opportunities and opportunities to improve their skills and, when they have jobs, they contribute less to aggregate productivity growth (Saane and Baker 2018). The reported growth in participation in ALE in the region is welcome news, because it can provide out-of-school adults, early dropouts, adults with no access to education, and adults who received poor-quality education a second chance to benefit from basic and specialized education programs, to adjust and adapt to the changing nature of work.

Evidence shows, however, that ALE programs have had only minimal impacts on improving business knowledge and the productivity of beneficiaries, and no impact on massive employment creation. In Peru, a female adult entrepreneurship program aimed

(continued next page)

at training female entrepreneurs was hugely successful in improving the business skills of participants, but the program had no significant impact on increasing employment among program participants (UIL 2017; World Bank 2019). In Brazil, ALE programs significantly increased the earnings of participants. The program also increased the probability of being employed but had no effect on actual employment because jobs may not have existed to absorb the program participants even with their improved skills (Soares, Rocha, and Ponczek 2011). In the Dominican Republic, a youth and employment program rolled out in the country improved noncognitive skills and job formality for beneficiaries of the program but did not increase employment. In Turkey, a vocational training program had no significant impact on overall employment. And, although the program improved employment quality, this effect was short-lived.

the platform learning best agricultural practices (on weather, market prices, and inputs). The platform also collects information for buyers, governments, and other partners. Last year, the company launched its new product, CocoaLink Services, a free mobile app that enables smartphone-empowered farmers to acquire actionable knowledge on how to run a profitable agribusiness and succeed as entrepreneurs, while making agriculture an attractive, entrepreneurial, and profit-making profession for youth in the region (World Bank 2019).[6]

In Kenya, the World Bank Group and the Korean World Bank Facility, together with other development partners, are investing in mentoring and providing financial support to create an innovation ecosystem of new start-ups and entrepreneurs and innovators in agritech. The aim is to connect a million Kenyan farmers to disruptive agricultural digital technologies and scale up the impact of these digital technologies to boost the productivity, market links, and financial inclusion of smallholders and women farmers. The program also aims to increase the scale and speed of agricultural transformation in Kenya.[7] Digi Cow, a digital technology from Kenyan Farmingtech Solutions Ltd., provides a mobile-based service delivery platform that links small livestock owners to veterinary and artificial insemination services, feed suppliers, and business enterprises. It has resulted in a significant increase in milk productivity in the country. Other digital technologies, such as Digital Green, Farmers Pride, Precision Agriculture for Development, and SunCulture, provide large numbers of smallholder farmers with agricultural extension advisory services, personalized agricultural advice through video-enabled approaches and mobile phones, and smart irrigation systems to increase crop productivity. In addition, digital technologies such as M-Shamba, Tru Trade Africa, Tulaa, ACRE Africa, Agri-Wallet, and Arifu help to address the market failure problems that smallholder farmers face, by providing them with links to markets and fair prices for their produce, loans and finance, and index insurance to safeguard farmers from weather shocks.[8]

The level of skills required to use many types of digital technologies may be low, and potential users and beneficiaries often find ways to adapt and use the technologies once they deem those technologies useful. The potential benefits or advantages that consumers receive from adopting digital technologies could serve as drivers of adoption and diffusion. Figure 2.9 illustrates that, despite having low education levels and receiving no structured skill upgrading, a large share of adults (ages 15+) in Sub-Saharan Africa use mobile phones and the internet to access their financial accounts.

Digital Technologies for New and More-Productive Low-Skill Jobs

Digital technologies can help generate new formal private sector jobs adapted to the current stock of skills. This pathway is similar to the generation of new activities observed in the rest of the world, especially in developed countries. It too will require a massive drive to invest and create a critical mass of potential

Figure 2.9 Use of Mobile Phone and Internet to Access Financial Accounts

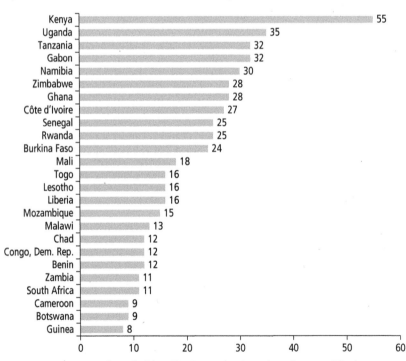

Share of adults with primary education or less who use mobile phones or the internet to access accounts, ages 15+ (%)

Source: World Bank elaboration based on 2017 data from the Global Findex (Financial Inclusion) database, https://datacatalog.worldbank.org/dataset/global-financial-inclusion-global-findex-database.

digital entrepreneurs and to address critical constraints such as the funding of start-ups at their early stages.

Innovation in digital technologies has often been based on a complex platform allowing, for example, millions to make a living by knowing only how to drive a car and follow instructions on the screen or how to accept a booking request online and then open their doors to host guests for a fee (for example, Uber, Airbnb, and similar platforms). Launched in Sub-Saharan Africa in 2013, the San Francisco–based Uber has created thousands of driver jobs (12,000 in South Africa, 7,000 in Nigeria, 5,000 in Kenya, 3,000 in Ghana, and 1,000 in Tanzania and Uganda) and has served about 1.8 million riders in the region. Ride-sharing companies like Taxify (now rebranded as Bolt) have joined the ride-sharing market to compete with Uber in the region by charging lower commissions to the drivers (15 percent compared with Uber's 25 percent commission) (*Quartz Africa* 2017). In South Africa, Airbnb reported generating an estimated US$678 million for the South African economy, creating 22,000 jobs and an estimated US$260 million for hosts across the country (African News Agency 2018). In Nigeria, e-commerce leader Jumia employs about 3,000 workers across the region, and 100,000 more workers who help customers make orders (Ng'weno and Porteus 2018). Despite the short-term nature of some of these jobs, digital technologies help create jobs for a significant share of low-skilled workers in the region, helping them to save and later use those savings to start their own firms—mostly formal firms. A typical example of this phenomenon is when MTN Ghana introduced credit transfer technology that allowed people to buy a SIM card, load it with money (credit), and sell the credits in smaller units to customers. Over time, many credit sellers were able to save and transform their businesses into larger, formal telecommunication support businesses, sometimes even selling mobile phones.

Digital Technologies, Human Capital Formation, and Jobs in the Health and Education Sectors

Health workers play an all-important role in the provision and delivery of health services. The global distribution of health workers is, however, unequal between and within countries. Fewer health workers are found in poorer countries and areas where health needs are most severe. Their numbers remain insufficient to meet the health needs of Sub-Saharan Africa, which has only 2 percent of the world's doctors (Bastos de Morais 2017). For instance, in Malawi, a country that has consistently recorded one of the worst ratios of health workers to population, the average number of physicians for 100,000 people is 2.2; and about 50 percent of the country's nursing posts are unfilled. Most countries in the region do not have the human resources to provide quality health care. More often than not, lower-level staff members take on the responsibility of performing high-skill functions. Many factors are cited as having contributed to this problem, including but not limited to low pay and poor staff benefits for government health workers, poaching of government health workers to work in private health facilities, and migration of health workers to countries where the payoff for their services is comparably higher (Liese and Dussault 2004; WHO 2006).

Digital technologies can help make up for the shortage of health care workers by increasing the efficiency and productivity of health care staff. Given the low supply of health care workers and that many people in the region must travel a long distance to receive health care, digital technologies will have more of an enabling and gap-filling effect than a disruptive one. In most cases, digital technologies will not significantly increase employment in the health sector but will affect the execution of jobs in the sector and help increase the efficiency and productivity of employed health staff. Remote diagnostics and telemedicine have been estimated to be able to address 80 percent of health issues of patients in rural parts of the region, where most understaffed health posts are found (Manyika et al. 2013). Digital technologies can also help centralize and synchronize the public and private health systems through proper patient electronic record keeping, thereby making patient admissions and treatment possible with a smaller workforce. Health care wastage could also be reduced. For instance, with access to proper patient electronic records, the use and scale-up of mobile health services could allow the few health practitioners in the region to work with clients from remote locations, review clients' medical histories, and write prescriptions.

In Ghana, the Novartis Foundation and its partners have developed a telemedicine system to expand the reach of medical expertise to deprived communities through the use of digital technologies. Started as a pilot project in 2011 in one district covering 30 communities of about 35,000 people, the telemedicine system was selected by the Ghana Health Service for implementation across the nation because of the project's success. The system uses digital technologies to connect community health workers (with relatively less knowledge, experience, and expertise) to medical specialists via 24-hour teleconsultation centers. The medical specialists (doctors, nurses, and midwives) in the teleconsultation centers "provide coaching services to the community health workers and advise on the treatment of their patients, helping them manage emergency cases that are beyond their capacity and avoiding unnecessary referrals, reducing transport times and cost while improving the quality of health care."[9]

In South Africa, the messaging platforms MomConnect and NurseConnect, part of an initiative of the South African National Department of Health, support and deliver better maternal and child health care through the use of cell phone–based technologies. All pregnant women can voluntarily register electronically in the public health system at a very early stage of pregnancy to receive targeted health promotion messages that will improve their health and that of their children. The platform also allows pregnant women to provide feedback on the quality of services received. NurseConnect, an extension of

MomConnect, supports nurses and midwives in their daily work by allowing them access to targeted support messages, in-depth information, and advice on maternal and child health.[10] About 466,000 users have reportedly adopted the MomConnect service, and 19,524 had registered to use NurseConnect by 2017 (Bastos de Morais 2017).

In Uganda, the mTrac digital technology initiated by the government is being used to digitize the transfer of Health Management Information System data via mobile phones. The mTrac digital technology tracks the stock of medicine across the country, disease outbreaks, and health care delivery challenges, while empowering district health teams by providing timely information for action.[11] About 27,000 government health workers in Uganda use mTrac (Bastos de Morais 2017).

Digital technologies have the potential to reinforce learning, increase access to education, offer access to high-quality materials where teachers lack the needed skills, and deliver high-quality education and learning outcomes in the region. In any region, a sufficient supply and quality of teaching staff at all levels of education are fundamental for human capital development. Having an over-crowded class or lecture room limits a teacher's ability to provide proper and equal attention to all students. Much worse are overcrowded, poorly resourced class or lecture rooms run by less qualified teaching staff. Class size is an impor-tant determinant of student performance. A high pupil-to-teacher ratio will harm not only children's test scores in the short run but also their long-run human capital formation (Schanzenbach 2014). For these reasons, the number and quality of teaching staff should be two of the most important areas for concern when designing and implementing policies to increase access to qual-ity education. Unfortunately, many countries in Sub-Saharan Africa have over-crowded classrooms—although some countries have lower class sizes. At the tertiary level the pupil-to-teacher ratio is 52:1 in Cameroon, 43:1 in Mauritania, 33:1 in Togo and Kenya, but only 9:1 in Cabo Verde. At the primary education level, the pupil-to-teacher ratio is 58:1 in Rwanda, 52:1 in Mozambique, 50:1 in Angola and Burundi, but only 14:1 in Seychelles.[12]

As in the health sector, digital technologies have the potential to be an enabler rather than a disrupter in education, creating new jobs in the sector. The impact on overall employment in the sector is likely to be marginal, however, and pupil-to-teacher ratios are likely to remain unchanged for at least the next few years. Instead, digital technologies are expected to have significant effects on the effi-ciency of the delivery of teaching and learning. In many ways, digital technolo-gies provide a way for learning models to become increasingly personalized. It is expected that adaptive learning software will increasingly replace textbooks and other learning materials in the classroom. The future of schooling will be an education system that trains students to study and learn on their own with computer-assisted programs that adapt to their needs. The use of digital tech-nologies to teach will create agency in the classroom: students will assume more responsibility for their own learning, which will improve and increase their motivation to learn. Digital technologies will offer access to high-quality materials when students need to develop skills that their teachers lack or do not teach. In Uruguay, evidence shows that videoconferencing with English speakers from the Philippines helped improve learning among first-graders. In Mumbai, India, fourth-graders are reported to have benefited from the Khan Academy's independent learning approach to math teaching (World Bank 2016).

Despite the benefits of digital technologies, using them effectively in education will still require that teachers play an important role, namely, as part of a technology-saturated teacher workforce (Perera and Aboal 2019). Giving teachers appropriate skills training on how to use digital technologies in the delivery of teaching, creating computer-assisted learning platforms for teachers and students, and addressing logistical and infrastructure constraints will allow teachers to assist students in overcrowded and poorly resourced classrooms with few textbooks—through the use of e-books, affordable tablets, and computerized learning platforms for learning in the classroom and at home. But these innovations can reach the classrooms across Sub-Saharan Africa only if governments, the private sector, nongovernmental organizations, parents, and other stakeholders work together to pool resources (Manyika et al. 2013).

A recent study in Uruguay examined the impact of the Mathematics Adaptive Platform (Plataforma Adaptativa de Matemática, or PAM), a digital technology learning tool, on students' performance by using mathematics test scores for beneficiary primary school students of the country's One Laptop per Child program. The PAM platform offers a variety of teaching and learning activities that give personalized assistance to each student and teacher user by adapting to each user's level of knowledge and skill. Students who use the platform get immediate feedback on completed exercises and are provided with the solutions to the exercises they get wrong. The results show a positive and significant impact of PAM on students' math test scores. The results also show that, with higher use of PAM in the class, student gains on math test scores are higher, suggesting the crucial role of teachers and group learning strategies (matching students with a similar skill level to work together) in ensuring the success of the program (Perera and Aboal 2019). Finland, one of the best-performing countries in educational testing and also one of the most connected, uses very little technology in the classroom but instead invests in improving the quality of teachers. To this end, the proposal for Sub-Saharan Africa is that technology be used to closely guide teaching, only as a second-best option to improve learning outcomes at a modest cost where teacher training is unlikely to improve quickly (World Bank 2016).

In Sub-Saharan Africa, companies such as Eneza Education in Kenya, Obani in South Africa, the social enterprise Ubongo in Tanzania, and Togo's OkpaBac all use digital platforms to promote the development of education infrastructure. Aside from anecdotal reports of the success of these digital plat-forms in improving the educational performance of beneficiary students, there is no proper evidence of their comparative effectiveness in generating learning and the other social skills that schooling is meant to provide (World Bank 2016).

Overall, digital technology is an enabler with the potential to positively and significantly transform and revolutionize the region's health care and edu-cational systems by addressing the acute shortage of health and educational human resources. Digital technology also affects the nature of work for health and educational workers in the region, making them more efficient and pro-ductive. Such improvements are possible only with the right complementary incentives and resources in place (box 2.7).

BOX 2.7

Unlocking Technological Entrepreneurship in Sub-Saharan Africa: The Rise of Tech Startups, Tech Hubs, and Innovation Ecosystem

The number of technology hubs in Sub-Saharan Africa has grown by over 50 percent, from 314 in 2016. The technology investment ecosystem across the region is also attracting more capital and expertise. Not only has the volume of funding raised by tech start-ups across the continent soared, but also new ecosystem cities, such as Abidjan in Côte d'Ivoire and Accra in Ghana, have joined traditional frontrunner tech hub and ecosystem cities such as Cape Town in South Africa, Lagos in Nigeria, and Nairobi in Kenya as internationally attractive technology centers (Bayen 2018). Top-tier countries remain the premier tech investment destinations on the continent in 2019 (map B2.7.1). Nigeria surpassed South Africa to emerge as a premier investment desti-nation with 85 active tech hubs in 2019, compared with 80 in South Africa (Guiliani and Ajadi 2019). Overall, the region's tech start-ups attracted about US$334.5 million in tech investment in 2018 (Disrupt Africa 2018).

A host of other countries in the region also show signs of joining and becoming internationally attractive tech centers. Kigali in Rwanda is one such city: the Kigali Innovation City is gradually positioning itself as an attractive tech investment destina-tion with the government's US$1.9 billion digitization project that aims to build a vibrant tech ecosystem of technology clusters of universities and industries. Further to these aims, the country is hosting major regional tech events such as the African Tech Summit in 2020. Rwanda has also introduced entrepreneurship in its secondary school teaching curriculum, which will better prepare its youth to improve their livelihoods through work while addressing the country's youth unemployment problems.[a] Other countries, such as Zambia and Zimbabwe, have recorded sizable growth in active tech hubs over the years, from 2 to 6 in Zambia and from 6 to 13 in Zimbabwe over the period 2016–18 (map B2.7.1). And countries where tech hubs were previously

(continued next page)

Box 2.7 (continued)

nonexistent (Cabo Verde, Chad, Djibouti, Eswatini, and Mauritania) can boast at least one active tech hub. With increasing government support, with the region's tech ecosystem showing signs of maturity (leading tech hubs in the region have an average half a decade of activity), and with growing synergy between investors, industry, and universities, the future looks promising for the region's technology ecosystem. This improvement is timely, but the region needs to speed up its connectivity to take full advantage of digital technologies (figure 2.10).

Map B2.7.1 Growth of Africa's Tech Hubs Landscape, 2019

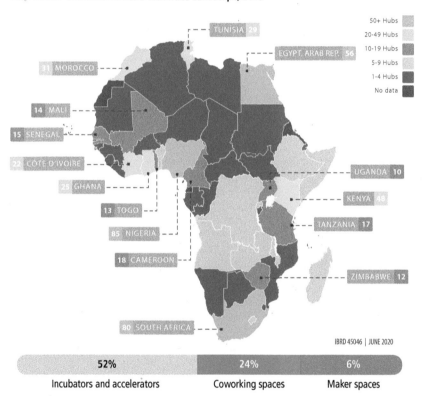

Source: Guiliani and Ajadi 2019. © GSMA and Briter Bridges. Reproduced with permission from GSMA and Briter Bridges; further permission required for reuse.
Note: Numbers in circles show the number of tech hubs in each country. Percentages show the share of tech hubs that are incubators and accelarators, share coworking spaces, or maker spaces. Incubators focus on and specialize in growing new and early-stage tech business. Accelerators focus on scaling up tech businesses by connecting start-ups with mentors, guidance, resources, and funding.

a. See the Innovations for Poverty Action's overview of teacher training and entrepreneurship in Rwanda at https://www.poverty-action.org/study/teacherz-training-and-entrepreneurship-education-evidence -curriculum-reform-rwanda.

Figure 2.10 Shares of Individuals Using the Internet in Sub-Saharan Africa

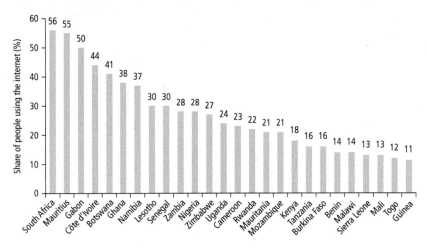

Source: World Bank elaboration based on 2017 data from the ITU (International Telecommunication Union) database.

The Importance of Grassroots and Bottom-Up Innovation

In Sub-Saharan Africa, governments have mostly relied on the top-down model to power innovation and technological development in the region, by creating the enabling business environment, investing in R&D, and providing the needed analog complements. Although the approach has yielded some success, notable adaptive innovations and inventions have emanated from the bottom-up model, often enabled by development partners and implemented by entrepreneurs or the private sector operating in an entrepreneurial mode. Risk and failure are accepted parts of the model (figure 2.11). Countries in Sub-Saharan Africa need to embrace a bottom-up approach to unlock the power of technological entrepreneurship. The region has often neglected bottom-up initiatives, yet they are a key component of success.

The region is growing more connected, and digital development is accelerating. As of 2013, 13 percent of the population in the region used the internet, compared with 36 percent globally (Hjort and Poulsen 2019). By 2018, the share of the population using the internet in Sub-Saharan Africa had reached almost 30 percent—or 24 percent in terms of unique users, counting only one user for those with multiple connections (Bayen 2018). This growth presents a unique opportunity to explore the ability of the region's increasing digitization to create conditions for new jobs. Creating those conditions will require critical interventions, starting with a coherent, pragmatic national ICT strategy; building infrastructure that supports the digital economy; and, most important,

Figure 2.11 Top-Down and Bottom-Up Framework for Sub-Saharan Africa's Innovation Ecosystem

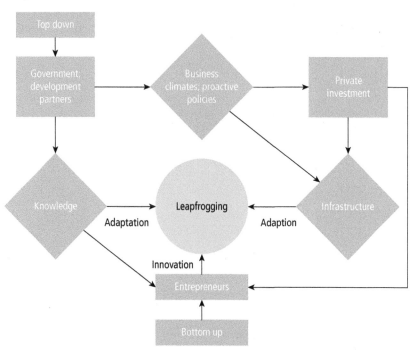

Source: World Bank 2017.

producing a large pool of digital entrepreneurs and high-skilled youth with a strong ICT skills base. Presently, countries in the region rank low in ICT-related human capital and in an ICT skills base, primarily as a result of low quality and quantity of human capital at the tertiary education level in STEM-related programs. It will take a workforce of qualified high-end skilled professionals in science, technology, and business to make this happen. Developing this workforce depends on factors such as the quality and quantity of math, science, and business education and enrollment rates in these fields at the tertiary level (Manyika et al. 2013).

In line with this priority, a study examined the readiness of countries in the region to exploit the opportunities offered by the internet (Internet Foundation Index-i5F; see Manyika et al. 2013) using five pillars, namely, national ICT strategy, business environment, infrastructure, financial capital, and ICT skills base. The study finds that most countries in the region lack the capacity of an ICT skills base ready to use and reap the benefits of the internet. All countries in the region except South Africa scored below 30 percent on their ICT skills base readiness to leverage the opportunities of the internet. The score for the ICT skills base variable was the lowest among all the variables used in constructing the index (figure 2.12) (Manyika et al. 2013). More recent data from the International Telecommunication Union (ITU) and the World Economic Forum[13] further confirm this low skills base. The ITU ICT Development Index ranks most countries in the region at the bottom of the global ICT skills base distribution. In the rankings of 176 countries, Sub-Saharan African countries occupy positions 153 through 176 (except position 163, occupied by Haiti).[14] A combination of factors has contributed to the region's low scores on its ICT skills base, but more important are the low quality and quantity of math and science education, low tertiary enrollment in these fields, and inadequate availability of scientists and engineers.

The analysis in table 2.1 shows a positive and significant correlation between expenditures on R&D, skills (proxied by enrollment in higher levels of education), knowledge production (proxied by patents), employment, and job creation. Of particular interest is the knowledge production generated by residents of countries in the region (resident patents) that is used in this analysis. The results show a strong positive correlation between R&D investment and knowledge production (0.88), and between skills and knowledge production (0.69 for

Figure 2.12 **ICT Readiness Determined by Five Key Variables, Selected Countries in Sub-Saharan Africa**

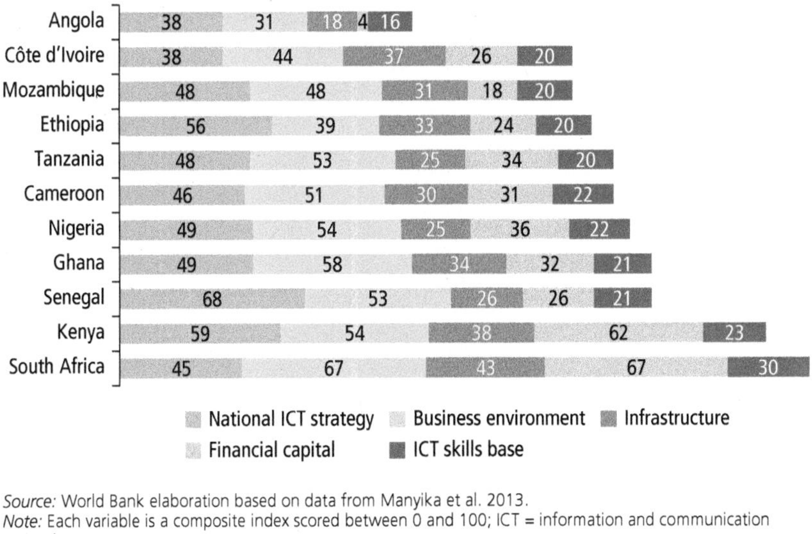

Source: World Bank elaboration based on data from Manyika et al. 2013.
Note: Each variable is a composite index scored between 0 and 100; ICT = information and communication technology.

Table 2.1 **Investment in Skills, Knowledge Production, and Job Creation in Sub-Saharan Africa**

	Patent	R&D
Patent	1.00	0.88***
R&D	0.88***	1.00
Secondary school enrollment	0.69***	0.51***
Tertiary school enrollment	0.44***	0.42***
Job creation		
Services	0.19*	0.48***
Manufacturing	−0.05	0.25*
Mining, utilities, and construction	0.47***	0.55***
Employment		
Services	0.41***	0.76***
Manufacturing	0.48***	0.72***
Mining, utilities, and construction	0.83***	0.80***

Sources: World Bank calculations based on data from World Intellectual Property Organization, World Bank World Development Indicators, Penn World Table 9.0 database, and Mensah and Szirmai 2018.

Note: Job creation by sector: $JC_{gt} = \Sigma_{g \in J} EW_{gt} \left(\Delta PE_{gt} / \overline{I}_{gt} \right)$; where JC_{gt} is the job creation effect of sector g belonging to economy J in year t, ΔPE_{gt} is the sum of positive employment changes in an expanding sector over time, $\overline{I}_{gt}$ is the sector's average employment over time and is given by $\overline{I}_{gt} = 0.5 \, (I_{gt} + I_{g0})$, and EW_{gt} is the sector employment weight and is given by the average employment of sector g divided by the average employment of the economy (Bartelsman 2013; Haltiwanger, Scarpetta, and Schweiger 2014). R&D = research and development.

Significance level: *** = 1 percent, ** = 5 percent, * = 10 percent.

secondary education and 0.44 for tertiary). Knowledge production is positively and significantly associated with job creation in services (0.19) and in mining, utilities, and construction (0.47). Knowledge production is also positive and significantly associated with employment in services (0.41), manufacturing (0.48), and mining, utilities, and construction (0.83). What these results suggest is that investments in high-end skills have the potential to produce the knowledge (technology) needed to create the conditions for new jobs in the region (box 2.8).

The result is in line with recent findings that show that fast internet, a product of investment in knowledge production, has a large and positive effect on employment rates in the region for the highly skilled and the less educated. More important, the study finds that the arrival of fast internet in the region reduced employment inequality by generating comparable magnitudes of positive employment effects for all educational attainment levels (primary, secondary, and tertiary). The large positive employment effects from the arrival of fast internet are generated through a substantial increase in the entry of new firms that use ICT extensively, and through increases in the productivity of existing firms and exports (Hjort and Poulsen 2019).

BOX 2.8

Pathways to Better Job Creation: The Role of Human Capital in Developing Countries

In 2018, a World Bank jobs diagnostics study explored the various pathways to better job creation that can drive inclusive growth and development in International Development Association countries (Moretto, Weber, and Aterido 2018). In terms of job creation, the study reveals four key stylized facts. First, a few large firms account for a large share of jobs and sales (figure B2.8.1). Second, most businesses in developing countries are made up of micro firms that persist but cannot expand employment (figure B2.8.2). They usually cannot grow beyond 10 workers. Third, employment growth is negatively correlated with firm age. And, fourth, new and young firms are the primary source of jobs. These new and young firms tend to be smaller, however, and smaller firms face a lower survival rate (figure B2.8.3).

Figure B2.8.1 Share of Employment, by Size of Firm, Sub-Saharan Africa

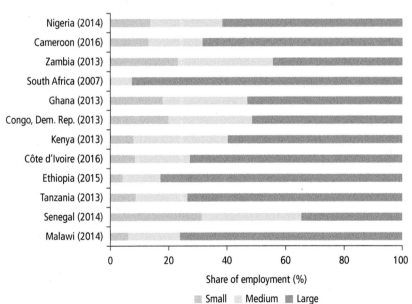

Share of employment (%)

Small   Medium   Large

Source: World Bank calculations based on data from internal Enterprise Surveys.
Note: Small (and micro) firms = fewer than 20 workers; medium firms = 20–100 workers; large firms = 100 or more workers.

(continued next page)

The findings of the study suggest that, going forward, Africa will have to grow more large firms that will create the large number of jobs needed to absorb a sizable amount of the region's labor force. Because, as noted, most businesses in the region are micro firms that cannot grow jobs, human capital efforts should focus on producing high-end skilled digital entrepreneurs who will develop the technology that will create the large firms.

Figure B2.8.2 Firm Size in Sub-Saharan Africa

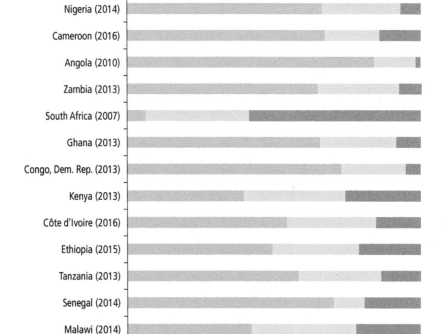

Source: World Bank calculations based on data from internal Enterprise Surveys.
Note: Small (and micro) firms = fewer than 20 workers; medium firms = 20–100 workers; large firms = 100 or more workers.

(continued next page)

Box 2.8 (continued)

Figure B2.8.3 **Survival Rates of Firms in Selected Countries, by Firm Age and Size**

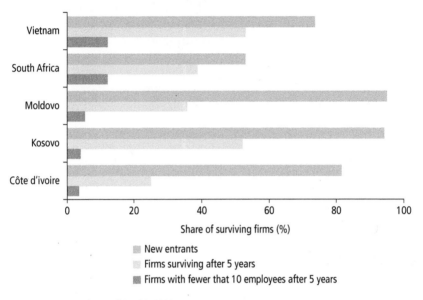

Share of surviving firms (%)

- New entrants
- Firms surviving after 5 years
- Firms with fewer that 10 employees after 5 years

Source: Moretto, Weber, and Aterido 2018.

Results from the econometric analysis further corroborate these findings. On average, a 1 percentage point increase in R&D expenditures leads to a 7.6 percent increase in knowledge production, all other things being equal. To show why the increase in investment in high-end skills is critical for the production of knowledge for job creation, R&D is interacted with the tertiary school enrollment rate (a proxy for skill provision). On average, increasing R&D investments in high-end skilled workers by 1 percentage point leads to a 0.3 percent increase in knowledge production, other things being equal.

Policy Implications and Future Research Agenda

Sub-Saharan Africa must invest in physical infrastructure expansion and improvements in the regulatory environment, as recommended by WDR 2019, to create the conditions for formal private sector jobs creation. In addition, it must act fast to create the human capital conditions needed to leverage the opportunities of digital technologies for job creation in the region. The center-piece of the strategy is training and enabling a critical mass of inventors and entrepreneurs to develop and scale digital technologies to boost the productivity of all workers, especially low-skilled workers in current and new occupations, and strengthening the delivery of education and health services. The current supply of STEM graduates in the region falls short of the numbers needed to generate the momentum for innovation. Evidence shows that it costs students in the region about 20–30 percent more to enroll in STEM-related programs at universities than it costs for other fields such as humanities and social sciences. And, not surprisingly, most tertiary enrollment is recorded in non-STEM fields. The cost of STEM field education is high not only for students but also for institutions. At the university level, running a quality STEM program requires a huge investment in resourcing lecture rooms, libraries, laboratories, and above all recruiting highly skilled experts with the capacity to teach STEM programs at a level that meets recognized international standards. Enabling universities to develop quality STEM programs will require huge and expensive capital invest-ment by governments and other stakeholders. And governments will have to bear part of the financial burden of students who enroll in STEM-related pro-grams. Given the limited fiscal space in the tertiary educational budgets of most countries in the region, and the inadequate supply of human capital resources to develop quality STEM field education across the region, investments will have to be strategic and targeted.

Evidence and experience from around the world offer some avenues to address this issue. For example, the region could learn from the success of Brazil's targeted tertiary STEM expansion program. In the short term, policies could focus on developing small, high-quality STEM programs at the ter-tiary level, establishing high-quality STEM research centers and technological hubs, and targeting investment that will enhance the potential of exceptionally bright STEM students. In the medium to long term, scaling up such programs and investment is desirable to cover other students enrolled in STEM-related programs, while paying attention to equity in the distribution and building of foundational skills, the lack of which often deters many students from enroll-ing in STEM-related programs at the tertiary level. Governments in the region will also have to design attractive incentive packages (such as higher remuner-ation, better conditions of work, research grants, and grants for international research collaboration) to attract and retain qualified STEM field experts and professors.

Certain scholarship schemes can provide incentives to students to return home after completing their studies and help tap into the diaspora skills pool. Initiatives such as The Returning Experts Program run by the German Development Cooperation and the Centre for International Migration and

Development encourage students to return to their home country after their studies by offering support (including a monthly income allowance to help students settle in when back home) and work in a development-related capacity.[15] Governments will have to partner with such organizations to share the cost of such programs. In South Africa, Homecoming Revolution[16] recruits and places globally experienced talent with reputable organizations working in various sectors, including technology, media, telecommunication, education, and health care. Established in 2003 and launched in 2004, Homecoming Revolution initially aimed to encourage South African expats abroad to return home, in an attempt to reverse the country's brain drain problem. Homecoming Revolution has now been expanded across other countries in the region—including Ghana, Kenya, Tanzania, and Uganda—to bring the region's top skills back home. Between 2009 and 2013, about 400,000 professional South Africans returned home through the initiative. Homecoming Revolution is now a full-fledged pan-Africa recruitment firm, serving as a leader in skills repatriation. The region needs more such initiatives. It will also need to get the diaspora involved by tapping into the diaspora skills pool, especially those trained in STEM-related fields. Highly skilled migrants have been found to exhibit high return rates (OECD 2008); however, for the region to harness that potential would require policies that encourage returnees and make efficient use of their skills, supported by proper labor market reintegration programs.

Finally, the region must address critical constraints such as funding start-ups in their early stage and must incorporate entrepreneurship into the mainstream educational curriculum. Although the latter holds a key to job creation, it is happening in only a few countries in the region. Even in those countries, the program has yet to produce "entrepreneurs that can succeed in enterprise creation that yields proportionate returns in expected areas such as job creation" (*Forbes Africa* 2019). A study examined entrepreneurship education programs in secondary and tertiary education institutions in three countries in the region, namely, Botswana, Kenya, and Uganda, and found that students who completed the program could not start their own businesses immediately after completion. Unlike technical and vocational education programs whose graduates are more likely to start their own businesses within a few years after graduation (Farstad 2002), the low quality of entrepreneurship programs in the region means that, after completing them, students must still go through the traditional route to self-employment, starting with an initial period of apprenticeship or wage employment to gain practical experience and build professional self-confidence before setting out to start a new business (Adams, Johansson de Silva, and Razmara 2013). Quality entrepreneurship education needs more space in the region's education curriculum. Grooming students to become successful job-creating entrepreneurs will require a well-planned, structured, and systematic change of existing curricula.

Going forward, additional knowledge is needed on several questions to help guide policies. First, there is a need for a better understanding of how to identify, empower, and train transformational inventors and entrepreneurs, especially those with high talents and low incomes. Second, although digital technologies can promote access to human capital services, a better understanding is needed of the extent of the impact of digital technologies on the quality of human capital service delivery. Would digital technologies mainly complement already high-performing human capital workers, allowing them to perform better, or can they improve the performance of low-performing workers? Will digital technologies enable better access to public education and health services for marginalized populations, people in rural areas, ethnic minorities, the elderly, and the disabled; or will they exacerbate these inequalities? How can the prospects of a digital divide be mitigated and addressed? Third, a real risk exists for rapid obsolescence of acquired digital skills and educational curricula in the face of accelerated technological change. It will be important to understand the challenges of ensuring education systems, teacher training, pedagogical styles, and learning materials keep up with the pace of technological advancements. Finally, adequate measurements are needed on many fronts, including better measures of the quality of education, innovator and entrepreneurial skills, and worker skills, especially soft skills and skills for adaptation. A limitation in the computation of the Human Capital Index is that the test scores used to construct the quality of education measure, for instance, are measured infrequently and available for few countries. Additionally, the test scores from different international testing programs must be harmonized into common units of learning outcomes. There is also the issue of the sample representation of test takers, including whether their numbers are sufficient to represent all students in respective countries, their ages, and the subjects covered, which vary across testing programs. The combination of all these limitations makes it difficult to establish accurate cross-country comparisons of the quality of educational systems.

This chapter focuses above all on the importance of building a critical mass of high-skilled inventors and entrepreneurs to help the large stock of low-skilled people in the region take advantage of the opportunities provided by digital technologies. Given that most people in Sub-Saharan Africa earn their incomes in the informal economy, the next chapter explores in greater detail the challenges and productivity potential of informal enterprises.

Notes

1. More than 30 percent of children under age five are stunted in 10 countries in the region—Botswana, Cameroon, Guinea, Lesotho, Liberia, Malawi, Rwanda, South Sudan, Sudan, and Tanzania. In Burundi, the share is more than 50 percent, and it is over 40 percent in Niger and Nigeria (World Bank 2019).

2. There may be some additional learning on the job, which will contribute to closing the productivity gaps, as workers are reallocated across sectors. This chapter does not ignore that factor; however, and as shown in extant literature, it is difficult to isolate the single contribution of additional learning to the productivity change in structural decomposition exercises that explore the contribution of within and between effects to productivity change. Intuitively, the contribution of additional learning to productivity change is assumed to be captured in the within effect (see, for instance, Mensah et al. 2018).

3. For more information on the different rankings, see https://www.timeshighereducation.com/world-university-rankings and https://www.topuniversities.com/university-rankings/world-university-rankings/2020.

4. Data from the World Intellectual Property Organization.

5. For an overview of how Africa is addressing systemic gaps in skills and knowledge in priority STEM fields, see the World Bank video "Creating a Critical Mass of Highly Skilled Science and Technology Professionals in Africa" at http://www.worldbank.org/en/news/video/2017/09/22/creating-a-critical-mass-of-highly-skilled-science-and-technology-professionals-in-africa.

6. For more information on how Farmerline is using inclusive digital technology to increase the productivity of farmers in Africa, see its page about CocoaLink, https://farmerline.co/2018/05/24/farmerline-launches-new-cocoalink-service-a-free-mobile-app-that-puts-the-power-of-mobile-technology-in-farmers-hands/.

7. For more on what the World Bank Group and other partners are doing to scale up disruptive digital technologies use in the agricultural sector in Africa, see information about the Disruptive Agricultural Challenge and Conference, https://www.worldbank.org/en/events/2019/04/05/disruptive-agricultural-technology-challenge-and-conference.

8. For more on FarmLINK Kenya's programs to connect farmers, see http://www.farmlinkkenya.com/program-launched-to-help-kenyan-farmers-access-agri-tech-by-2022/.

9. For more on how Ghana is using digital technology to deliver better and more inclusive health care, see the Novartis Foundation web page at https://www.novartisfoundation.org/our-work/reimagining-healthcare-through-digital-technology/ghana-telemedicine.

10. For more on how South Africa is using digital technology to deliver better maternal and child health care services, see the Department of Health Republic of South Africa web page at http://www.health.gov.za/index.php/mom-connect.

11. For more on how Uganda is using digital technology to deliver better health care services, see the Ugandan Ministry of Health mTrac web page at http://www.mtrac.ug/.

12. UNESCO Institute of Statistics (UIS). Current available year (2012–17) data are used for each country.

13. For more on digital-savvy country rankings, see the World Economic Forum's Networked Readiness Index at http://reports.weforum.org/global-information-technology-report-2016/networked-readiness-index/.

14. For more on the ITU's ICT Development Index, see https://www.itu.int/net4/itu-d/idi/2017/index.html.

15. For more on labor market integration programs for returning skilled Africans in the diaspora, see the German Alumniportal website at https://www.alumniportal -deutschland.org/en/study-continuing-education/programmes/returnees-from -abroad/.

16. For more on other labor market integration programs for returning skilled Africans in the diaspora, see the Homecoming Revolution website at http://homecomingrevolution .com/about-us/.

References

Adams, A. V., S. Johansson de Silva, and S. Razmara. 2013. *Improving Skills Development in the Informal Sector: Strategies for Sub-Saharan Africa*. Washington, DC: World Bank.

African News Agency. 2018. "Airbnb Supports 22,000 Jobs across South Africa." IOL Business Report, September 12. https://www.iol.co.za/business-report/companies /airbnb-supports-22-000-jobs-across-south-africa-17029508.

Arias, O., D. Evans, and I. Santos. 2019. *The Skills Balancing Act in Sub-Saharan Africa: Investing in Skills for Productivity, Inclusion and Adaptability*. Africa Development Forum Series. Washington, DC: World Bank.

Bartelsman, E. J. 2013. "ICT, Reallocation and Productivity." Economic Paper 486, European Commission, Brussels.

Bashir, S., L. Marlaine, E. Ninan, and T. Jee-Peng. 2018. *Facing Forward: Schooling for Learning in Africa*. Washington, DC: World Bank.

Bastos de Morais, J.-C. 2017. "Digital Technologies Can Deliver Better Healthcare to Sub-Saharan Africa. Here's How." World Economic Forum Agenda, October 19. https://www.weforum.org/agenda/2017/10/digital-paths-for-better-healthcare-in-sub -saharan-africa/.

Bayen, M. 2018. "Africa: A Look at 442 Active Tech Hubs of the Continent." *Mobile for Development* (blog), March 22. https://www.gsma.com/mobilefordevelopment /programme/ecosystem-accelerator/africa-a-look-at-the-442-active-tech-hubs-of-the -continent/.

Benjamin, N. C., and A. A. Mbaye. 2012. "The Informal Sector, Productivity, and Enforcement in West Africa: A Firm-Level Analysis." *Review of Development Economics* 16 (4): 664–80.

Böhme, M., and R. Thiele. 2012. "Is the Informal Sector Constrained from the Demand Side? Evidence for Six West African Capitals." *World Development* 40 (7): 1369–81.

Bold, T., D. Filmer, G. Martin, B. Stacy, and C. Rockmore. 2017. "Enrollment without Learning: Teacher Effort, Knowledge, and Skill in Primary Schools in Africa." *Journal of Economic Perspectives* 31 (4): 185–204.

Cadot, O., J. de Melo, P. Plane, L. Wagner, and M. Woldemichael. 2016. "Industrialization and Structural Change: Can Sub-Saharan Africa Develop without Factories?" *Revue d'économie du développement* 24 (2): 19–49.

Disrupt Africa. 2018. *African Tech Startups Funding Report 2018*. https://disrupt-africa. com/funding-report/.

Cassim, A., K. Lilenstein, M. Oosthuizen, and F. Steenkamp. 2016. "Informality and Inclusive Growth in Sub-Saharan Africa: Evidence and Lessons from Latin America (ELLA) Regional Evidence Paper." Working Paper 201602, Development Policy Research Unit, University of Cape Town, South Africa.

Cornell University, INSEAD, and WIPO (World Intellectual Property Organization). 2017. *The Global Innovation Index 2017: Innovation Feeding the World*. Geneva: WIPO.

Fagerberg, J., and B. Verspagen. 2002. "Technology-Gaps, Innovation-Diffusion and Transformation: An Evolutionary Interpretation." *Research Policy* 31 (8–9): 1291–304.

Farstad, H. 2002. "Integrated Entrepreneurship Education in Botswana, Uganda and Kenya: Final Report." Review commissioned by the World Bank. National Institute of Technology, Oslo.

Forbes Africa. 2019. "African Curricula That Mean Business." March 27. https://www .forbesafrica.com/entrepreneurs/2019/03/27/african-curricula-that-mean-business/.

Garcia, M., A. Pence, and J. L. Evans. 2008. *Africa's Future, Africa's Challenge: Early Childhood Care and Development in Sub-Saharan Africa*. Directions in Development Series. Washington, DC: World Bank.

Gelb, A., C. Meyer, and V. Ramachandran. 2013. "Does Poor Mean Cheap? A Comparative Look at Africa's Industrial Labor Costs." Working Paper 325, Center for Global Development, Washington, DC.

Guiliani, D., and S. Ajadi. 2019, "618 Active Tech Hubs: The Backbone of Africa's Tech Ecosystem." *Mobile for Development* (blog), July 10.

Halliwell, J. E. 2012. "Centres of Excellence as a Tool for Capacity Building–Canada Case Study." OECD Publishing, Paris.

Haltiwanger, J., S. Scarpetta, and H. Schweiger. 2014. "Cross Country Differences in Job Reallocation: The Role of Industry, Firm Size and Regulations." *Labour Economics* 26 (116): 11–25.

Hjort, J., and J. Poulsen. 2019. "The Arrival of Fast Internet and Employment in Africa." *American Economic Review* 109 (3): 1032–79.

ILO (International Labour Organization). 2018. *World Employment Social Outlook: Trends 2018*. Geneva: ILO.

Liese, B., and G. Dussault. 2004. "The State of the Health Workforce in Sub-Saharan Africa: Evidence of Crisis and Analysis of Contributing Factors." Africa Region Human Development Working Paper Series, World Bank, Washington, DC.

Manyika, J., A. Cabral, L. Moodley, S. Yeboah-Amankwah, S. Moraje, M. Chui, J. Anthonyrajah, and A. Leke. 2013. "Lions Go Digital: The Internet's Transformative Potential in Africa." McKinsey & Company.

McKenzie, D., and Y. S. Sakho. 2010. "Does It Pay Firms to Register for Taxes? The Impact of Formality on Firm Profitability." *Journal of Development Economics* 91 (1): 15–24.

Mensah, E. B., S. Owusu, N. Foster-McGregor, and A. Szirmai. 2018. "Structural Change, Productivity Growth and Labour Market Turbulence in Africa." Working Paper 2018-025,

Maastricht Economic and Social Research Institute on Innovation and Technology, Maastricht, The Netherlands.

Mensah, E. B., and A. Szirmai. 2018. "African Sector Database: Expansion and Update." Working Paper 2018-020, Maastricht Economic and Social Research Institute on Innovation and Technology, Maastricht, The Netherlands.

Moretto, D., M. Weber, and R. Aterido. 2018. "Pathways to Better Jobs in IDA Countries: Findings from Jobs Diagnostics." World Bank, Washington, DC.

Ng'weno, A., and D. Porteus. 2018. "Can Africa Show How Gig Workers Get a Fair Share in the Digital Economy?" *Center for Global Development* (blog), October 15. www.cgdev.org /blog/can-africa-show-how-gig-workers-get-fair-share-digital-economy.

OECD (Organisation for Economic Co-operation and Development). 2008. "Return Migration: A New Perspective." In *International Migration Outlook 2008*, 161–222. Paris: OECD.

Perera, M., and D. Aboal. 2019. "The Impact of a Mathematics Computer-Assisted Learning Platform on Students' Mathematics Test Scores." Working Paper 2019-007, Maastricht Economic and Social Research Institute on Innovation and Technology, Maastricht, The Netherlands.

Quartz Africa, (A. L. Dahir). 2017. "Uber's Four-Year Journey through Africa's Fast-Changing Cities Has Been Bumpy, but Disruptive." September 30. https://qz.com /africa/1090738/uber-is-marking-four-years-in-africa/.

Rodrik, D. 2016. "Premature Deindustrialization." *Journal of Economic Growth* 21 (1): 1–33.

Roser, M., and E. Ortiz-Ospina. 2020. "Tertiary Education." Our World in Data, Global Change Data Lab, University of Oxford. https://ourworldindata.org /tertiary-education.

Saane, Z., and M. Baker. 2018. "Improving Productivity and Job Quality of Low-Skilled Workers in the United Kingdom." Economics Department Working Paper 1457, Organisation for Economic Co-operation and Development, Paris.

Schanzenbach, D. W. 2014. "Does Class Size Matter?" Policy Brief, National Education Policy Center, School of Education, University of Colorado, Boulder.

Soares, M., D. B. Rocha, and V. Ponczek. 2011. "The Effects of Adult Literacy on Earnings and Employment." *Economics of Education Review* 30 (4): 755–64.

Szirmai, A., and B. Verspagen. 2015. "Manufacturing and Economic Growth in Developing Countries, 1950–2005." *Structural Change and Economic Dynamics* 34 (September): 46–59.

UIL (UNESCO Institute for Lifelong Learning). 2013. *Second Global Report on Adult Learning and Education: Rethinking Literacy.* Hamburg: UIL.

———. 2016. *Third Global Report on Adult Learning and Education: The Impact of Adult Learning and Education on Health and Well-Being, Employment and the Labour Market, and Social, Civic and Community Life.* Hamburg: UIL.

———. 2017. *The Status of Adult Learning and Education in Sub-Saharan Africa: Regional Report.* Hamburg: UIL.

WHO (World Health Organization). 2006. *The World Health Report 2006: Working Together for Health.* Geneva: WHO.

World Bank. 2016. *World Development Report 2016: Digital Dividends*. Washington, DC: World Bank.

———. 2017. "Leapfrogging: The Key to Africa's Development? From Constraints to Investments in New Opportunities." World Bank, Washington, DC.

———. 2018. *World Development Report 2018: Learning to Realize Education's Promise*. Washington, DC: World Bank.

———. 2019. *World Development Report 2019: The Changing Nature of Work*. Washington, DC: World Bank.

Chapter 3

Increasing Informal Sector Productivity

Pierre Nguimkeu and Cedric Okou

Introduction

About 82 percent of Sub-Saharan Africa's poor people still live in rural areas, earning their living primarily in farming. Relative to other world regions, the informal labor market and the number of informal enterprises are the largest and have been most prevalent in Sub-Saharan Africa. In most Sub-Saharan African countries, about 89 percent of total employment from 2000 to 2016 was in informal work, with Senegal at 89 percent, Chad at 81 percent, and Togo at 63 percent. Entrepreneurship remains predominantly informal, at about 90 percent of all businesses; according to the 2016 enterprise census, 97 percent of enterprises are informal in Senegal.[1] The sheer size of the region's informal economy implies several challenges. Compared with those in the formal sector, farms, firms, and workers in the informal sector have poor access to information on input, knowledge, and output markets; suffer from lower productivity; and have limited revenues. To tackle the challenges of informality, the 2019 *World Development Report* (WDR 2019) advocates for the creation of stable, formal sector private jobs for the poor (World Bank 2019d). Following this recommendation, made from a global and long-term perspective, has had limited success and may not fully account for the immediate needs and challenges of informal firms and workers in Africa.

Against this backdrop, this chapter aims to address the following questions:

- What are the specific features of the informal economy in Sub-Saharan Africa compared with other regions?

- How can informality-related policies better focus on Sub-Saharan African circumstances, beyond the longer-term pro-formalization reforms articulated in WDR 2019?

- How can digital technologies be leveraged to address the challenges and harness the potential of informal firms and workers in Sub-Saharan Africa?

The chapter complements and contextualizes the policies presented in WDR 2019. In addressing the challenges of informality in Sub-Saharan Africa, the analysis takes a multiple time–horizon perspective. It distinguishes between formalization policies aimed at inducing the transition of informal firms and workers into the formal economy, which have had limited success so far, and short- to medium-term policies focused on upgrading the productivity of small firms, farms, and unskilled workers in the informal sector. Implementing productivity-enhancing policies in the informal sector appears more realistic in the short to medium term. In the long run, more productive informal firms will likely seek to formalize as they grow and perceive the benefits of becoming formal.

WDR 2019 broadly discusses the creation of stable jobs in the formal sector and formalization policies—including reducing registration costs, streamlining taxation, nurturing human capital, investing in training, and using e-payroll—as solutions to the issues of the informal economy, often referred to as the shadow economy. The primary goal of common pro-formalization reforms is to achieve the transition of informal labor and production units to the formal sector using a range of incentives and enforcement tools. Nonetheless, the empirical evidence suggests that formalization policies implemented in developing countries in general and in Sub-Saharan Africa in particular have delivered only modest beneficial impacts at best relative to their costs. For instance, one-stop-shop formalization reforms led to, at most, a 5 percent increase in business registrations in Colombia and Mexico, whereas these formalization policies reduced the number of firms registering in Brazil (Bruhn and McKenzie 2014). In a recent randomized experiment study, Benhassine et al. (2018) document that a full formalization package—including registration incentives, business advisory support and training, and tax and banking support—raised the formalization rate in Benin by a modest 16.3 percent relative to prohibitively high intervention costs.

To understand the rather limited success of formalization reforms, formalization should be viewed as a gradual process rather than as a one-off experiment. Many formalization actions are reversible, as firms and workers constantly weigh the trade-off between formalization gains and incentives in terms of increased market access, eased funding conditions, and additional support services relative to their costs and deterrents, namely, taxation, associated licensing costs, and registration of employees. The informal sector in Sub-Saharan Africa comprises small and large firms that operate informally. In this regard, formalization will probably take time to materialize in Sub-Saharan Africa and might not be broad-based, although it can be effective for large informal firms even in the medium term, as documented by Benjamin and Mbaye (2012a). Therefore, a key development question is what actionable policies can be implemented meanwhile, that is, in the short to medium term. Given the ubiquity of informality in Sub-Saharan Africa and the roadblocks to formalization, this chapter takes the view that policy interventions focusing more on leveraging low-productivity units are likely to be more successful at unlocking the potential of the informal economy. In the short to medium run, pro-productivity policy interventions can help boost the productivity of informal firms, in addition to policies to enhance the skills of workers, as covered in chapter 2. Moreover, better enforcement can stimulate the transition of large informal firms to the formal sector. In the long run, a supportive business environment and evenhanded enforcement will likely help some productive informal firms to grow and ultimately become formal, as they perceive a beneficial trade-off between the gains and the costs of operating formally (Grimm, Knorringa, and Lay 2012).

WDR 2019 does not thoroughly discuss the barriers to credit that small businesses in Sub-Saharan Africa typically face, or how digital technologies can be leveraged to circumvent these hurdles. Digital technologies are inherently disruptive, and they are heralded as a key to catalyzing economic growth. The adoption of digital technologies offers a potentially very different trajectory in high-income and emerging market countries where the population is fully literate and has at least minimum numeracy skills, in contrast to low-income Sub-Saharan African countries where a significant share of the population is still functionally illiterate, with low or no numeracy skills.

The digital economy offers Sub-Saharan African businesses and workers, including those in informal sectors, an opportunity to realign markets by minimizing information asymmetry, which has multidimensional benefits, including making formalization easier. By connecting more informal businesses with consumers, digital technologies can strengthen the backbone of Sub-Saharan African economies. In low-income environments, low-skill-biased digital technologies—through instructional videos, voice-activated tactile screens, and simple-to-use applications—can empower low-skilled informal workers to perform higher-skilled tasks and learn as they work. Such technologies can enable workers who lack collateral but can make small savings to access credit and insurance products based on their recorded savings and purchase histories, and to be matched to better jobs over time. Digitization is already creating new opportunities for the smallest informal entrepreneurial firms and farms to access larger networks and markets. In Kenya, women working informally can get mobile credit, buy food products to resell in the local markets from a wider network of farmers, and thus invest and save more. The use of social media platforms such as Instagram, Twitter, and WhatsApp to advertise goods and services to a wider range of customers at minimal cost relative to brick and mortar shops is another example.

To complement the long-term policy target of formalization, this chapter explores other pathways that, in the short to medium term, can realistically focus more on upgrading the productivity of workers and firms in the informal sector.

The investigation is anchored in the digital economy, which can unleash substantial productivity gains. The chapter provides an overview of labor and business markets in Sub-Saharan Africa that are characterized by a large informal sector, highlighting the barriers and opportunities. It documents the key trends of the demand and supply sides of the labor market amid high informality in the region. Doing so refines our understanding of the role of digital technologies in increasing the productivity of informal firms. The chapter explores how digitization can unlock the entrepreneurial potential of informal units, fostering sustainable and inclusive growth in Sub-Saharan Africa. Given that access to credit is one of the key barriers to entrepreneurship in Sub-Saharan Africa, the chapter examines how the adoption and diffusion of digital technologies, such as mobile phones, mobile money, and accounting apps, can enable subsistence workers without any collateral, but with the ability to make small savings, to access credit and insurance products. These workers can rely on their recorded savings and purchase histories to get small loans and grow their businesses or be matched to better jobs over time. In addition, the chapter discusses the importance of mutually reinforcing policies in enhancing productivity while mitigating new labor market risks. Indeed, although digitization may facilitate the creation of new formal technology-driven firms (for example, YouTube and Instagram influencers who earn their income by advertising other firms' products), it brings to governments in low-income Sub-Saharan African countries the challenge of harnessing the tax base for such jobs. The rest of the chapter is organized as follows. It first reviews the various dimensions of informality and provides an overview of informal firms and farms in Sub-Saharan Africa. The chapter then discusses the role of digital technologies for the future of informal work in Sub-Saharan Africa. Finally, the last section discusses recommended related policy interventions and concludes.

Overview of Formal and Informal Farms and Firms

This section summarizes the recent literature and documents stylized facts related to the roots and challenges of informality in Sub-Saharan Africa. It reviews the potential sources of informality, explores various correlates, and discusses the interactions between the formal sector and the informal economy.[2] It also provides a portrait of the informal economy by highlighting the salient characteristics that shape the productivity of informal workers, firms, and farms. In the section, Sub-Saharan Africa and Africa are used interchangeably.

What Do We Know about Informality?
Informality is a multifaceted and subtle concept. Broadly, it refers to the production of legal goods and services by firms and workers that do not comply with business or labor market regulations. Various definitions or typologies

of informality exist along different dimensions, such as participation motives (survival, evasion, exclusion) and margins (firms, workers). Three major views explain the sources of informality (Boly 2018; Kanbur 2017; Loayza 1996; World Bank 2019c). First, low-productivity firms may be forced to operate informally as a survival strategy (La Porta and Shleifer 2014). "Survivors" encompass low-skilled individuals and subsistence entrepreneurs who would be best allocated as workers in growing firms if such an option were available. Second, heavy-handed regulations may push potentially productive firms to hide from the regulators (de Soto 1989). These "held-back establishments" are hampered by high costs of entry and other regulations. Third, firms can also choose to operate in the shadow economy on the basis of a rational profit-maximizing assessment of compliance (de Mel, McKenzie, and Woodruff 2011). These "free riders" could be as productive as formal firms but choose not to formalize to save on regulation costs and taxes. Ulyssea (2018) shows how these complementary views reflect heterogeneous firms' responses to their institutional environment, in a model where formal firms can decide to pay (or not) for formalization and may choose how many employees to report or leave "off the books." Against this backdrop, the following questions are addressed:

- Which criteria are commonly used to define informality?
- How is the informal sector connected to the formal economy?
- What are the salient dimensions of the informal sector in Africa?

There is no unique definition for informal activities. A generally accepted way to define informality is by considering employees and firms that engage in activities that are not taxed or registered by the government. For instance, WDR 2019 defines an informal worker as a person who "does not have a contract, social security and health insurance, and is not a member of a labor union" (World Bank 2019d, 27). In contrast, the 17th International Conference of Labour Statisticians (ICLS) recommends a sharper definition of informal employment as "all remunerative work (both self-employment and wage employment) that is not registered, regulated or protected by existing legal or regulatory frameworks, as well as nonrenumerative work undertaken in an income-producing enterprise" (ILO 2013). In addition, ICLS defines informal firms as production units comprising unincorporated enterprises owned by households, including informal own-account enterprises and enterprises of informal employers (typically small and nonregistered enterprises). Overall, the informal economy encompasses worker and enterprise perspectives, as shown in table 3.1.

In the context of Sub-Saharan Africa, relevant criteria to define formal firms may include one or more of the following:

Table 3.1 Conceptual Framework of the Informal Economy

Production units by type	Jobs by status in employment								
	Own-account workers		Employers		Contributing family workers	Employees		Members of producers' cooperatives	
	Informal	Formal	Informal	Formal	Informal	Informal	Formal	Informal	Formal
Formal sector enterprises					1	2			
Informal sector enterprises[a]	3		4		5	6	7	8	
Households[b]	9					10			

Source: ILO 2013.

Note: Cells colored deep yellow refer to jobs, which by definition do not exist in the type of production unit in question. Cells colored pale yellow refer to formal jobs. White cells represent the various types of informal jobs.

a. As defined by the 15th ICLS resolution (excluding households employing paid domestic workers).

b. Households producing goods exclusively for their own final use and households employing paid domestic workers.

Informal employment: Cells 1 to 6 and 8 to 10
Employment in the informal sector: Cells 3 to 8
Informal employment outside the informal sector: Cells 1,2,9, and 10.

- Registration with the national or local business registry
- Registration with the national tax authorities (having a tax identifier)
- Compliance with tax obligations
- Compliance with accounting standards (for example, Organization for the Harmonization of Business Law in Africa regulations)
- Declaration of all employees with the relevant national or local authorities, and fulfillment of all related obligations

Appraising the level of informality is challenging because it is an endogenous feature of the economy. On the one hand, informality can shape the growth path of developing economies—for instance, by absorbing a large share of unskilled labor or constraining the fiscal space. On the other hand, the level of economic development—growth, poverty, and inequality—can also affect the size and composition of the informal sector (figure 3.1, panel a). In addition, trade policies and fiscal outcomes are key correlates of informality (figure 3.1, panel b). Trade reforms can shape the informal sector through competition. High levels of informality can also tilt fiscal policies toward trade-based taxation—rather than more broadly based corporate and labor taxation. Institutional quality also matters, because a conducive business environment and balanced enforcement of regulations can help reduce the level of informality (figure 3.1, panel c). Moreover, the degree of informality can vary across firms (Perry et al. 2007). Some firms can operate fully informally in product markets and labor markets

Figure 3.1 Key Correlates of Informality: Development Outcomes, Fiscal Indicators, and Governance

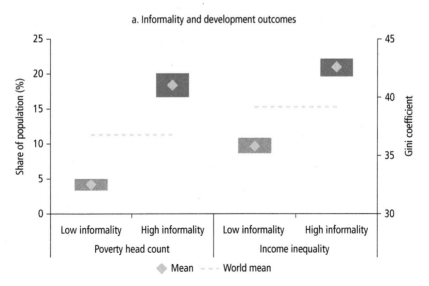

a. Informality and development outcomes

(continued next page)

Figure 3.1 **Key Correlates of Informality: Development Outcomes, Fiscal Indicators, and Governance (continued)**

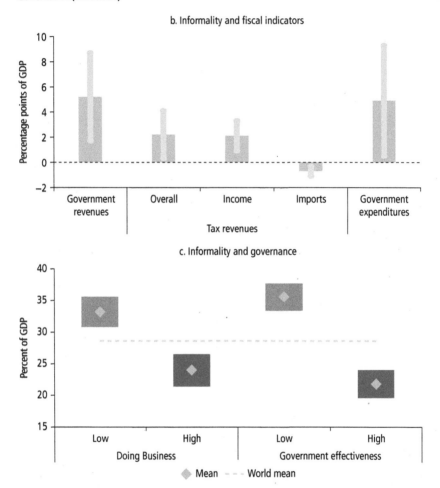

b. Informality and fiscal indicators

c. Informality and governance

◆ Mean   – – – World mean

Source: World Bank 2019c.
Note: Unweighted averages of data spanning 1990 to 2016. In panel a, group means (diamonds) and 95 percent confidence intervals (bars) are shown for the poverty head count ratio at $1.90 a day (2011 purchasing power parity, percent of population) and Gini coefficients. "High informality" and "Low informality" indicate countries with above-median and below-median informal output (dynamic general equilibrium–based estimates). Panel b shows differences in the 2000–16 average fiscal indicators among the one-third of emerging market and developing economies with the highest and lowest informality (measured by the share of dynamic general equilibrium–based informal output averaged during 2000–16). Vertical bars indicate 90 percent confidence intervals of the difference. The sample includes 70 non-energy-exporting emerging market and developing economies with populations above 3 million people. In panel c, group averages of informal output based on dynamic general equilibrium in percent of official gross domestic product (GDP) in 2016 are presented in diamonds, with bars representing 95 percent confidence bands. The world average is shown by a dashed line. "High" and "Low" indicate countries with above-median and below-median values in the following two measures: Doing Business distance-to-frontier and governance effectiveness (World Governance Indicators).

whereas other formally registered firms can employ, in part, informal labor. Thus, assessing the characteristics of the informal sector is often performed in a context-specific fashion, relying on correlations—rather than causal effects—and using model-based (multiple indicators, multiple causes frameworks; dynamic general equilibrium models), survey-based (household surveys, labor force surveys), or perception-based indicators (World Bank Enterprise Surveys, World Economic Forum indexes).

Over economic cycles, formal and informal sectors may have intertwined dynamics driven by existing links. During economic contractions, the informal sector can grow while the formal economy contracts. In this regard, the shadow economy may serve as a buffer or a safety net to support poor households' incomes (Loayza and Rigolini 2011). An informal economy may also evolve procyclically to support economic growth by providing more services and intermediate inputs to the formal economy during economic upturns; however, procyclical behavior of the informal sector may amplify the adverse effects of economic downturns (Chen 2005; Dell'Anno 2008; Meagher 2013). The short- and long-run dynamics of informality also matter. In the short run, informal activity can provide a safety net during business cycle fluctuations and labor market disruptions driven by major structural reforms such as trade liberalizations. Nonetheless, in the long term, the informal sector can impede development by potentially constraining the expansion of the tax base, thus limiting domestic resource mobilization for development (Dix-Carneiro et al. 2018; Docquier, Muller, and Naval 2017). The synchronization—or lack thereof—of the movement between the formal and informal sectors varies substantially across countries and depends on the degree of integration of formal and informal activity, sectoral composition, market structures, and rigidities. Trade, tax, and other regulatory policies that—purposely or unintentionally—affect informality account for important sources and dynamics of the shadow economy. Ultimately, these policies should strike a balance between regulation enforcement, market flexibility, and protection of the vulnerable segments of the population.

Estimates based on household surveys show that the share of the informal sector in gross domestic product has averaged 74, 49, and 54 percent since 2000 in Benin, Burkina Faso, and Senegal, respectively (Benjamin and Mbaye 2012a, 2012b). Informal activity is dominant in the primary sector across all three countries (figure 3.2, panel a). Secondary and tertiary sectors exhibit more heterogeneity. Nearly half of the value added in the secondary and tertiary sectors can be attributed to the shadow economy in Senegal. In Burkina Faso, the informal sector accounts for about half of secondary value added but one-quarter of tertiary output. In contrast, the informal sector produces more than 60 percent of secondary and tertiary output in Benin. Despite substantial sectoral heterogeneity across countries, this evidence points to the large prevalence of informality in the primary and tertiary sectors. The secondary (manufacturing) sector is

Figure 3.2 Share of Informal Activity for Three West African Economies

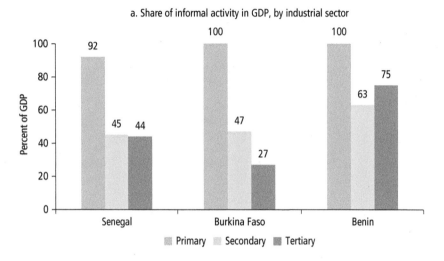

a. Share of informal activity in GDP, by industrial sector

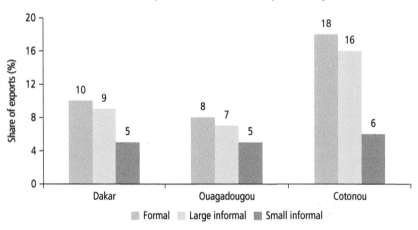

b. Share of exports in total sales in three capital cities, by sector

Source: Benjamin and Mbaye 2012a.
Note: Panel a shows informal activity as a percentage of gross domestic product (GDP) by industrial sector in Senegal, Burkina Faso, and Benin around 2009. Panel b shows proportion of exports in total sales by firms' informality status in capital cities (Dakar, Senegal; Ouagadougou, Burkina Faso; and Cotonou, Benin).

small or embryonic in many African economies. Looking at exports, it is clear that large, informal firms have comparable exports in percentage of total sales to formal firms (figure 3.2, panel b). Large, informal firms have a very different export profile, however, compared with small-scale informal firms (Benjamin and Mbaye 2012b).

Size and Features of the Informal Sector

Informality is a salient feature of most developing countries, with far-reaching socioeconomic implications for poverty-reducing and welfare-enhancing policies. Informality tends to be more acute in low-income agrarian economies with a high share of unskilled workers (Schneider and Enste 2002). Informal firms and farms absorb a substantial share of the unskilled labor force. Moreover, small start-ups often use the informal sector as an incubator to grow, become more productive, and eventually transition to the formal sector (Nguimkeu 2014). The informal sector is a key part of the fabric of many Sub-Saharan African countries and, as such, needs to be fully embraced in the design of economic policies.

This section describes the labor supply side amid widespread informality. In the next two decades, Africa is projected to have more people entering the labor force than the rest of the world (IMF 2017). This increase entails a higher demand for jobs than the formal sector is likely able to offer. In Sub-Saharan Africa, 89 percent of workers—about 20 percentage points higher than in emerging markets and developing economies (EMDEs)—are employed in the informal sector (figure 3.3, panels a and b). Informality is higher in West Africa, low-income countries, fragile states, and commodity exporters (figure 3.3, panels b and c). Moreover, young and older persons tend to face a higher level of informality. In Africa, 95 percent of young and older persons are informal workers (figure 3.4). This share is much higher than the average for EMDEs (85 percent) and worldwide (77 percent). Because education allows the acquisition of productive skills, it is a key determinant of human capital,

Figure 3.3 Pervasive Informal Labor in Africa

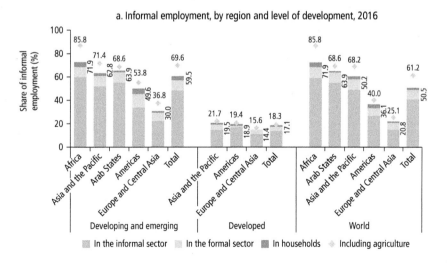

a. Informal employment, by region and level of development, 2016

(continued next page)

Figure 3.3 Pervasive Informal Labor in Africa (continued)

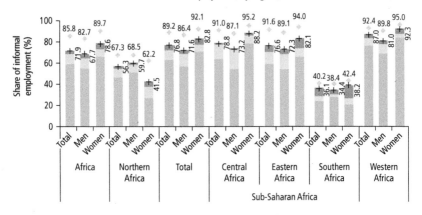

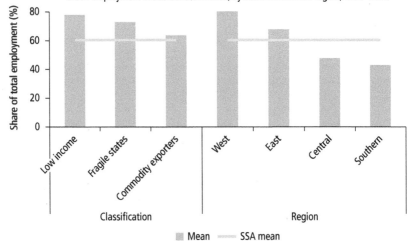

Sources: ILO 2018; World Bank 2019c.
Note: In panel a, the International Labour Organization's 2018 grouping for Africa includes countries in Northern Africa (the Arab Republic of Egypt, Morocco, and Tunisia) and Sub-Saharan Africa (SSA). Panel b shows regional estimates for Northern Africa and Sub-Saharan Africa (total) regions, with the latter broken down into Central, Eastern, Southern and Western Africa. Panel c shows estimates from World Bank (2019c) and uses World Bank country classifications.

as elaborated in chapter 2. As expected, informality is negatively correlated to the level of education (World Bank 2019c). Workers with secondary and tertiary education are less likely to be informally employed compared with low-skilled workers who have no education or completed only primary education. This evidence is more pronounced in Africa than in other regions (ILO 2018). Clearly, the workforce in Sub-Saharan Africa is overwhelmingly informal (Fox et al. 2013).

Figure 3.4 Formal Employment, by Worker Age and Economy's Level of Development, 2016

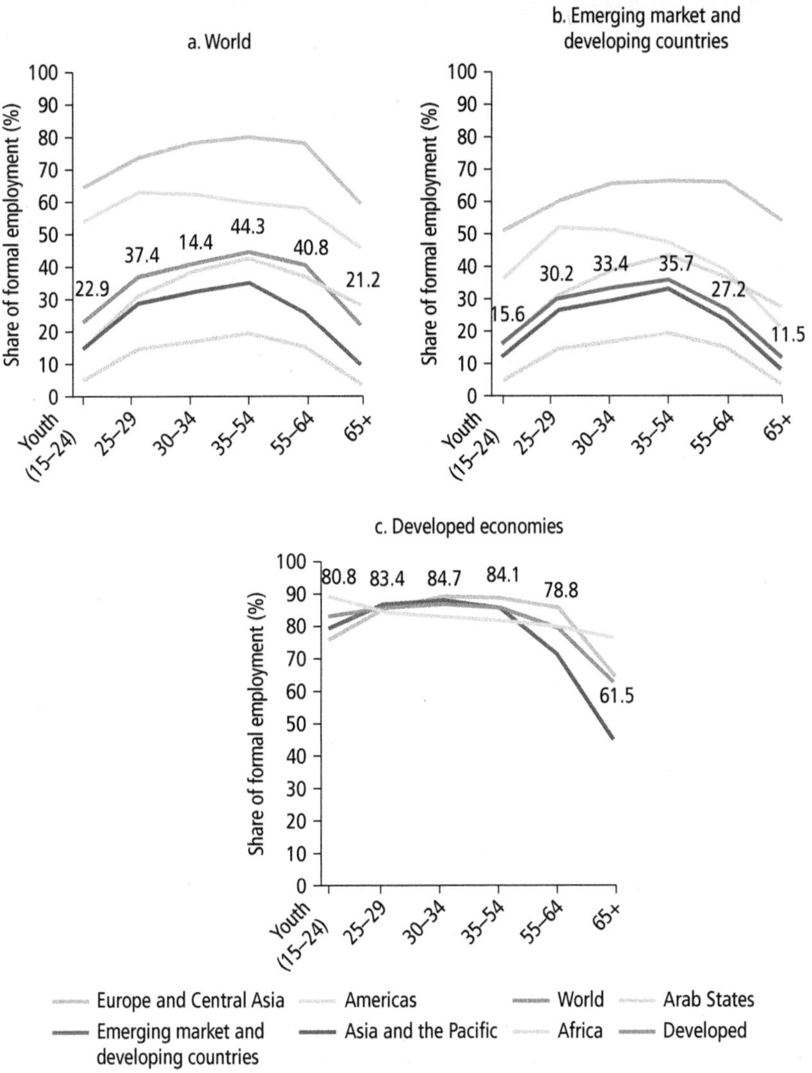

a. World

b. Emerging market and developing countries

c. Developed economies

Legend			
Europe and Central Asia	Americas	World	Arab States
Emerging market and developing countries	Asia and the Pacific	Africa	Developed

Source: ILO 2018.

Informal firms can be important engines of growth if they boost their productivity. Their estimated contribution to value added is already sizable, given their large numbers, averaging about 40 percent of gross domestic product (GDP) in Sub-Saharan Africa over 2010–14 (figure 3.5, panel a). Typical informal firms, which account for 90 percent of all businesses in the region, commonly use unskilled labor, are financially constrained, have limited access to markets, and are relatively small (Ali and Najman 2017; Perry et al. 2007; Xaba, Horn, and Motala 2002). Informal employment or self-entrepreneurship is a common option for unskilled or less educated people (Fox and Sohnesen 2012). Despite less conducive business conditions, Sub-Saharan Africa could benefit from more dynamic entrepreneurial attitudes (figure 3.5, panels b and c). Thus, skills upgrading and improving access to resources can help informal firms become more productive.

The productivity gap between formal and informal firms is much smaller for East African countries than for Southern African countries, possibly because of a weaker institutional environment in East Africa.[3] Similar findings from Benjamin and Mbaye (2012a) corroborate the negative correlation between informality and productivity of firms in West Africa. The shadow economy in Africa also includes large firms that operate informally yet compete—in scale and sophistication—with large formal sector firms. These large informal

Figure 3.5 Informality and Entrepreneurial Dynamism, Sub-Saharan Africa Relative to Other Regions and EMDEs

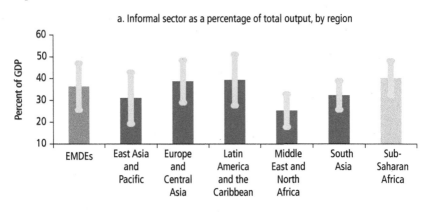

a. Informal sector as a percentage of total output, by region

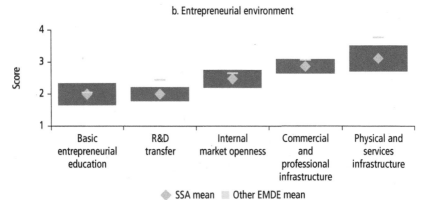

b. Entrepreneurial environment

◆ SSA mean   ▪ Other EMDE mean

(continued next page)

Figure 3.5 Informality and Entrepreneurial Dynamism, Sub-Saharan Africa Relative to Other Regions and EMDEs (continued)

c. Entrepreneurial behavior

◆ SSA mean ▨ Other EMDE mean

Source: World Bank 2019c.
Note: Panel a shows a multiple indicators, multiple causes model estimation of informal output. The green and blue bars indicate group means for 2006–16, with yellow vertical bars indicating +/– one standard deviation. In panel b, the score (ranging from 1 to 9) is based on the National Expert Survey of the Global Entrepreneurship Monitor. A higher score represents better perceived condition. Blue bars are +/– one standard deviation of the SSA (Sub-Saharan Africa) mean. Other EMDE (emerging market and developing economy) refers to all EMDEs except SSA (Sub-Saharan African) countries. In panel c, data come from the Adult Population Survey of the Global Entrepreneurship Monitor for 2001–16. Motivational index is the percentage of those who have recently started a business and were driven by opportunity divided by the percentage of those who were driven by necessity. A lower ratio indicates a higher proportion of necessity-driven businesses. Blue bars are +/– one standard deviation of the SSA mean. Other EMDE refers to all EMDEs except SSA countries. GDP = gross domestic product; R&D = research and development.

establishments are fundamentally different from typical small informal firms, because they exploit complex networks linking seemingly isolated informal micro firms (Benjamin and Mbaye 2012a). The existence of large informal firms suggests that the size and contribution of the shadow economy may be underestimated in much surveyed data. Africa also has a sizable amount of informal cross-border trade (ICBT), including smuggling and clandestine re-exports of goods to neighboring countries. Informal establishments involved in ICBT take advantage of cross-country differences in import taxes and quotas in the same subregion. The estimated ICBT flow vastly surpasses official cross-border trade figures. For instance, the ICBT estimate for domestically produced goods between Cameroon and Nigeria is US$240 million, six times the upper bound of officially recorded flows (Benjamin, Golub, and Mbaye 2015; Golub 2014).

Agriculture-led economies in Africa are dominated by small, labor-intensive farms with limited mechanization (Christiaensen and Demery 2018; ILO 2018). Agriculture absorbs a large share of the labor force in most African economies. Fox and Sohnesen (2012) show that the agriculture sector is by far the largest source of employment in many (13) Sub-Saharan African countries, accounting for 72 percent of primary employment. Many informal farms in Africa are small-scale and family-operated establishments. Using data from worldwide agriculture censuses, Lowder, Skoet, and Raney (2016) document that 9 percent of the estimated 570 million farms in the world are located in Africa and have an average size of less than 2 hectares (figure 3.6, panels a and b). The amount of land allocated to crop cultivation is relatively small, partly because

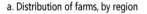

Figure 3.6 Distribution and Characteristics of Farms, Sub-Saharan Africa and Other Regions

a. Distribution of farms, by region

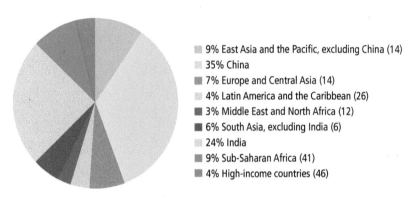

- 9% East Asia and the Pacific, excluding China (14)
- 35% China
- 7% Europe and Central Asia (14)
- 4% Latin America and the Caribbean (26)
- 3% Middle East and North Africa (12)
- 6% South Asia, excluding India (6)
- 24% India
- 9% Sub-Saharan Africa (41)
- 4% High-income countries (46)

b. Distribution of farmland in Sub-Saharan Africa

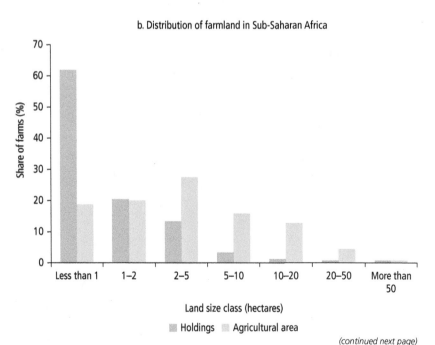

(continued next page)

Figure 3.6 **Distribution and Characteristics of Farms, Sub-Saharan Africa and Other Regions (continued)**

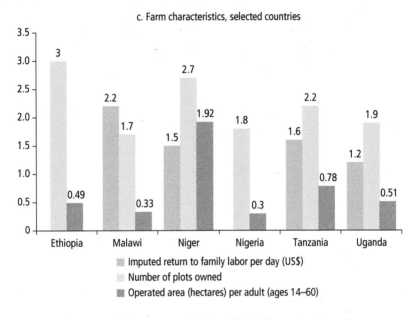

c. Farm characteristics, selected countries

- Imputed return to family labor per day (US$)
- Number of plots owned
- Operated area (hectares) per adult (ages 14–60)

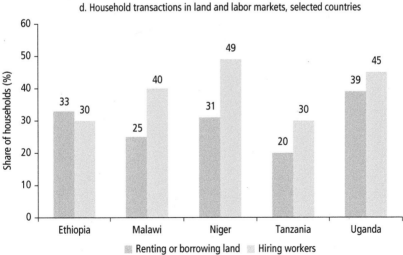

d. Household transactions in land and labor markets, selected countries

- Renting or borrowing land
- Hiring workers

Sources: Christiaensen and Demery 2018; Lowder, Skoet, and Raney 2016.
Note: Panel a shows the share of 570 million farms in 161 countries worldwide, by region. The number of countries included is shown in parentheses. Panel b shows the share in percent of the total number of farms by land size in Sub-Saharan Africa. Panel c shows variations in farm characteristics in some Sub-Saharan African countries. Panel d gives the proportion of rural households that transact in land and labor markets in some Sub-Saharan African countries. US$ = US dollar.

of fragmentation (Christiaensen and Demery 2018). In Ethiopia, for instance, the average household owns nearly three plots, and the operated area per adult (household members ages 14 to 60 years) is less than one-half a hectare (figure 3.6, panel c). Substantial variation also exists in the average daily return to family labor—a revenue-based proxy of farming productivity—ranging from US$1.20 in Uganda to US$2.20 in Malawi.

Moreover, and contrary to common wisdom, labor and land markets for agricultural activities in Sub-Saharan Africa are relatively deep. A large share of households operate in agricultural markets by transacting labor (hiring workers during the farming cycle) and land (renting or borrowing plots). In Uganda, for example, instead of just relying on household labor and owned land, 45 percent of households hire help for farming and 39 percent of farmers rent or borrow land (figure 3.6, panel d). The depth of agricultural labor and land markets coupled with the existence of disparities in land distribution and productivity offer a unique opportunity for Sub-Saharan African economies (Christiaensen and Demery 2018). Transactions on agricultural labor and land markets can help equalize endowments and boost the productivity of these economies. To this end, it is crucial to promote sustainable land management, to foster efficiency-enhancing transfers, to curb information asymmetries by facilitating access to clear and detailed records on land ownership, and to ensure property rights that effectively hedge against the risk of land loss.

Location matters in the analysis of informality patterns. In rural areas, informal activities relate mainly to agriculture and household work. By contrast, cities are typically economic hubs that offer agglomeration benefits: larger markets, better infrastructure to access markets and operate business, a larger pool of workers, and greater technology spillovers (Duranton and Puga 2004; Rosenthal and Strange 2004). The urban informal sector serves as a receptacle for the flow of rural migrants (Mbaye and Benjamin 2015). In assessing the spatial dimension of informality in Uganda, Hobson and Kathage (2017) identify clusters of informal firms located in the vicinity of potential customers in the Greater Kampala area. This finding is corroborated by survey data revealing that 97 percent of informal firms transact directly with individuals or households, and that 84 percent of informal firms sell to customers within a 30 minute walk. Thus, informal firms tend to operate near densely populated areas for easy access to customers.

Moreover, urban informal activities typically take place on streets and in public places and are often seen as eyesores and undesirable by authorities. For instance, informal street vendors and transport providers are often criticized for exacerbating city congestion. African countries are experiencing rapid urbanization amid high informality; from a spatial perspective, authorities try to apply rules and regulations and keep their cities clean, whereas urban informal sector activities need space. If not addressed, this situation may lead to tensions between local authorities, formal businesses, and informal operators. The urban informal sector is vital to provide livelihoods to poor households living in cities. As market accessibly emerges as a key determinant for the viability of informal firms, local governments can work closely with informal sector operators to zone land specifically for trading.

Challenges and Opportunities of Informality

Challenges of Informality

Cumbersome regulation, excessive taxation, poor governance, lengthy procedures, and high registration costs are often cited as key culprits of informality in Africa (Distinguin, Rugemintwari, and Tacneng 2016; Djankov et al. 2002; World Bank 2019c). Although regulation is necessary for raising tax revenues and ensuring compliance with minimum labor, health, environmental, and quality standards, excessive regulation effectively increases the cost of entry and operation in the formal sector. This high cost may contribute to the sheer size of the informal economy and raise important development issues. Table 3.2 presents the list of countries at the opposite ends of the World Bank's 2019 Ease of Doing Business rankings. No African economy appears among the top-10 performers, whereas 8 African countries are among the bottom-10 performers, along with Haiti and República Bolivariana de Venezuela. Moreover, the average costs of regulation in registration costs, number of days and administrative procedures, and tax rates as a proportion of gross national income (GNI) per capita are considerably higher in Sub-Saharan Africa than in other regions. For example, the entry cost in Sub-Saharan Africa is an estimated 225 percent of GNI, compared with 8 percent in Organisation for Economic Co-operation and Development countries (a ratio of 28 to 1), 45.4 percent in South Asia, 47.1 percent in East Asia and Pacific, 51.2 percent in the Middle East and North Africa, and 60.4 percent in Latin America and the Caribbean.

Heavy-handed regulations and the less conducive business climate in Sub-Saharan Africa can impede the productivity of most firms, pushing them to operate informally. Nguimkeu (2016) analyzes the roles of skills, collateral-based lending, and institutional constraints—registration costs and taxation—on entrepreneurship and informality in Africa. He finds that barriers to entry provide incentives to less productive entrepreneurs to self-select into informality. The results also show that the likelihood to formalize is U-shaped in the entrepreneur's level of education; the likelihood to formalize decreases with lower levels of education to a certain threshold, after which the likelihood starts to increase. Informality is perceived as more profitable to less educated entrepreneurs, whereas highly educated ones find formality increasingly attractive. This finding points to the importance of multipronged policies that bundle mutually reinforcing reforms. More research is needed to understand the types of contexts where digital technologies together with specific types of complementary support could help boost the productivity of informal enterprises,

Table 3.2 Top 10 and Bottom 10 Economies on Ease of Doing Business Rankings, 2019

Country	Ease of doing business rank	Starting a business	Dealing with construction permits	Getting electricity	Registering property	Getting credit	Protecting minority investors	Paying taxes	Trading across borders	Enforcing contracts	Resolving insolvency
Top 10 of the world											
New Zealand	1	1	6	45	1	1	2	10	60	21	31
Singapore	2	3	8	16	21	32	7	8	45	1	27
Denmark	3	42	4	21	11	44	38	9	1	14	6
Hong Kong SAR, China	4	5	1	3	53	32	11	1	27	30	44
Korea, Rep.	5	11	10	2	40	60	23	24	33	2	11
Georgia	6	2	27	39	4	12	2	16	43	8	60
Norway	7	22	22	19	13	85	15	30	22	3	5
United States	8	53	26	54	38	3	50	37	36	16	3
United Kingdom	9	19	17	7	42	32	15	23	30	32	14
North Macedonia	10	47	13	57	46	12	7	31	29	37	30
Bottom 10 of the world											
Chad	181	186	153	177	134	144	161	188	172	153	154
Haiti	182	189	180	142	181	178	188	147	86	124	168
Central African Republic	183	181	181	184	172	144	149	187	163	183	154
Congo, Dem. Rep.	184	62	165	174	156	144	165	180	188	178	168
South Sudan	185	177	169	187	179	178	180	66	180	85	168
Libya	186	160	186	136	187	186	185	128	128	141	168
Yemen, Rep.	187	175	186	187	81	186	132	83	189	139	157
Venezuela, RB	188	190	152	186	138	124	180	189	187	148	165
Eritrea	189	187	186	187	180	186	174	152	189	103	168
Somalia	190	188	186	187	152	186	190	190	164	114	168

Source: World Bank's Doing Business database, 2019 data.

by overcoming interlocking state failures (high transaction costs for registration) and market failures (scarcity of information on creditworthiness and business banking history).

Formalization reforms have had little success in curbing the prevalence of informality. Using data from Brazil, Ulyssea (2018) shows that most informal businesses (52.6 percent) are low-productivity survivors that will likely remain informal even when the formal sector's entry costs are removed.[4] This observation echoes the evidence documented in the literature that maps the composition of the informal sector to the limited performance of formalization reforms in developing economies in general and in Africa in particular. Easing entry costs has had a very limited—or no—impact on the formalization of existing informal firms, especially for tax registration in Bangladesh, Brazil, Colombia, Mexico, Peru, and Sri Lanka (Alcázar, Andrade, and Jaramillo 2010; Bruhn and McKenzie 2014; de Giorgi and Rahman 2013; de Mel, McKenzie, and Woodruff 2013).

Focusing on Africa, Lince (2011) analyzes the "open-air market" formalization scheme for local vendors and fishers introduced in 2004 in Uganda. This reform promoted the transition of informal firms to the formal economy by highlighting the advantages of formalization—greater prosperity and increased involvement in local governance. This reform led to adverse economic effects, however, that worsened the welfare of the informal business owners. In a related work, Grimm, Knorringa, and Lay (2012) study the behavior of informal firms facing the prospect of formalization across seven West African countries. Their findings suggest that low- to medium-potential informal firms—combining "survivalists" and "constrained gazelles"—account for nearly 90 percent of the population of informal enterprises in those countries. But less than 44 percent of these informal enterprises would consider formalizing.[5] This share represents an upper threshold, because the actual formalization rate is expected to be much lower.

In Malawi, Campos, Goldstein, and McKenzie (2015) show that focusing exclusively on information and assistance has limited impact on tax registration. Moreover, business registration (formalization) has no material effect on levers of firm productivity such as financial access and usage. Benhassine et al. (2018) conduct a randomized experiment based around the introduction of the "entreprenant" legal status in Benin. The authors use monthly administrative data on formalization to map out the effectiveness of three formalization schemes—basic, intermediate, and full package. They find that a full formalization scheme bundling registration incentives, business advisory support and training, and tax and banking support increased the formalization rate in Benin by only 16.3 percent, but it had substantially high intervention costs. The limited performance of pro-formalization schemes calls for a paradigm shift for effectively addressing the challenges of the informal economy in Africa, by focusing more policy interventions on upgrading the productivity of firms in the informal sector.

Opportunities of Informality in Africa: Beyond the Formalization Dichotomy
This paradigm shift in policy priorities is needed to harness the potential of the informal sector in Africa. Since the beginning of the 21st century, most policies addressing informality in Africa were intended to stimulate informal firms and workers to formalize. As mentioned previously, formalizing the informal sector may prove to be elusive as an objective, at least in the short run. The outcomes of several policy assessments show that, despite a strong push for formalization reforms, most firms remain informal (Bruhn and McKenzie 2014). A range of reasons may explain the limits to formalization (Campos, Goldstein, and McKenzie 2018). The formalization process is gradual rather than a one-off experiment. It is reversible and implies potentially slow changes in institutional and business environments. Along the formalization path, businesses and workers constantly assess the trade-off between formalization incentives (increased market access, eased funding conditions, and additional support services) and deterrents (taxation, associated licensing costs, and registration of employees).

To some extent, pro-formalization policies take a "misallocation angle" by providing incentives for the reallocation of production factors from a low-productivity informal sector toward a more productive formal sector. In this regard, formalization reforms reflect a "between" answer to the challenge of informality. In contrast, a "within" approach to informality focuses on raising informal firms' productivity, by upgrading their internal capabilities such as entrepreneurial mindset, managerial skill, technology absorption capability, workforce skill, and innovation capacity (Campos et al. 2017; Cusolito and Maloney 2018). A pathway to achieve this objective is to refocus policies and reforms on boosting the productivity of most small-scale, low-productivity firms and enhancing the skills of informal workers. Targeted formalization and improved enforcement schemes can help large informal firms make the transition to the formal sector.

The Future of Informal Work under the Digital Economy

This section discusses how digital technologies can shape the premium to different skills for people in the informal sector. It provides a summary of the latest examples of technology adoption by—and potential impact on—informal firms and farms. The section also highlights the impact of digital technologies largely on informal labor markets, given that formal labor contracts cover only a small share of workers in Africa.

Technology Acquisition, Diffusion, and Impact on Informal Labor Markets

How do small and informal firms in Africa access and use new technologies? Despite growing consensus on the role that digital technologies play in the

Table 3.3 Uses of ICTs by Informal Businesses in Selected East African Countries
percent

		Uganda	Tanzania	Rwanda	Kenya
ICT uses by businesses	Mobile phones for business purposes	67.9	44.4	53.4	67.4
	Own computers	2.0	0.1	0.7	3.0
	Working internet connection	3.2	2.8	2.0	3.5
	Working fixed-line phone	6.9	1.0	1.3	0.1
If the businesses use SMS or text messages	Sends	27.2	77.3	63.9	78.1
	Receives	18.1	37.4	33.3	55.3
Why businesses do not use mobile phones	Too expensive	37.1	41.7	55.3	5.5
	No need	48.7	55.8	33.1	20.2

Source: Deen-Swarray, Moyo, and Stork 2013.
Note: ICT = information and communication technology; SMS = short message service.

enhancement of business activities and in economic development in general, there is still little evidence on the uptake and usage of these technologies by informal firms. Although evidence shows wide use of mobile phones among informal businesses, little is known about the use of other information and communication technologies (ICTs). Deen-Swarray, Moyo, and Stork (2013) explore the use of mobile phone and related digital technologies—such as mobile internet, mobile money, and mobile applications—and examine how those technologies can enhance the way informal businesses conduct their activities.

Table 3.3 displays ICT usage for four East African countries. It shows that mobile phones remain the most important and commonly used ICT device among informal businesses. This technology could therefore be a channel through which businesses can improve their growth and sustainability.

Table 3.3 also shows that informal businesses do not use mobile phones mainly because they find no need to do so. This lack of need would typically be the case for subsistence activities, which are very limited in their scope (for example, street vending); activities that are not susceptible to automation; or activities for which business owners lack skills or awareness of the services and potential benefits offered through a mobile phone. Chapter 1 gives detailed statistics on key digital technology developments and trends in Sub-Saharan Africa.

Formalization of informal firms has always been one of the main objectives of governments (OECD 2016). Governments have considered several policies to induce a transition from informal to formal, such as simplifying business registration procedures while reducing taxes. These policies have shown limited success in many countries (Ulyssea 2010), and the process of formalization has not been successful in any of the economies in Africa, which will likely remain the case. Moreover, for many activities in Africa, business owners do not feel that registration or tax reforms will give them any clear advantage. One example is the case of African traditional spiritualists, whose activities are confined mainly to the informal sector.[6] Unlike those engaged in other types of informal activities, these individuals are not likely to enter the formal sector because of socio-cultural restrictions and the secrecy that surrounds their activities, not because they lack the resources or skills.

Drawing on Global Findex data, Berkmen et al. (2019) investigate how digital financial services can encourage formalization of informal firms and discuss risk mitigation policies.[7] They describe the financial technology landscape by documenting the evolution of the number of informal firm owners who make digital payments, use savings products, and borrow money, as well as informal firm owners' access to mobile phones and the internet. On the one hand, given the evidence that the informal sector constantly uses retail electronic payment systems, virtual savings, and virtual credit supply platforms, the digitization process (involving easy payment platforms and accessibility to markets) could allow informal markets in Africa to join the realm of formal transactions. Therefore, inconsistent taxation of digital technologies (as with over-the-top regulations in Uganda and Zimbabwe) has led to less access, which is detrimental to this process. For example, the Ugandan Communication Commission estimated that the number of internet users dropped by nearly 30 percent between March and September 2018, indicating severe consequences of the over-the-top tax imposed by the Ugandan government.[8] Moreover, the economic cost of the social media tax is predicted to be a reduction of US$750 million in GDP growth and US$106 million in forgone taxes in Uganda (Stork and Esselaar 2018).

On the other hand, to the extent that formalization is associated with skills acquisition, greater access to multipurpose technologies may provide more information and resources as well as easy-to-use applications that can thus help reduce informality. More research is needed, however, to show that those digital technologies that facilitate access to financial services can effectively increase compliance with formal business requirements. These findings therefore raise questions about whether formalizing the informal sector is elusive as an explicit policy goal for Africa, given that it has been tried and failed in this region. A more realistic objective (which is also useful for formalization) may be to focus on boosting the productivity of informal enterprises across activities, given that firms will not formalize unless they grow. This objective could be achieved by adopting digital technologies that enable these businesses to overcome information constraints through social media and reach more customers, and to overcome financial constraints by adopting productivity-boosting technologies such as apps that facilitate access to mobile money.

Agricultural technologies have been emerging rapidly across the region, driven by lower costs, better connectivity, and advanced analytics (World Bank 2019b). Specifically, digital technologies appear to be currently at an inflection point where the falling cost allows scalable innovations. For instance, cellular subscriptions are skyrocketing—with 420 million unique mobile subscribers in Sub-Saharan Africa and mobile internet penetration reaching 240 million people (26 percent penetration) in 2016. Although cellular subscriptions and internet penetration have increased across the continent, they are constrained by digital access (figure 3.7). Rural internet penetration is 10 percent in Africa, and it varies with age, gender, and income.

The rapid evolution of disruptive agricultural technologies caters to the characteristics of Africa's food system (box 3.1). One of the characteristics of Africa's food system is inequality in access to technologies, information, skills, and markets. A wide array of technology models is being developed to deliver services to all types of farmers and specifically to farmers who lack resource and information access. For certain types of services, farmers are willing to pay if digital technologies are customized to their needs and address their agricultural challenges. Digital agricultural information platforms or mobile solutions can level the playing field for marginalized groups, such as women, who traditionally have lower access to information and markets.

Complementary Benefits from Digital Technologies

Chapter 1 discusses the broader benefits of digital technologies. This section focuses on the benefits of digital technologies for informal sectors. Recent conceptual frameworks of skilled-biased technologies (Acemoglu 1998; Aghion 2002; Violante 2008) can be adapted to emphasize four types of complementary

Figure 3.7 Internet in Africa, by Demographic and Socioeconomic Characteristics, 2011–12

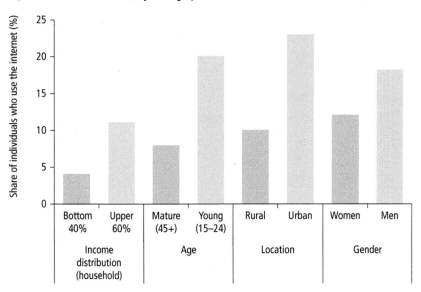

Source: World Bank.

BOX 3.1

E-Extension Increases Productivity for Smallholders in Sub-Saharan Africa

E-extension in agriculture is the use of modern information and communication technologies to easily and quickly extend relevant information to farmers. By ensuring that smallholders have real-time access to pertinent agronomic information to make informed decisions, e-extensions promote agricultural productivity, increase food security, and improve rural livelihoods. Smallholder farmers often represent a low-skill user base with limited access to technology. Innovations designed to cater to this segment include the following:

- *8028 Farmer Hotline.* In Ethiopia, the Agricultural Transformation Agency—in collaboration with the Ministry of Agriculture and Livestock Resources, the Ethiopian Institute of Agricultural Research, and Ethio Telecom—offers a platform to deliver information directly to farmers through mobile phones. The technology used is an Interactive Voice Response and Short Message Service system, which does not require data connectivity, only access to feature phones with simple instructions to follow.

- *Precision Agriculture for Development (PAD).* PAD is a development organization that operates in Ethiopia, Kenya, and Rwanda and covers more than 6 million farmers. It focuses on sending Short Message Service to smallholders with agricultural advice to increase yields.

- *Farm.ink.* Farm.ink is based on a peer-to-peer learning platform and is supported by the CGIAR Research Program on Livestock. Farm.ink operates as an active online community through a mobile chatbot service where farmers can ask questions. Machine learning classifiers provide tailored answers to smallholders' questions. The chatbot can work with a low-cost smartphone and basic internet connection.

- *Digital Green.* Digital Green's video-enabled approach is an adaptable, scalable, cost-effective solution to reach large numbers of smallholder farmers with agricultural extension advisory services. Partnering with existing extension providers in Ethiopia, Kenya, and Malawi has allowed Digital Green to tap into trusted networks operating in remote rural communities, enabling rapid scale-up. Extension providers produce, disseminate, and monitor the impact of short, locally relevant videos. These locally relevant videos are often customized according to farmers' needs and capabilities.

Source: Kim et al., forthcoming.

benefits of digital technologies that may be particularly important for improving growth and inclusion outcomes for farms and firms in the informal sector: complementary effects to existing capital, inclusion gains, efficiency gains, and innovation gains.

Technology adoption and diffusion has effects complementary to existing capital and helps alleviate credit constraints and improve financial inclusion.

For example, that a large percentage of business owners have mobile phones can be used as a way to enhance credit access. Indeed, one of the main barriers to credit is the asymmetry of information between informal businesses and financial institutions. When businesses have neither a business plan nor a transaction history, banks have no means to assess the viability of an investment for which a loan is sought. It is therefore difficult for them to demonstrate the profitability of a business (McCormick 2012). Banks usually require collateral as the alternative to assessing a loan application, which excludes initially poor (although possibly talented) entrepreneurs and creates significant frictions, as found by Nguimkeu (2014). The administration of microcredit creates other challenges that are well documented (Ivatury 2009).[9] The increasing popularity of mobile money could provide a platform to address most of these issues, because it enables the movement of money between different parties. Because individuals and firms also use technology for payments in exchange of goods or services, data from these money transactions generate an electronic trail (for example, amounts, frequencies, and reasons for transactions) that provides a rich data set useful for a wide range of financial analytics. Moreover, because operators have data that link transactions to actual user locations, the combination of mobile money transaction data with other operator data provides a powerful platform for tracking informal business behavior across time and space. Such information can be used for better risk management within banks and to the benefit of both parties.

Inclusion gains occur through overcoming information asymmetries to create, expand, and bring the excluded into larger and more transparent input and output markets (for example, greater arbitrage opportunities from more integrated input and output markets at the local, national, and global levels; more efficient coordination; and matchmaking). For example, a quasi-experimental study by Annan and Sanoh (2018)—which exploited the exogenous introduction of the 2013 national mandatory SIM registration reform in Niger—found that moving a household with mobile use activity to an environment with no mobile use activity because of SIM deactivation resulted in a decline of roughly 33.1 percentage points in the likelihood that the household would engage in nonagricultural business enterprises. Digital technologies such as digital payments and e-governance offer pathways to financial inclusion (box 3.2).

The impressive growth in financial inclusion in Sub-Saharan Africa over the past decade has been driven primarily by mobile money and agent banking. Mobile money allows transactions between peers and between mobile devices and can store money and credit and debit cards (Diniz, de Albuquerque, and Cernev 2011). This technology is perceived as a stepping-stone to the financial inclusion of those who lack access to formal financial services like savings, credit, and insurance (for example, Comninos et al. 2009). As mobile money distribution expands beyond agents to include bank ATMs, cards, and online platforms for cash-in and cash-out

BOX 3.2

Services Increasing Farmers' Financial Inclusion

Innovations designed to increase financial inclusion among smallholder farmers include the following:

- *Arifu*. Arifu is a personalized digital platform and education marketplace catering to the needs and information accessibility of farmers. It provides financial literacy and interactive training to increase the uptake and usage of new savings and borrowing products among rural populations. Farmers in rural areas are often unaware of the benefits of credit, savings, and insurance and the process for applying.

- *Apollo Agriculture*. An average Apollo customer is a remote, rural farmer supporting a family of five to seven people by growing maize and other crops on about two acres of land. Apollo Agriculture builds credit profiles for unbanked smallholders using machine learning models that process large volumes of customer data, including satellite data of customers' fields. Satellite data allow the inference of characteristics, such as yield, crop type, and evidence of livestock, and incorporate these insights into a credit assessment model. Apollo Agriculture has also built automated, digital processes for each step in the customer life cycle, from customer acquisition, to training, to collecting repayment. Together, these innovations allow the delivery of proven agricultural tools to rural, remote smallholder farmers.

Source: Kim et al., forthcoming.

transactions, there may be some form of interaction between using mobile money and subsequently having access to a bank account. Other detailed evidence of the role digital access plays in financial inclusion in Africa can be found in IFC (2018). Specifically, working along with 14 microfinance institutions, banks, mobile network operators, and payment service providers across the continent, a joint initiative between the International Finance Corporation and the Mastercard Foundation to support the growth of digital finance in Africa has resulted in 7.2 million new digital financial services users (that is, a 250 percent increase from the baseline), 45,000 new banking agents, and US$300 million in monthly transactions (IFC 2018). It is important to emphasize that digital transactions leave a footprint that provides information that can put firms on creditors' and regulators' radar screens. In the case of the former, such attention can help expand access to credit and increase financial inclusion. In the latter, it may expand the gray area where firms do not fully comply with regulations and taxes because they can be tracked or regulated in some aspects of their transactions. This apparent trade-off calls for tailored and even-handed regulations that foster the gains but lower the perceived costs of digitization.

Efficiency gains occur through improved access to knowledge and the resulting upgrading of productivity within informal farms and firms (for example, better investment decisions, lower production costs, and higher quality facilitated by extension advice about better seeds and fertilizers appropriate for prevailing soil and weather conditions, access to better planting, harvesting, and business process knowledge; and continuous learning from business management software and other productivity tools). For example, Cole and Fernando (2016) conduct a randomized controlled trial to examine how a mobile phone–based agricultural advice service provided to farmers affects agricultural productivity in India. Offering agricultural advice has helped change practices and increase yields of cumin (28 percent) and cotton (8.6 percent) for a subgroup receiving reminders. Positive peer effects also result, as nontreated farmers learn better practices from treated peers and lose less to pest attacks. By the same token, Kirui, Okello, and Nyikal (2012) use a propensity score matching technique to gauge the impact of mobile money technology on households in rural areas in Kenya. They find that mobile transfer services markedly raise household farms' annual input use by US$42, agricultural commercialization by 37 percent, and incomes by US$224.

Clearly, mobile money technology helps alleviate agricultural market failures, boosts production outcomes, and improves welfare, especially in rural areas. A detailed review of the impact assessment of digitization on farmers' livelihoods in Sub-Saharan Africa can be found in Clark et al. (2015). Efficiency gains from digitization can be captured in terms of improved human capital and welfare. Vasilaky et al. (2016) examine the effectiveness of mediated video-based training on individuals' adoption rates of a new agricultural technology. They find a higher probability of adoption after tailored and mediated video-based trainings relative to standard training (a 50 percent increase between treatment and control groups).

Innovation gains occur through enabling new processes and products, including lower-cost access to customers and services through digital platforms across supply chains, logistics, and financial services (for example, improved supply chain management; better product quality, including food safety and traceability; and faster, safer, and verifiable e-payments facilitating more secure payments, and access to savings, credit, and insurance products for the previously unbanked) (Deichmann, Goyal, and Mishra 2016).[10]

Innovation from digitization takes advantage of the opportunities of generating more income in an excess capacity environment by creating more jobs rather than destroying them (Spiezia and Vivarelli 2000), which enables an overall net increase in job creation. For example, as online shopping platforms gain ground in many African countries (such as Jumia, Nuria, Kilimall, and Lynk in Kenya), physical shopping malls occupied mainly by supermarkets and market stalls for small traders continue to flourish across towns and cities. Although customers continue to visit shops, traders now reach more customers through online shopping platforms and deliver their purchased products to them. This shift also generates increased opportunities for people to join the distribution sector and benefit from door-to-door delivery services. Innovation ecosystems are already impacting agricultural outcomes in Kenya and Nigeria, where smallholder farmers appear to be reaping various benefits by harnessing disruptive agricultural technology innovations (see box 3.3). Overall, the innovation ecosystem in these countries is improving market transparency, enhancing farm productivity, and enabling efficient logistics.

BOX 3.3

Potential Impact of Agricultural Innovation Ecosystems in Kenya and Nigeria

Of the surveyed active disruptive agricultural technology firms in Sub-Saharan Africa, one-half are located in Kenya and Nigeria. These two countries have the most advanced agri-tech ecosystems on the continent. These vibrant agriculture innovation ecosystems show how these two countries excel along six dimensions: culture, density, finance, human capital, infrastructure, and regulatory environment (see Kim et al., forthcoming. appendix B).

By harnessing disruptive agricultural technology innovations, smallholder farmers in Kenya and Nigeria have recognized the advantages to be gained, with the top expected benefits including reduced travel hours; reduced cost of doing business; increased collective action via stronger farmer networks; faster access to price, market, and farming information; increased adaptability to situational changes; and increased farmer leverage during negotiations with wholesalers, traders, and transport providers.

Overall, the innovation ecosystem in these countries appears to be achieving the following:

- Improving market transparency by providing greater arbitrage opportunities, reducing spatial price dispersion, and lowering wastage. It also offers greater market participation in remote areas through more efficient coordination, as well as increased farm gate prices through improved bargaining power with intermediaries.

- Enhancing on-farm productivity by facilitating adoption of improved inputs through the provision of advice and weather forecasts at a lower cost, improving household food security, income, and value of assets through enhanced management practices. Estimations from survey data reveal that mobile money technologies help farmers improve their production and welfare. Users of mobile money use more agricultural inputs, market a larger proportion (about 19 percent more) of their output, and reap 35 percent higher profits than nonusers (Kikulwe, Fischer, and Qaim 2014).

- Enabling efficient logistics by optimizing supply chain management, transportation coordination, product delivery, and capacity utilization. Traceability from point of origin to consumers ensures greater food safety in agricultural product chains. Easy and secure means of payment allows fast and safe transfer of funds to pay for products and inputs, agricultural subsidies, or remittances.

Source: Kim et al., forthcoming.

Challenges and Risks

Various challenges and risks could impede countries' ability to achieve the outcomes mentioned in the previous sections. Those challenges and risks involved in the adoption of digital technologies include the absence of needed accompanying assets, new labor market risks, and political economy challenges.

In addition to the necessary digital infrastructure, increasing the use of digital technologies requires physical capital–based infrastructure, such as electricity, transport, and logistics; human capital, including digital skills and literacy levels; and supporting institutional infrastructure, including for the broadly defined business environment. The widespread use of digital IDs not only would increase benefits but also could facilitate formalization. Unfortunately, many countries still face issues related to the quality of mobile connections and telecom infrastructure. The risks of a worsened broadband internet access divide are still very present (urban/rural, primary/secondary cities, within-city divides, gender and young/old divides, and others). Other dimensions of basic supporting institutional infrastructure are also insufficient in many African countries. For example, decades of conflict and fragile development in the Democratic Republic of Congo have created infrastructure challenges such as the lack of national ID documents and legal procedures to endorse traditional collateral. These challenges have restrained the development of the financial sector. Challenges for digitization are bigger in rural areas and among farmers. A major challenge in the digitization of the cocoa value chain in Côte d'Ivoire (the world's largest cocoa producer) is that many farmers often lack a valid ID. According to IFC (2018), just over half of the Ivorian population has a birth certificate or other ID, which is a limiting factor for enrolling farmers in bank and mobile accounts.

Digital technologies also bring new types of labor market risks, such as insufficient competition, job insecurity, technological unemployment, data privacy and cybersecurity, and consumer protection issues related to fraud, manipulation, and deception (Artecona and Chau 2017). Although digitization can facilitate the creation of new, formal technology-driven firms, it raises new challenges for governments in low-income African countries in terms of their ability to harness the tax base for such jobs, as discussed in chapter 4. Another two-margin situation exists with, on the one hand, an extensive margin that involves registering and paying entry fees to achieve formal status and gain credibility from outside partners, and, on the other hand, an intensive margin where these new businesses decide how much of their taxable income to report under existing tax law. In the digital domain, products and services are bought and sold, uploaded, downloaded, and used without any product or person physically crossing international borders. Significant profits are often generated from sources within countries without establishing a physical presence in those countries.

Digital technologies bring a wide range of political economy challenges (Autor 2015). As social media and the internet continue to gain considerable power and agency around the world, many governments may see them as an existential threat that must be contained, despite the consequences doing so may have on other sectors. In most cases, the desire to control the digitization process could be rooted in governments' determination to control the political narrative, which includes blockage by those perceiving that they will lose from rapid changes related to digital technology. For example, the internet could be seen as a threat because it disrupts traditional forms of government political control, particularly control of the production and dissemination of information, which has been an invaluable political tool for many African governments.

Policy Implications and Future Research Agenda

This section surveys policy interventions that facilitate access to bundles of support services across the input, knowledge, and output markets that are essential to build the productive capacity of credit-constrained, low-skill informal farms and firms (box 3.4). The goal is effective implementation of an encompassing

BOX 3.4

Policies Implemented to Address Informality

Countries have undertaken a range of policy reforms with intended and unintended effects on informality (World Bank 2019c). Compared with other regions, Sub-Saharan African countries have implemented more high-paced reforms (figure B3.4.1, panel a). Nonetheless, the bulk of these reforms appears not to be directly aimed at informality (figure B3.4.1, panel b), which highlights the need for an overarching development strategy that is carefully tailored to country circumstances while accounting for specific sources, types, and challenges of informality.

Among the implemented policies, reforms addressing the challenge of informality have focused mostly on formalization. The main challenge in helping informal establishments make the transition to the formal economy is finding the right policy mix that corresponds to the diversity of characteristics and drivers of informality. Fiscal reforms that streamline tax collection, management, and government procurement systems can lead to lower informality in some economies. Conducive business environments that support entrepreneurship and bolster productivity—by leveling the playing field for all workers and firms through increased flexibility for the labor market and better governance—can help curb the level of informality. Adaptable rules, even-handed enforcement of regulations, reliable delivery of public services, and balanced social protection of the most vulnerable segments of the labor force can also enhance the

(continued next page)

Box 3.4 (continued)

Figure B3.4.1 Policy Reforms to Curb Informality, Sub-Saharan Africa and Other Regions

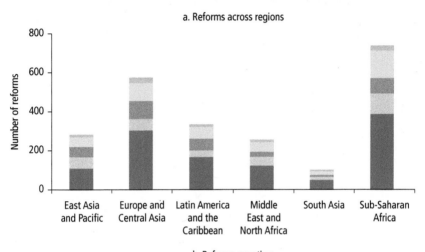

a. Reforms across regions

b. Reforms over time

Sources: World Bank 2019a, 2019c.
Note: Doing Business ratings for 2008–18. Panel a depicts the number of policy reforms that have been implemented since 2008 and are regarded as "improvement" in the ease of doing business or "neutral" (which only applies to "labor market regulation") by Doing Business 2008–18. Panel b depicts the annual average number of policy reforms that were implemented during 2008–10 compared with the annual average number of reforms conducted during 2016–18 (shown in bars).

(continued next page)

Box 3.4 (continued)

working conditions in the informal sector and facilitate a smoother transition from the informal sector to the formal sector. These formalization policies can leverage digital technologies to boost productivity (Nguimkeu 2016).

In light of the limited success of formalization reforms in Africa, policies that focus on low-skill-biased technologies—incentives and subsidies to foster low-skill-biased technology development—can empower informal low-skilled workers and firms to achieve higher productivity and inclusive growth (Bruhn and McKenzie 2014). Catalytic improvements in governance can further boost these positive complementary effects. More research is warranted to identify the effectiveness of these policy reforms and design the appropriate policy mix to address the challenges of informality in Sub-Saharan Africa.

digital strategy for agricultural and nonagricultural informal firms—to help informal firms and workers reap the technological gains of the digital economy.

In a nutshell, most policy reforms, which have aimed to formalize firms and workers, have had limited success, despite their relatively high implementation costs. On the one hand, more realistic short- to medium-term policies should focus on pro-productivity and skills-upgrading interventions for small informal firms and unskilled workers. On the other hand, formalization policies should be more targeted toward larger informal firms that aggressively compete with formal firms. Digital technologies can be leveraged to boost productivity, job creation, access to credit, and financial inclusion in the informal sector, while also making formalization easier in this region over time.

Complementary Policies for Increased Access to Credit

Given the above discussions, policy makers should see digital financial inclusion as a tool to facilitate development goals and not necessarily as a bludgeon to force formalization (Klapper, Miller, and Hess 2019). Policies to enhance access to credit and insurance start with an improvement in institutional infrastructure that facilitates the adoption and diffusion of digital financial technologies. Apart from the previously mentioned needs for energy, roads, and transportation infrastructure, a critical complementary infrastructure is the provision of affordable internet access—that is, expanding network coverage and building network capacity, both of which are imperative in countries with low population densities, low literacy rates, and a lack of local digital content. Other efforts include the improvement and implementation of an effective individual ID system across countries. Finally, the combination of mobile money transaction data with other network operator data provides a powerful platform for tracking informal business behavior across time and space that can be used for better risk management within banks. This improvement could benefit both parties by alleviating information asymmetry, which is a critical step toward a more efficient credit market.

Channeling the Gains from Digital Technologies

The question asked here is how African workers can get a fair share of the innovation benefits from digital technologies. African governments face the challenge not only of designing policies to formalize businesses across all sectors but also of finding new ways for workers to get their fair shares from the efficiency and productivity gains that digitization brings. As argued by Ng'weno and Porteous (2018), one way for governments to channel the gains from digitization is to start by recognizing that digitally supported employment could become an important source of livelihoods in these countries. Policy makers should therefore prescribe that "platform providers open their systems to allow workers to register for government benefits and private services rather than creating an entire range of poorly-enforced regulations" (Ng'weno and Porteous 2018). Governments should also improve the reliability of payments and design a strategy to fight against fraud. For example, many digital transactions go through unsupervised payments from buyers to sellers that may come late or be diverted without punitive consequences. Governments and businesses should therefore work together to prioritize the improvement of payments in the digital economy. Finally, despite the challenges involved (including developing good track records of economic activities), it is possible for governments to tax the digital economy and return the profits in the form of improved government services, especially from international digital platforms.

Beyond the Current Evidence: New Research Avenues

Evidence that digital technologies are likely to disrupt the future of work in Africa opens new avenues for more in-depth research for better understanding the opportunities and challenges for informal firms and farms. Some directions to consider are the following:

- Collect harmonized and high-quality data on the use of digital technologies in the informal sector in African countries.
- To understand and quantify how various policies toward adoption and diffusion of digital technologies can influence the (mis)allocation of skills and resources across sectors, build a model to rationalize and elicit the channels through which the taste for digitization can shape occupational choices and entrepreneurship amid informality.
- Assess the extent to which major development strategies for Africa, such as the 2030 Sustainable Development Goals and Agenda 2063, accounting for pervasive informality on the continent.

- Identify and discuss the refinements (if any) that are warranted to improve the effective implementation of these strategies in achieving the ambitious development goals in Africa.
- Explore how digital business incubators and joint ventures can help African firms internationalize and boost their exports.

This chapter begins by highlighting the poverty challenges faced by workers in the informal sector. The next wave of higher-productivity informal jobs will require more targeted social protection to help workers adjust to new risks. More social protection also will be needed as digital technology entrepreneurship increases; as people experiment and try to produce new goods and services, and produce better existing goods and services, they will face more market-related risks. The next chapter argues that, given the reality of the low levels of resources available for social protection coverage to address these work-related risks, the focus of social protection in Sub-Saharan Africa over the short to medium term should be on increasing the efficiency of domestic resource mobilization and social protection policies, rather than on broadening their scope.

Notes

1. Informality, as defined in this chapter, includes workers and enterprises (see box 3.1). Enterprise census data are from the 2016 "Rapport global du Recensement général des Entreprises" of the Ministère de l'économie, des finances, et du plan du Sénégal.
2. The chapter highlights the underlying reasons for enterprise informality (survival, evasion, exclusion) with a specific focus on the socioeconomic context of Africa. Benjamin and Mbaye (2012a), for instance, highlight the major role that large informal firms play in some sectors in francophone Africa, notably commerce. Data on informal enterprises are largely based on registration, because it is difficult to understand the scope of tax compliance from standard enterprise surveys. This is an area, among others, where the report's forward-looking recommendations emphasize the need for improved data collection and analyses.
3. See Gelb et al. (2009), who use survey data from Southern and Eastern African countries.
4. Ulyssea (2018) estimates that 35.9 percent of informal firms are free riders and 11.5 percent are held-back entrepreneurs.
5. Table 4 in Grimm, Knorringa, and Lay (2012) shows that only 44 percent of constrained gazelles would register, and only 22 percent of survivalists would consider formalizing.
6. African traditional spiritualists are people who perform indigenous spiritual practices for their customers. They include all people who use spiritual powers, knowledge, and inherited skills to assist other people in solving problems that defy physical remedies. Examples are priests and priestesses of ancestral deities, fortune tellers,

spiritual healers, psychotherapists, herbalists, bone setters, diviners, mediums, magicians, and rain makers (Truter 2006).

7. The Global Financial Inclusion (Global Findex) database provides country-level indicators of financial inclusion for more than 140 countries. The Global Findex database is available at https://datacatalog.worldbank.org/dataset/global-financial-inclusion-global-findex-database.

8. This new tax on the ICT sector was imposed by the Ugandan government in July 2018 in the form of excise duties on social media use and mobile money services. It consisted of a mobile money tax of 1 percent on the transaction value of payments, transfers, and withdrawals and a social media tax of 200 Ugandan shillings per day (Stork and Esselaar 2018).

9. For example, microcredit is labor intensive and expensive for banks to offer to informal businesses.

10. These digital technology benefits for informal and formal enterprises lead to poverty reduction outcomes for households through four main economic channels: (1) better consumption opportunities for poor people (from lower-priced and higher-quality goods and services including health, education, and social protection services enabled by the associated productivity increases), (2) more labor income (through more jobs and higher wages with differential effects depending on whether the technology is high-skill or low-skill biased), (3) more profit income (from entrepreneurial farms and firms and other owners of capital, to the extent that they are lower-income people), and (4) more income transfers (from digital technology-related efficiencies, increased integrity in the collection of tax revenues, and more transparent and accountable allocation and targeting of public resources).

References

Acemoglu, D. 1998. "Why Do New Technologies Complement Skills? Directed Technical Change and Wage Inequality." *Quarterly Journal of Economics* 113 (4): 1055–89.

Aghion, P. 2002. "Schumpeterian Growth Theory and the Dynamics of Income Inequality." *Econometrica* 70 (3): 855–82.

Alcázar, L., R. Andrade, and M. Jaramillo. 2010. "Panel/Tracer Study on the Impact of Business Facilitation Processes on Enterprises and Identification of Priorities for Future Business Enabling Environment Projects in Lima, Peru—Report 5: Impact Evaluation after the Third Round." Report to the International Finance Corporation, World Bank Group, Washington, DC.

Ali, N., and B. Najman. 2017. "Informal Competition, Firms' Productivity and PR Policy Reforms in Egypt." In *The Informal Economy: Exploring Drivers and Practices*, edited by I. A. Horodnic, P. Rodgers, C. C. Williams, and L. Momtazian, 229–254. New York: Routledge.

Annan, F., and A. Sanoh. 2018. "Social Protection in Niger: What Have Shocks and Time Got to Say?" Policy Research Working Paper 8455, World Bank, Washington, DC.

Artecona, R., and T. Chau. 2017. "Labour Issues in the Digital Economy." Studies and Perspectives 17, United Nations Economic Commission for Latin America and the Caribbean, Washington, DC.

Autor, D. 2015. "Why Are There Still So Many Jobs? The History and Future of Workplace Automation." *Journal of Economic Perspectives* 29 (3): 7–30.

Benhassine, N., D. McKenzie, V. Pouliquen, and M. Santini. 2018. "Does Inducing Informal Firms to Formalize Make Sense? Experimental Evidence from Benin." *Journal of Public Economics* 157 (1): 1–14.

Benjamin, N., S. Golub, and A. A. Mbaye. 2015. "Informality, Regional Integration and Smuggling in West Africa." *Journal of Borderland Studies* 30 (3): 381–94.

Benjamin, N., and A. A. Mbaye. 2012a. "Informality, Productivity, and Enforcement in West Africa: A Firm-Level Analysis." *Review of Development Economics* 16 (4): 664–80.

———. 2012b. *The Informal Sector in Francophone Africa: Firm Size, Productivity, and Institutions.* Washington, DC: World Bank.

Berkmen, P., K. Beaton, D. Gershenson, J. Arze del Granado, K. Ishi, M. Kim, E. Kopp, and M. Rousset. 2019. "Fintech in Latin America and the Caribbean: Stocktaking." Working Paper 19/71, International Monetary Fund, Washington, DC.

Boly, A. 2018. "On the Short- and Medium-Term Effects of Formalisation: Panel Evidence from Vietnam." *Journal of Development Studies* 54 (4): 641–56.

Bruhn, M., and D. McKenzie. 2014. "Entry Regulation and the Formalization of Microenterprises in Developing Countries." *World Bank Research Observer* 29 (2): 186–201.

Campos, F., M. Frese, M. Goldstein, L. Iacovone, H. C. Johnson, D. McKenzie, and M. Mensmann. 2017. "Teaching Personal Initiative Beats Traditional Training in Boosting Small Business in West Africa." *Science* 357 (6357): 1287–90.

Campos, F., M. Goldstein, and D. McKenzie. 2015. "Short-Term Impacts of Formalization Assistance and a Bank Information Session on Business Registration and Access to Finance in Malawi." Policy Research Working Paper 7183, World Bank, Washington, DC.

———. 2018. "How Should the Government Bring Small Firms into the Formal System?" Policy Research Working Paper 8601, World Bank, Washington, DC.

Chen, M. 2005. "Rethinking the Informal Economy: Linkages with the Formal Economy and the Formal Regulatory Environment." Research Paper 2005/10, Expert Group on Development Issues and United Nations University World Institute for Development Economics Research, Helsinki.

Christiaensen, L., and L. Demery. 2018. *Agriculture in Africa: Telling Myths from Facts.* Directions in Development Series. Washington, DC: World Bank.

Clark, C., K. P. Harris, P. Biscaye, M. K. Gugerty, and C. Leigh Anderson. 2015. "Evidence on the Impact of Rural and Agricultural Finance on Clients in Sub-Saharan Africa: A Literature Review." Brief 307/Learning Lab Technical Report 2, Evans School of Public Policy and Governance, University of Washington, Seattle.

Cole, S. A., and A. Fernando. 2016. "'Mobile'izing Agricultural Advice: Technology Adoption, Diffusion and Sustainability." Working Paper 13-047, Harvard Business School, Cambridge, MA.

Comninos, A., S. Esselaar, A. Ndiwalana, and C. Stork. 2009. "Airtime to Cash: Unlocking the Potential of Africa's Mobile Phones for Banking the Unbanked." In *IST-Africa 2009 Conference Proceedings IIMC,* edited by P. Cunningham and M. Cunningham, 1–16. Dublin: International Information Management Corporation.

Cusolito, A. P., and W. F. Maloney. 2018. *Productivity Revisited: Shifting Paradigms in Analysis and Policy.* Washington, DC: World Bank.

Deen-Swarray, M., M. Moyo, and C. Stork. 2013. "ICT Access and Usage among Informal Businesses in Africa." *Info* 15 (5): 52–68.

De Giorgi, G., and A. Rahman. 2013. "SME's Registration: Evidence from an RCT in Bangladesh." *Economics Letters* 120 (3): 573–78.

Deichmann, U., A. Goyal, and D. Mishra. 2016. "Will Digital Technologies Transform Agriculture in Developing Countries?" Policy Research Working Paper 7669, World Bank, Washington, DC.

Dell'Anno, R. 2008. "What Is the Relationship between Unofficial and Official Economy? An Analysis in Latin American Countries." *European Journal of Economics, Finance and Administrative Sciences* 12 (October): 185–203.

De Mel, S., D. McKenzie, and C. Woodruff. 2011. "What Is the Cost of Formality? Experimentally Estimating the Demand for Formalization." Working Paper, University of Warwick, Coventry, UK.

———. 2013. "The Demand for, and Consequences of, Formalization among Informal Firms in Sri Lanka." *American Economic Journal: Applied Economics* 5 (2): 122–50.

De Soto, H. 1989. *The Other Path: The Invisible Revolution in the Third World.* New York: Harper & Row.

Diniz, E. H., J. P. de Albuquerque, and A. K. Cernev. 2011. "Mobile Money and Payment: A Literature Review Based on Academic and Practitioner-Oriented Publications (2001–2011)." In *Proceedings of SIG Global Development Fourth Annual Workshop,* 1–35, Shangai, December 3.

Distinguin, I., C. Rugemintwari, and R. Tacneng. 2016. "Can Informal Firms Hurt Registered SMEs' Access to Credit?" *World Development* 84 (August): 18–40.

Dix-Carneiro, R., P. Goldberg, C. Meghir, and G. Ullyssea. 2019. "Trade and Informality in the Presence of Labor Market Frictions and Regulations." https://site.stanford.edu /sites/g/files/sbiybj8706/f/5151-trade_and_informality_in_the_presence_of_labor _market_frictions_and_regulations.pdf.

Djankov, S., R. La Porta, F. Lopez-de-Silanes, and A. Shleifer. 2002. "The Regulation of Entry." *Quarterly Journal of Economics* 117 (1): 1–37.

Docquier, F., T. Müller, and J. Naval. 2017. "Informality and Long-Run Growth." *Scandinavian Journal of Economics* 119 (4): 1040–85.

Duranton, G., and D. Puga. 2004. "Micro-Foundations of Urban Agglomeration Economies." In *Handbook of Regional and Urban Economics*, vol. 4, edited by V. Henderson and J. F. Thisse, 2063–117. Amsterdam: Elsevier.

Fox, L., and T. Sohnesen. 2012. "Household Enterprises in Sub-Saharan Africa: Why They Matter for Growth, Jobs, and Livelihoods." Policy Research Working Paper 6184, World Bank, Washington, DC.

Fox, L., A. Thomas, C. Haines, and J. Huerta Munoz. 2013. "Africa's Got Work to Do: Employment Prospects in the New Century." Working Paper 13/201, International Monetary Fund, Washington, DC.

Gelb, A., T. Mengistae, V. Ramachandran, and M. K. Shah. 2009. "To Formalize or Not to Formalize? Comparisons of Microenterprise Data from Southern and East Africa." Working Paper 175, Center for Global Development, Washington, DC.

Golub, S. 2014. "Informal Cross-Border Trade and Smuggling in Africa." In *Handbook on Trade and Development: Africa*, edited by O. Morrissey, R. A. López, and K. Sharma, 179–209. Cheltenham, UK: Edward Elgar.

Grimm, M., P. Knorringa, and J. Lay. 2012. "Constrained Gazelles: High Potentials in West Africa's Informal Economy." *World Development* 40 (7): 1352–68.

Hobson, E., and A. Kathage. 2017. "From Regulators to Enablers: Role of City Governments in Economic Development of Greater Kampala." World Bank, Washington, DC.

IFC (International Finance Corporation). 2018. "Digital Access: The Future of Financial Inclusion in Africa." IFC, Washington, DC.

ILO (International Labour Organization). 2013. *Measuring Informality: A Statistical Manual on the Informal Sector and Informal Employment*. Geneva: ILO.

———. 2018. *Women and Men in the Informal Economy: A Statistical Picture,* 3rd ed. Geneva: ILO.

IMF (International Monetary Fund). 2017. *Regional Economic Outlook: Sub-Saharan Africa—Restarting the Growth Engine*. Washington, DC: IMF.

Ivatury, G. 2009. "Using Technology to Build Inclusive Financial Systems." In *New Partnerships for Innovation in Microfinance*, edited by J. Pischke and I. Matthäus-Maier, 140–64. Berlin: Springer-Verlag.

Kanbur, R. 2017. "Informality: Causes, Consequences and Policy Responses." *Review of Development Economics* 21 (4): 939–61.

Kikulwe, E. M., E. Fischer, and M. Qaim. 2014. "Mobile Money, Smallholder Farmers, and Household Welfare in Kenya." *PLOS ONE* 9 (10): e109804.

Kim, J., P. Shah, J. C. Gaskell, A. Prasann, and A. Luthra. Forthcoming. *Scaling Up Disruptive Agricultural Technologies in Africa*. International Development in Focus Series. Washington, DC: World Bank.

Kirui, O. K., J. J. Okello, and R. A. Nyikal. 2012. "Impact of Mobile Phone-Based Money Transfer Services in Agriculture: Evidence from Kenya." Paper prepared for presentation at the International Association of Agricultural Economists (IAAE) Triennial Conference, Foz do Iguaçu, Brazil.

Klapper, L., M. Miller, and J. Hess. 2019. "Leveraging Digital Financial Solutions to Promote Formal Business Participation". World Bank, Washington, DC.

La Porta, R., and A. Shleifer. 2014. "Informality and Development." *Journal of Economic Perspectives* 28 (3): 109–26.

Lince, S. 2011. "The Informal Sector in Jinja, Uganda: Implications of Formalization and Regulation." *African Studies Review* 54 (2): 73–93.

Loayza, N. 1996. "The Economics of the Informal Sector: A Simple Model and Some Empirical Evidence from Latin America." *Carnegie-Rochester Conference Series on Public Policy* 45 (December): 129–62.

Loayza, N., and J. Rigolini. 2011. "Informal Employment: Safety Net or Growth Engine?" *World Development* 39 (9): 1503–15.

Lowder, S. K., J. Skoet, and T. Raney. 2016. "The Number, Size, and Distribution of Farms, Smallholder Farms, and Family Farms Worldwide." *World Development* 87 (November): 16–29.

Mbaye, A. A., and N. Benjamin. 2015. "Informality, Growth and Development in Africa." In *The Oxford Handbook of Africa and Economics: Volume 1 Context and Concepts*, edited by C. Monga and J. Y. Lin, 620–655. New York: Oxford University Press.

McCormick, D. 2012. "Risk and Firm Growth: The Dilemma of Nairobi's Small-Scale Manufacturers." Discussion Paper 291, Institute for Development Studies, University of Nairobi, Kenya.

Meagher, K. 2013. "Unlocking the Informal Economy: A Literature Review on Linkages between Formal and Informal Economies in Developing Countries." WIEGO Working Paper 27, Women in Information Employment Globalizing and Organizing, Manchester, UK.

Nguimkeu, P. 2014. "A Structural Econometric Analysis of the Informal Sector Heterogeneity." *Journal of Development Economics* 107 (March): 175–91.

———. 2016. "Some Effects of Business Environment on Retail Firms." *Applied Economics* 48 (18): 1647–54.

Ng'weno, A., and D. Porteous. 2018. "Let's Be Real: The Informal Sector and the Gig Economy Are the Future, and the Present, of Work in Africa." CGD Note October, Center for Global Development, Washington, DC. https://www.cgdev.org/publication/lets -be-real-informal-sector-and-gig-economy-are-future-and-present-work-africa.

OECD (Organisation for Economic Co-operation and Development). 2016. "Automation and Independent Work in a Digital Economy." Policy Brief on the Future of Work, OECD Publishing, Paris.

Perry, G. E., W. F. Maloney, O. S. Arias, P. Fajnzylber, A. D. Mason, and J. Saavedra-Chanduvi. 2007. *Informality: Exit and Exclusion*. Washington, DC: World Bank.

Rosenthal, S. S., and W. C. Strange. 2004. "Evidence on the Nature and Source of Agglomeration Economies." In *Handbook of Regional and Urban Economics*, vol. 4, edited by V. Henderson and J. F. Thisse, 2119–71. Amsterdam: Elsevier.

Schneider, F., and D. H. Enste. 2002. "Shadow Economies: Size, Causes, and Consequences." *Journal of Economic Literature* 38 (1): 77–114.

Senegal, Ministry of Economy, Finance and Planning. 2016. "Rapport global du Recensement général des Entreprises." Ministry of Economy, Finance and Planning, Dakar.

Spiezia, V., and M. Vivarelli. 2000. "The Analysis of Technological Change and Employment." In *The Employment Impact of Innovation: Evidence and Policy*, edited by M. Pianta and M. Vivarelli, 12–25. London: Routledge.

Stork, C., and S. Esselaar. 2018. "ICT Sector Taxes in Uganda: Unleash, Not Squeeze, the ICT Sector." Policy Brief, Research ICT Solutions, North Vancouver, Canada. https://researchictsolutions.com/home/wp-content/uploads/2019/01/Unleash-not -squeeze-the-ICT-sector-in-Uganda.pdf.

Truter, I. 2006. "African Traditional Healers: Cultural and Religious Beliefs Intertwined in a Holistic Way." *South African Pharmaceutical Journal* 74 (8): 56–60.

Ulyssea, G. 2010. "Regulation of Entry, Labor Market Institutions and the Informal Sector." *Journal of Development Economics* 91 (1): 87–99.

———. 2018. "Firms, Informality, and Development: Theory and Evidence from Brazil." *American Economic Review* 108 (8): 2015–47.

Vasilaky, K., K. Toyama, T. Baul, and D. Karlan. 2016. "Learning Digitally: Evaluating the Impact of Farmer Training via Mediated Videos?" Working Paper, Jameel Poverty Action Lab, Cambridge, MA.

Violante, G. L. 2008. "Skilled Biased Technical Change." In *The New Palgrave Dictionary of Economics*, 2nd ed., edited by L. Blume and S. Durlauf. London: MacMillan.

World Bank. 2019a. *Doing Business 2019: Training for Reform*. Washington, DC: World Bank.

———. 2019b. "Future of Food: Harnessing Digital Technologies to Improve Food System Outcomes." World Bank, Washington, DC.

———. 2019c. *Global Economic Prospects, January 2019: Darkening Skies*. Washington, DC: World Bank.

———. 2019d. *World Development Report 2019: The Changing Nature of Work*. Washington, DC: World Bank.

Xaba, J., P. Horn, and S. Motala. 2002. "The Informal Sector in Sub-Saharan Africa." Working Paper on the Informal Economy 2002/10, International Labour Organization, Geneva.

Chapter 4

Extending Social Protection Coverage

Zainab Usman

Introduction

This chapter identifies and analyzes the range of social protection and labor (SPL) policies to help Sub-Saharan African countries respond to the changing world of work. The future of work in Sub-Saharan Africa will be shaped by disruptions from the diffusion and adoption of digital technologies. This digital revolution is occurring not in isolation, but within the context of other disruptive trends such as acceleration of economic integration, climate change and fragility, and rapid demographic changes. The interaction of digital innovations with other disruptive forces will result in high levels of labor transitions across rural-urban spaces, jobs, industries, sectors, and borders. These transitions will not only create risks but also provide opportunities for expanding social protection coverage in Sub-Saharan Africa. The following questions guide the chapter:

- What risks to labor markets do Sub-Saharan African economies face in the changing world of work?
- What social protection policies should African governments consider in preparing for the future of work, and how can they finance those policies?

This chapter argues that the labor transitions in Sub-Saharan Africa induced by the digital revolution within the context of other trends will require more responsive social protection and risk management strategies. This responsive social protection in the changing world of work in African economies should entail (1) rebalancing traditional SPL programs with more focus on workers in transition, especially in the informal sector; (2) leveraging new solutions around social protection that turn these risks into opportunities; and (3) optimizing resources to increase investments in social protection for workers in transition through fiscal reforms to raise domestic revenue, addressing inefficiencies in social spending, and navigating the political economy of public policies.

The chapter has a heavy but not exclusive emphasis on social safety nets as the most prevalent form of social protection in Sub-Saharan Africa.

SPL systems, policies, and instruments help individuals manage risk and volatility and protect them from poverty and destitution by improving equity, resilience, and opportunity (World Bank 2012). Equity is enhanced through instruments that help protect against chronic poverty and destitution. Resilience is "the ability of countries, communities, and households to manage change by maintaining or transforming living standards in the face of shocks or stress" without compromising long-term prospects (Alfani et al. 2015, 4; DFID 2011). Programs can promote resilience by minimizing the negative effects of economic shocks and natural disasters on individuals and families. Related to resilience, shock readiness is the extent to which SPL systems can meet the anticipated needs of vulnerable populations resulting from the impact of endogenous or exogenous shocks that adversely affect livelihoods and labor markets.[1] Finally, opportunity is enhanced through policies and instruments that contribute to building human capital and facilitating access to jobs and investments in livelihoods.[2] SPL systems provide a foundation for inclusive growth with transformative impacts on people's lives (World Bank 2012). The discussion in this chapter draws mainly on the resilience function and shock-readiness feature of SPL systems to manage risk and uncertainty in the changing world of work, which they achieve through instruments that fall into three categories, summarized in table 4.1 and outlined in more detail in annex 4A.

To address the risks associated with current and future labor markets, African governments need to rethink social protection systems (World Bank 2019b) while taking into account several issues. First, labor markets in the region face pronounced risks induced by the digital revolution and other global trends, resulting in large movements of workers across rural-urban spaces, jobs, industries, sectors, and borders. Thus, social protection policies will need to effectively manage a large set of risks for workers in transition. Second, given the low baseline of social protection coverage in most Sub-Saharan African countries, a comprehensive expansion of coverage would require more resources than are available over the coming years. Consequently, it will be crucial to account for the fiscal implications of expanding coverage in the Sub-Saharan Africa context. Third, given the low income level of most Sub-Saharan African countries, it will be important to identify ways to balance competing policy priorities such as education and health, infrastructure and security, and optimizing public investments.

The chapter is structured as follows. The next section identifies the disruptions to African labor markets from the digital revolution, which is occurring within the context of other trends, that will require social protection. That section also examines the fiscal and policy constraints to comprehensive social protection coverage in Sub-Saharan Africa. The chapter then illustrates several

Table 4.1 Social Protection and Labor Programs

Social protection and labor programs	Objectives	Types of programs
Social safety nets and social assistance (noncontributory)	Reduce poverty and inequality	• Unconditional cash transfers • Conditional cash transfers • Social pensions • Food and in-kind transfers • School feeding programs • Public works • Fee waivers and targeted subsidies • Other interventions (social services)
Social insurance (contributory)	Ensure adequate living standards in the face of shocks and life changes	• Contributory old-age, survivor, and disability pensions • Sick leave • Maternity and paternity benefits • Health insurance coverage • Other types of insurance
Labor market programs (contributory and noncontributory)	Improve chances of employment and earnings; smooth income during unemployment	• Active labor market programs (training, employment intermediation services, wage subsidies) • Passive labor market programs (unemployment insurance, early retirement incentives)

Source: World Bank 2019b.

social protection policy options to consider in responding to jobs uncertainty and transitions in the future of work. It also provides recommendations for overcoming the fiscal and policy constraints to providing more realistic levels of social protection coverage. The chapter concludes by outlining areas for future research.

Systemic Risks and Fiscal Constraints to Social Protection Coverage in Sub-Saharan Africa

The systemic disruptions to labor markets in Sub-Saharan Africa in a changing world of work are inducing the movement of workers across jobs, industries, sectors, and borders. These labor transitions will add to the already high levels of unmet needs for social protection and risk management in Sub-Saharan Africa. Starting with the digital revolution, the main focus of this book, this section identifies these disruptive factors, the risks they generate for the labor force in Africa, and the fiscal and policy constraints to expanding social protection coverage.

The Digital Revolution, Other Global Trends, and the Risks They Pose to African Labor Markets

Recent studies point to the systemic disruptions to formal labor markets by digitization and globalization as key determinants of the future of work (World Bank 2019b). These trends are likely to affect no more than 20 percent of workers in the region, however, because roughly 90 percent of workers in Sub-Saharan Africa operate in the informal economy, as chapter 3 discusses. The structure of Sub-Saharan African economies and their low levels of formalization mean that the region has a different starting point. As chapter 1 observes, most Sub-Saharan African countries do not have a large manufacturing sector (less than 10 percent of the workforce). Most employment is in agriculture (60–70 percent) and consumer services (20–30 percent) (IMF 2018b), often in the informal sector, and characterized by income volatility.

For most Africans, therefore, the interaction of digital innovations with other factors will induce job transitions across industries, sectors, and borders, generating both risks and opportunities for work. This subsection outlines these global drivers of disruption of labor markets. They include digital technology generation and adoption, which are taking place within an environment of greater economic integration; climate change and fragility; and demographic change in Africa.[3] These trends disrupt economies, diversify the world of work, and challenge norms such as the standard employment relationship around which risk-sharing SPL policies in industrialized countries developed beginning early in the twentieth century (World Bank 2019a). The risks they pose for Sub-Saharan African economies include shocks (earnings volatility, work disruption, outdated or unsought skills, and so forth) and market failures (uncertainty, coordination failures, market power, and so forth). According to the World Economic Forum, the impact for nearly all these drivers will occur by 2025, highlighting the urgency for adaptive action today (WEF 2016).

Digital Technologies

Digital technology innovations are transforming the nature of work, including in Sub-Saharan Africa. As discussed in chapter 1, adoption of digital technologies offers the potential for strong, positive net effects on jobs. Chapter 3 notes that adoption of digital technologies also has the potential to lead to higher productivity and jobs gains in the informal sector, with mobile technologies in sectors like financial services and agriculture likely to generate a significant number of jobs for low-skilled workers (IMF 2018b; Ng'weno and Porteous 2018; World Bank and China Development Bank 2017). As box 4.1 shows, however, digital technologies could have disruptive and jobs-displacing impacts in some sectors, such as mining in resource-rich countries and the public sector.

Digital Technologies and Disruptions to Work in Africa's Mining Sector

The nonrenewable resources sector is one of the main "old" sectors in many Sub-Saharan African countries set to be disrupted by the adoption of digital technologies, with implications for formal and informal jobs. Of the region's 48 economies, 19 can be considered rich in mineral resources, defined by the International Monetary Fund as having mineral rents contributing at least 25 percent of their exports (Lundgren, Thomas, and York 2013). Globally, it is estimated that robotic technologies in driverless vehicles, sensor-based sorting of minerals, and data analytics will reach their peak deployment in the mining sector through 2030. In the global mining industry, the adoption of digital technologies will mean a potential loss of 330,000 jobs, or nearly 5 percent of the workforce, with implications for Africa's mineral-rich countries. Despite a strong focus on the risk of job losses to automation, accompanying improvements in safety could result in a 10 percent decrease in lives lost and a 20 percent decrease in injuries through 2030 (WEF and Accenture 2017). In Sub-Saharan Africa, the mining sector contributes a small share of aggregate national employment despite contributing between 25 and 86 percent of exports in 19 mineral-rich economies, and accounting for 60–90 percent of foreign direct investment in many countries (figure B4.1.1).

Figure B4.1.1 **Contributions of Mining Sector to Exports and National Employment, Selected Sub-Saharan African Countries**

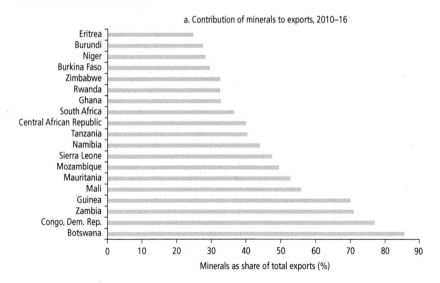

a. Contribution of minerals to exports, 2010–16

Minerals as share of total exports (%)

(continued next page)

Figure B4.1.1 **Contributions of Mining Sector to Exports and National Employment, Selected Sub-Saharan African Countries (continued)**

b. Contribution of mining sector to national employment, 1990–2014 versus 2005–18

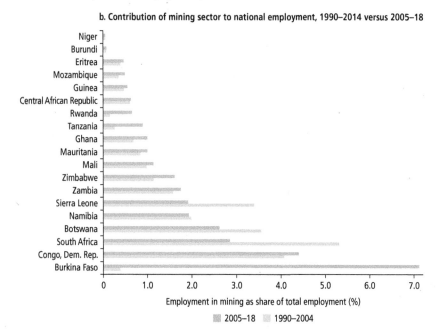

Employment in mining as share of total employment (%)

■ 2005–18   ▨ 1990–2004

Source: Usman et al., forthcoming.

In many countries, the number of people engaged in artisanal and mostly informal mining is three to six times higher than in formal direct jobs in the sector (figure B4.1.2). The sector constitutes a smaller share of national employment than agriculture, for instance. Employment in the sector has been stable, with notable exceptions. In countries like Burkina Faso and Mali, it has increased because of recent foreign direct investment flows and relatively new large-scale gold mining activity. Only South Africa has witnessed a steady decline in absolute employment in the sector, from a peak of more than 900,000 employees to fewer than 400,000 as of 2017, and it is one of the countries where large-scale adoption of digital technology could further disrupt employment.

In the academic and policy literature, debate is ongoing about the impact of digital technologies on work in the mining sector. The evidence so far is sketchy and presents a mixed portrait—on the one hand, promising to create beneficial outcomes for companies, communities, and governments, and, on the other hand, threatening to exacerbate the tension between productivity enhancement and equity concerns. Some of

(continued next page)

Figure B4.1.2 **Employment in Formal versus Artisanal Mining, Selected Sub-Saharan African Countries, 2017**

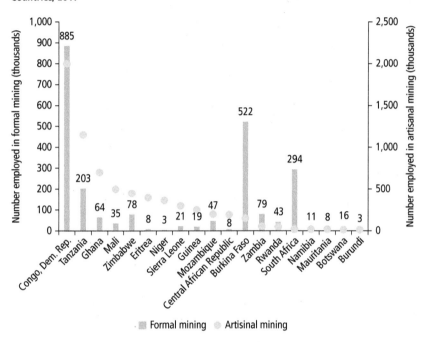

Source: Usman et al., forthcoming.
Note: Formal mining employment numbers based on estimates by the International Labour Organization.
Artisinal mining employment numbers based on estimates by the Intergovernmental Forum on Mining, Minerals, Metals, and Sustainable Development.

the questions raised include the following: Could the adoption of digital technologies result in massive labor displacement, especially at the lower-skill end of occupational profiles and routine tasks (see figure B4.1.3)? Could it eliminate hazardous occupational profiles—for example, in underground mines? Could it create new occupational profiles that are more inclusive of women, the elderly, and other marginalized groups? Could digital technologies enhance the productivity of artisanal miners, formalize their activities, and promote the development of small and medium-size enterprises in the sector through miniaturization of equipment? Could digital technologies enable the achievement of national development objectives in the sector beyond employment, through tax policy and enforcement and stronger social protection and labor interventions for mining communities? These are important policy debates for stakeholders in the mining sector, including governments, industry, and mining communities where employment in the sector is often the only major source of income.

(continued next page)

Box 4.1 (continued)

Figure B4.1.3 Mining Industry Employment by Occupational Category, South Africa and Zambia

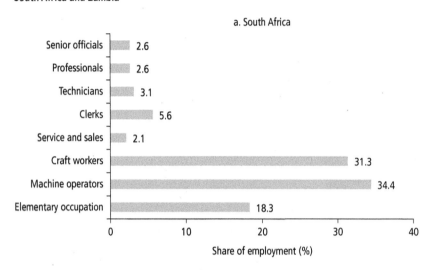

a. South Africa

Senior officials	2.6
Professionals	2.6
Technicians	3.1
Clerks	5.6
Service and sales	2.1
Craft workers	31.3
Machine operators	34.4
Elementary occupation	18.3

Share of employment (%)

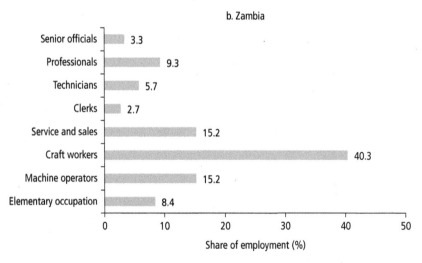

b. Zambia

Senior officials	3.3
Professionals	9.3
Technicians	5.7
Clerks	2.7
Service and sales	15.2
Craft workers	40.3
Machine operators	15.2
Elementary occupation	8.4

Share of employment (%)

Source: Usman et al., forthcoming.

Source: Based on Usman et al., forthcoming.

Despite the anticipated net aggregate gains in productivity and jobs that digital technologies can bring, policy makers will need to manage the transitional costs. The people moving from one job or set of tasks to others, or who are temporarily unemployed before finding alternate work, will require social protection. Policy makers will also need to mitigate the unequal distribution of these gains and potential disproportional impacts by gender, sector, and skill level (ILO 2017).

Global and Regional Economic Integration

The acceleration of trade integration in Sub-Saharan Africa characterizes the context of the digital revolution in the region. Trade integration will affect labor markets in profound ways because of new economic opportunities as well as resulting adjustment costs. Given the low levels of integration in Sub-Saharan Africa (figure 4.1), trade integration is accelerating and has almost tripled since the 1980s (IMF 2018b). Only about 17 percent of total exports is traded within Africa compared with 68 percent for Europe and 59 percent for Asia (figure 4.1). African countries have now ratified the African Continental Free Trade Area (AfCFTA), building on a history of subregional integration efforts.[4] Its implementation will change the trade and investment framework of countries in the region.[5] Estimates by the United Nations Economic Commission for Africa suggest that AfCFTA has the potential to boost intra-African trade by 52 percent from the elimination of tariffs alone (UNECA, African Union, and African Development Bank 2017). Further trade facilitation and elimination of nontariff barriers are expected to double the gains in intraregional trade. Recent analyses suggest that, because of economies of scale especially for smaller

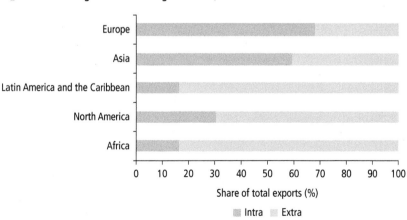

Figure 4.1 Extraregional and Intraregional Trade, 2017

Share of total exports (%)

Europe, Asia, Latin America and the Caribbean, North America, Africa

■ Intra   ■ Extra

Source: World Bank based on 2018 data from the United Nations Conference on Trade and Development database (UNCTADstat).

African economies, increased economic integration presents opportunities to create resilience to global shocks through diversifying exports (Brixiová, Meng, and Ncube 2015), supporting industrial growth (IMF 2019), enabling participation in global value chains, and increasing investment flows to the region (figure 4.2). AfCFTA is expected to increase competition, leading to efficiency gains and reduced costs and prices, and hence large welfare gains.

The structural transformation following AfCFTA will have implications for the future of work in the region. Still, the reallocation of factors of production within and across sectors and countries will impose adjustment costs. In the

Figure 4.2 Composition of Trade within Africa versus African Exports to the Rest of the World

a. Composition of intra-African trade

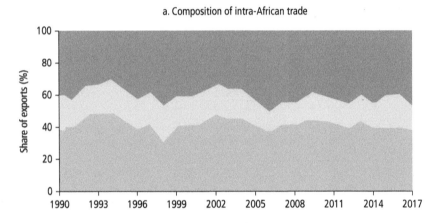

b. Composition of African exports to the rest of the world

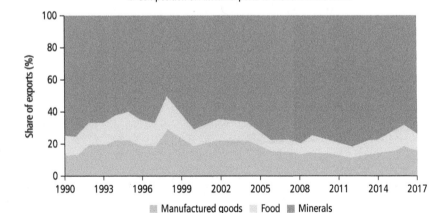

Manufactured goods   Food   Minerals

Source: World Bank calculations based on United Nations Comtrade data and International Monetary Fund data.

short run, job dislocations will occur across firms, sectors, and borders, as a reduction in trade barriers increases the substitutability of labor within and between countries. Despite expected economy-wide increases in investments and jobs, both investments and jobs will likely divert to more efficient locations. Without supportive public policies, those communities with preponderant employment in declining industries will likely see increased levels of poverty. In subsequent phases of the integration, ease of labor mobility may affect migration.

Figure 4.3 presents a simple representation of the costs of adjustment, defined as the value of output that is forgone in the transition to new, long-run production patterns because of the time taken to reallocate factors. The decline in the level of output during the initial phases of transition or adjustment follows a J-shaped curve (Francois, Jansen, and Peters 2011). More recent studies show that, depending on labor market frictions and the mobility of capital, the duration of the transition could be longer, and the magnitude of the adjustment costs could be larger (Dix-Carneiro 2014; Dix-Carneiro and Kovak 2017). In Brazil, regions that implemented tariff liberalization faced deteriorating labor market outcomes in the form of falling formal sector employment and earnings over a prolonged period: although on average households experienced net gains within each percentile of the income distribution, workers in some regions suffered earnings declines after 20 years that were three times larger than the declines after 10 years (Dix-Carneiro 2014).[6]

Overall, increased trade will have distributive implications with consequences for income, poverty, human development, and welfare. A large segment of the population in each country faces a high degree of vulnerability

Figure 4.3 Adjustment Paths Following Trade Liberalization

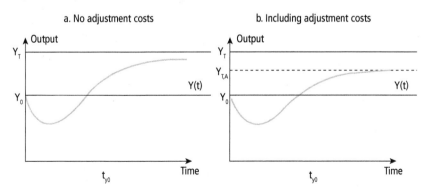

Source: Francois, Jansen, and Peters 2011.
Note: The long-run equilibrium path is represented by Y_T. If trade liberalization takes place at time t_{y0}, output would rise from Y_0 to Y_T in the absence of adjustment costs. With adjustment costs, however, output will instead follow a J-shaped curve, line $Y_{(t)}$, first declining below initial output Y_0 and gradually approaching Y_T. The discounted difference between Y_T and the curve $Y_{(t)}$ is the adjustment cost.

because of increasing regional competition, but there will be consumption gains. Complementary economic and social protection policies are needed to reduce trade costs and barriers to the free movement of factors and help workers adjust and benefit from new opportunities from regional integration.

Climate Change and Fragility

Climate and conflict drivers make up a second set of factors that define the environment within which digital innovations disrupt labor markets and result in worker transitions. Climate change causes asset losses (for example, through disability after floods or other natural disasters), crop losses (as a result of drought or crop disease), and food price shocks (World Bank 2016). Climate shocks are particularly acute in the region because of its heavy reliance on the agriculture sector for employment and subsistence, thereby placing many lives at risk of increased poverty and food insecurity (ILO 2018). Agrarian economies are especially vulnerable to unpredictable weather patterns and the resulting land-related conflicts. The impacts of climate change have already reduced yields by about 40 million tons of grain a year between 1981 and 2002 (World Bank 2016), and the losses are projected to reach 3 percent per year by 2030 (ILO 2017). Higher temperatures in tropical low-income countries have a long-lasting impact, particularly through the agriculture and manufacturing sectors, but also on labor productivity, mortality, health, and conflict (IMF 2017, 2018b). For the median low-income developing country with an average temperature of 25°C, the effect of a 1°C increase lowers growth by 1.2 percentage points (map 4.1).

Fragile and conflict situations also cause disruptions and the movement of large groups of people in African countries. The fragility framework of the

Map 4.1 **Effect of a 1°C Increase in Temperature on Real per Capita Output, Grid Level**

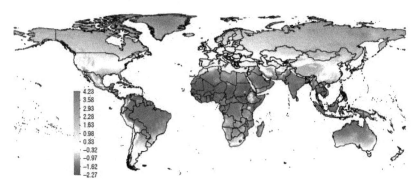

4.23
3.58
2.93
2.28
1.63
0.98
0.33
−0.32
−0.97
−1.62
−2.27

Source: IMF 2017. © International Monetary Fund. Reproduced with permission from the International Monetary Fund; further permission required for reuse.
Note: C = Celsius.

Organisation for Economic Co-operation and Development (OECD) identifies 58 fragile contexts, 35 of which are in Sub-Saharan Africa (OECD 2018b).
Incidents of conflict and violence have increased, from fewer than 10,000 in
2000 to about 50,000 in 2019. Conflict-related deaths have increased, from
about 2,500 in 2002 to nearly 15,000 in 2019. The number of internally displaced
persons due to conflict and violence is at an all-time high of about 14 million
(figure 4.4). Of the nine countries in extreme fragility in active armed conflict,
five are in Africa. These fragile situations are increasingly transnational and

Figure 4.4 Conflict Events Worldwide and Internally Displaced Persons in Africa

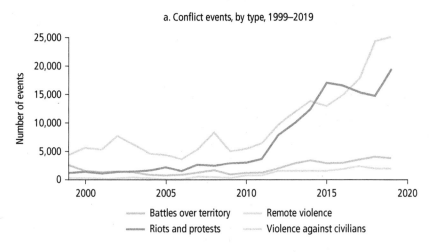

a. Conflict events, by type, 1999–2019

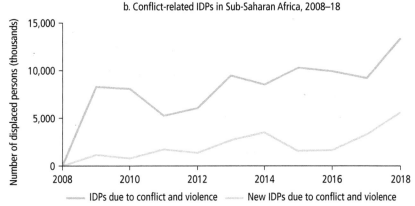

b. Conflict-related IDPs in Sub-Saharan Africa, 2008–18

Sources: World Bank calculations based on Armed Conflict Location and Event Data Project (ACLED),
www.acleddata.com (panel a); Internal Displacement Monitoring Center database, www.internal-displacement.org
(panel b).
Note: IDP = internally displaced person.

have intersecting drivers, including competition for political power, violent extremism, intercommunal conflicts, climate change, rising inequality, resource scarcity, demographic pressures, new technologies, and illicit financial flows (United Nations and World Bank 2018). Violent conflict scatters populations and disrupts incomes. According to the United Nations High Commissioner for Refugees, by the end of February 2019, more than 2.5 million internally displaced persons had settled in the Lake Chad Basin, including about 2 million in Nigeria, 246,000 in Cameroon, 126,000 in Chad, and 104,000 in Niger.[7] In Central Africa, conflict has triggered forced displacement of about 641,000 internally displaced and about 591,000 refugees in Cameroon, Chad, and the Democratic Republic of Congo. In East Africa, there are 806,680 Somali refugees living mainly in Ethiopia, Kenya, and the Republic of Yemen. The forceful ejection of people from their homes and communities frames the broader context of the digital revolution in payments systems, mobile technology, and other innovations in many parts of Sub-Saharan Africa.

Rapid Demographic Changes

A rapid demographic transition is the third factor that defines the environment within which digital technologies will affect the future of work in Sub-Saharan Africa. This changing demography is characterized by a youth bulge, rapid urbanization, and rising migration flows. The region's population is projected to nearly double in the next two decades, from approximately 900 million in 2015 to 1.7 billion in 2040 (figure 4.5, panel a) (IMF 2018b). More than half of the anticipated growth in global population between now and 2050 is expected to occur in Africa (UNDESA 2017). With half of Sub-Saharan Africa's population under 25 years of age, the labor supply in the region is estimated to increase by 198 million between 2017 and 2030 (ILO 2018), and 11 million young Africans are expected to enter the labor market each year for the next decade. As the labor force increases, there is a need to create 20 million jobs each year (IMF 2018b).

Furthermore, the region's growing population is urbanizing fast, but with low incomes and high engagement in the informal sector. Sub-Saharan Africa's urban population doubled since the mid-1990s, reaching almost 400 million in 2016, rising from 31 percent in 2000 to 38 percent in 2016 (Hommann and Lall 2019). Nearly three-fourths (72 percent) of the region's urban population resides in urban areas outside the largest city of each country. But the region is urbanizing at a much lower income level than other regions historically (figure 4.5, panel b). Today, 40 percent of the Sub-Saharan African population lives in an urban area with an average per capita income of about US$1,000. In comparison, when the Middle East and North Africa region reached the 40 percent mark in 1968, its per capita income was US$1,800; and per capita income in East Asia and Pacific was US$3,617 reached the same point in 1994 (Hommann and Lall 2019).

Figure 4.5 Demographic Transition and Urbanization in Sub-Saharan Africa

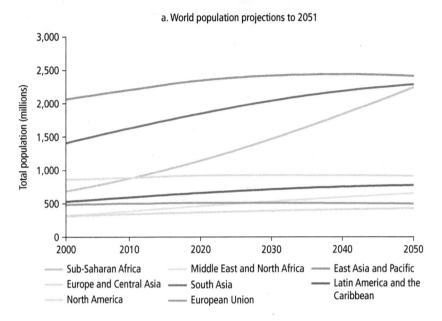

a. World population projections to 2051

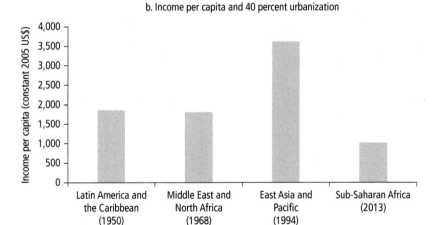

b. Income per capita and 40 percent urbanization

Sources: World Bank calculations based on World Development Indicators database; Hommann and Lall 2019.
Note: In panel b, years in parentheses indicate the year each region reached the 40 percent benchmark.
US$ = US dollar.

These low urban incomes suggest that Sub-Saharan Africa's urbanization does not come with good and productive jobs. The low quality of jobs in Africa's growing cities is attributable to insufficient infrastructure investments in physical capital (transport and housing) and human capital (schools, health clinics, and so forth) that undermine the agglomeration benefits of cities, raise the costs of doing business, and make cities uncompetitive. Most Sub-Saharan African countries have not seen a large reallocation of economic activity from subsistence agriculture toward the more productive industrial and service sectors, and this lack of reallocation has resulted in urbanization without growth.

Figure 4.6 **Destinations and Reasons for Emigration by Africans**

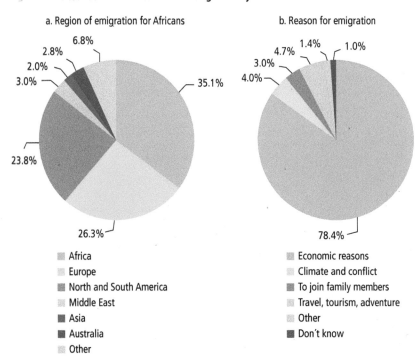

a. Region of emigration for Africans

6.8%
2.8%
2.0%
3.0%
35.1%
23.8%
26.3%

- Africa
- Europe
- North and South America
- Middle East
- Asia
- Australia
- Other

b. Reason for emigration

1.4%   1.0%
4.7%
3.0%
4.0%
78.4%

- Economic reasons
- Climate and conflict
- To join family members
- Travel, tourism, adventure
- Other
- Don't know

Source: World Bank calculations based on 2019 data from the Afrobarometer database.

Finally, Africa's population growth is linked to increased levels of migration, especially within the continent. Since 1990, the total number of migrants from Africa has increased by almost 80 percent, reaching 36.3 million people in 2017 (Mo Ibrahim Foundation 2019). African migrants represented only about 14 percent of the global migrant population, however, much less than the shares from Asia (41.0 percent), Europe (24.0 percent), and Latin America (14.6 percent) in 2017. More than 70 percent of Sub-Saharan African migrants move within the continent (figure 4.6, panel a). Almost 80 percent of African migrants are driven by the hope for better economic or social prospects (figure 4.6, panel b). According to Afrobarometer data, contemporary African migrants are mostly young, with about 60 percent of irregular migrants younger than age 35 years. The intersection of the population boom, youth bulge, urbanization, and migration will therefore have significant implications for work, especially in cities and urban areas in African countries. Unlike other regions, Sub-Saharan Africa has a rapidly growing population that is moving to cities and is increasingly engaged in the informal sector.

Fiscal Constraints to Social Protection Coverage in Sub-Saharan Africa

In a world of rising risks requiring greater levels of social protection, the baseline of coverage in Sub-Saharan Africa is low, fragmented, and underpinned by fiscal and policy constraints.[8] SPL systems cover less than 20 percent of Sub-Saharan Africa's population (figure 4.7, panel a). Most African countries have recently established social safety net (SSN) programs to protect the poor and vulnerable (Beegle, Coudouel, and Monsalve 2018). The number of countries with SSN programs rose to 18 in 2000, 36 in 2010, and 45 in 2017 (figure 4.7, panel b). By 2016, 32 African countries had established national social protection strategies or policies, with SSN as a core pillar. The average number of programs per country is 15, ranging from 2 each in the Republic of Congo and Gabon to 56 in Burkina Faso. Despite increasing establishment of SSNs, social protection coverage more broadly remains very low for various reasons, including fiscal constraints.

SSN programs in particular cover more people than social insurance and other SPL instruments. Of the Sub-Saharan African populations that have coverage, 78 percent have access only to SSN programs, and only 17 percent are covered by social insurance (figure 4.8). The SSN instruments vary. In the region, cash transfers, conditional and unconditional, account for almost 41 percent of the SSN budget; public works constitute 12 percent; and in-kind transfers account for 11 percent. Of countries in the region, Burundi, the Central African Republic, Ethiopia, and Liberia spend the highest share of gross domestic product (GDP) on public works (Beegle, Coudouel, and Monsalve 2018; World Bank 2018d). Social pensions are more prevalent in upper-middle-income countries and in Southern Africa. In Central Africa and fragile states, SSNs are widely used as a response to shocks, and emergency and food-based programs are the most common types of programs.

Figure 4.7 Social Protection Coverage and Number of Programs

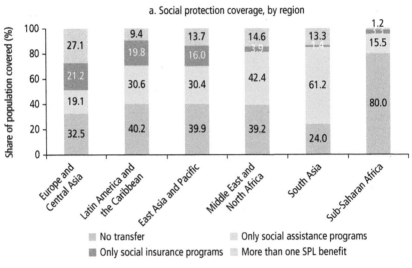

a. Social protection coverage, by region

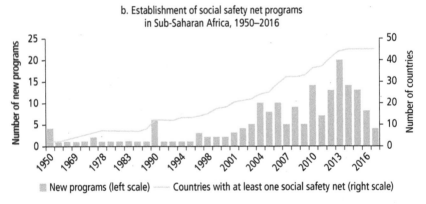

b. Establishment of social safety net programs
in Sub-Saharan Africa, 1950–2016

Sources: World Bank Atlas of Social Protection Indicators of Resilience and Equity (ASPIRE) database; Beegle, Coudouel, and Monsalve 2018.
Note: SPL = social protection and labor.

Social insurance programs in Africa target the elderly, and SSN programs predominantly target children, directly or indirectly, by assisting households with children (Beegle, Coudouel, and Monsalve 2018). Of all the SSNs directly targeting children through nutrition interventions, 29 percent target the benefits to orphans and other vulnerable children and include school feeding programs, provision of school supplies, and education benefits (figure 4.8). Of the 31 percent of the programs that target households more broadly, 19 percent target working-age individuals; 6 percent target the elderly; and

Figure 4.8 Social Safety Net Coverage of Population Groups, by Region and Program Type

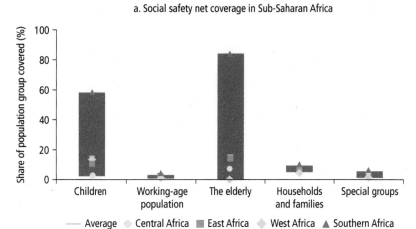

a. Social safety net coverage in Sub-Saharan Africa

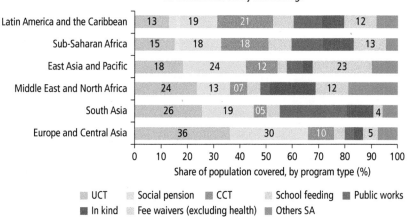

b. Global social safety net coverage

Sources: Beegle, Coudouel, and Monsalve 2018; World Bank 2018d.
Note: CCT = conditional cash transfer; SA = social assistance; UCT = unconditional cash transfer.

14 percent target other population segments, including the disabled, refugees, and internally displaced people. Old-age and veterans' social pensions vary from 7 percent in upper-middle-income countries and 9 percent in Southern Africa to less than 1 percent in low-income countries.

The low level of SPL coverage in Sub-Saharan Africa and the various risks for African populations on the move in a changing world of work would challenge the comprehensive implementation of social assistance packages such as those recommended in the 2019 *World Development Report*, referred to hereafter as WDR 2019, which are outlined in annex B. A universal basic income (UBI) is, for instance, put forward as an important option for expanding social assistance.[9] The fiscal implications of such a UBI for a basic social assistance package could amount to 9.6 percent of GDP in low-income countries, 5.1 percent in lower-middle-income countries, and 3.5 percent in upper-middle-income countries (figure 4.9). A comprehensive package could

Figure 4.9 **Social Assistance Packages and the Cost of Universal Basic Income**

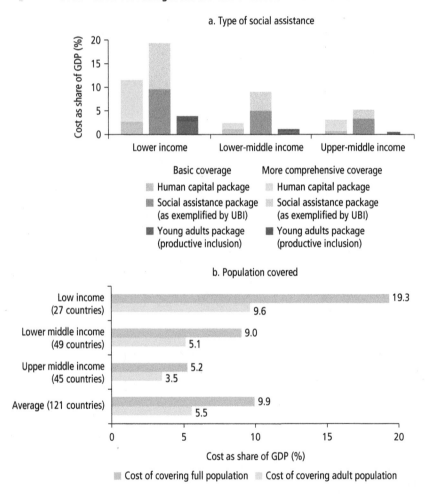

Source: World Bank 2019b.
Note: GDP = gross domestic product; UBI = universal basic income.

reach 19.3 percent of GDP for the poorest countries (World Bank 2019b). Implementing these UBI and other social minimum recommendations would be challenging in Sub-Saharan Africa because of the constraints of insufficient public investment, low levels of revenue mobilization, and competing policy priorities.

Insufficient Public Investment in SPL Systems

In most of Sub-Saharan Africa, insufficient resources are devoted to social protection. This situation can be attributed to low levels of social spending, dependence on foreign donor funding, and inefficiencies.

In aggregate, public expenditures on social protection in Sub-Saharan Africa are tilted toward pensions for formal workers. According to available data for some countries, SPL spending amounts to 1.7 percent of GDP in Côte d'Ivoire, 1.8 percent in Cameroon, and 2.4 percent in Tanzania (figure 4.10). As a percentage of total expenditures, that spending amounts to 6.3 percent in Côte d'Ivoire, 6.6 percent in Cameroon, and 12 percent in Tanzania. Looking more closely at the distribution of SPL expenditures by program type reveals a heavy concentration around pensions. These programs account for 93.9 percent of the total in Côte d'Ivoire, 66.7 percent in Cameroon, and 51.1 percent in Tanzania. SSN programs come in a distant second, at 27 percent of total spending in Côte d'Ivoire and 19.4 percent in Tanzania. Cameroon and Tanzania spend more on general subsidies than on labor market programs.

Figure 4.10 Social Protection and Labor Programs in Cameroon, Côte d'Ivoire, and Tanzania

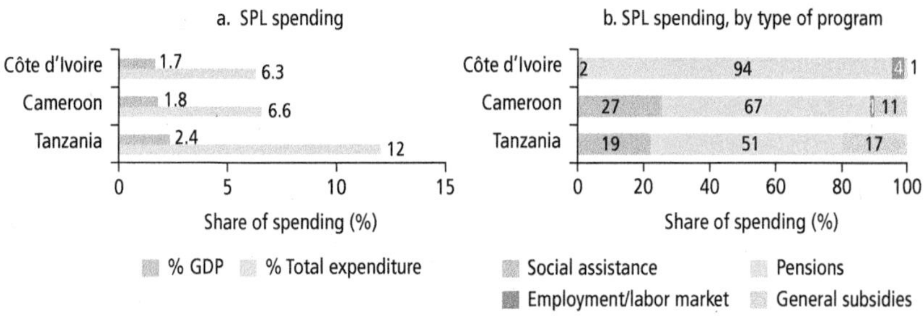

Source: World Bank calculations based on public expenditure reviews.
Note: GDP = gross domestic product; SPL = social protection and labor.

In the case of SSN programs, for example, spending as a share of GDP in Sub-Saharan Africa is similar to the global average for developing countries but lower in per capita terms. Countries in Sub-Saharan Africa, like other developing countries, spend on average 1.5 percent of GDP on SSN programs excluding general price subsidies (World Bank 2018d). Drawing on a sample of 124 countries, figure 4.11 shows how the region compares with other parts of the

Figure 4.11 Average Social Safety Net Spending, by Region

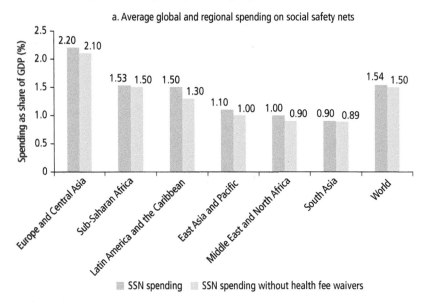

a. Average global and regional spending on social safety nets

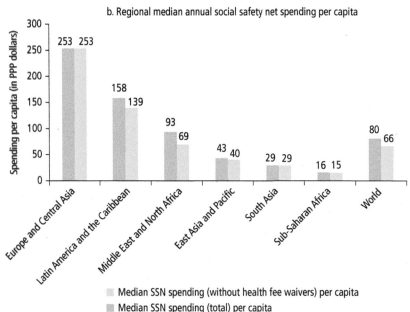

b. Regional median annual social safety net spending per capita

Source: World Bank 2018d.
Note: GDP = gross domestic product; PPP = purchasing power parity; SSN = social safety net.

developing world. Similarly, median SSN spending of 0.7–0.8 percent of GDP in Sub-Saharan Africa is comparable to that in East Asia and Pacific, the Middle East and North Africa, and South Asia (World Bank 2018d). Although Sub-Saharan Africa is the second-largest spending region in the world in relative terms, it is last in absolute terms. Countries in Latin America and the Caribbean spend $158 (in purchasing power parity [PPP] dollars), whereas African countries spend PPP$16 per person (World Bank 2018d).

Heavy donor dependence for the limited SSN programs available could also undermine sustainability. Since the beginning of the twenty-first century, many countries in Sub-Saharan Africa have introduced flagship SSN programs and are rapidly expanding coverage, but these programs are largely donor funded. Development assistance through bilateral and multilateral organizations represents an average of 55 percent of SSN financing in most African countries (figure 4.12) (Beegle, Coudouel, and Monsalve 2018). About two-thirds of the United Nations High Commissioner for Refugees' budget is allocated to programs in Africa, and this humanitarian assistance is counted as SSN spending (World Bank 2018d). Although South Sudan spends 10 percent of its GDP on SSN programs, the highest across Sub-Saharan Africa, it has only two emergency assistance programs, both of which are fully financed by donors. Some programs in the region have made the transition from full funding by development partners at inception to increased support by domestic resources. For instance, Kenya has committed to supporting SSN programs with domestic resources through its National Safety Net Program, which fully funds some programs and covers more than one-half the cost of others. Nevertheless, SSN programs are still mostly funded by external financing.

Figure 4.12 Share of Donor-Funded Safety Nets in Sub-Saharan African Countries

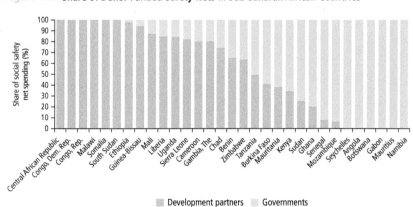

Source: Beegle, Coudouel, and Monsalve 2018.

Inefficiencies in SPL expenditure also contribute to the low levels of coverage. Administrative costs represent an estimated average of 17 percent of SSN program spending (Beegle, Coudouel, and Monsalve 2018), reflecting the cost of the initial investments in systems and the small size of many programs. As programs increase in size, average administrative costs are likely to fall. For instance, the administrative costs of the Social Safety Nets Project in Cameroon accounted for 65 percent of program spending at launch in 2015 but fell to 23 percent in 2016, while the number of beneficiaries quadrupled. In Mali, the administrative costs of the Jigisemejiri (Tree of Hope) Safety Nets Project fell from 41.8 percent to 11.9 percent of program costs in 2014–16, and the number of beneficiaries grew from about 30,000 to more than 375,000 people.

Challenges in Revenue Mobilization to Expand Social Protection Coverage
The second dimension of the limited SPL coverage and spending in Sub-Saharan African countries is the low levels of domestic revenue mobilization (DRM). WDR 2019 notes that expanding social assistance would require a significant mobilization of revenue by governments worldwide (World Bank 2019b). Low-income economies, like those in Sub-Saharan Africa, have the lowest tax-to-GDP ratio, at 14 percent in 2016, below middle-income economies (18 percent) and high-income economies (23 percent) (figure 4.13). Although revenue collection has improved overall, some resource-rich economies, including the Democratic Republic of Congo, Equatorial Guinea, and Nigeria, experienced reversals (figure 4.14). In the Democratic Republic of Congo, for instance, government tax and nontax revenues have been declining since 2012, amounting to just 8.1 percent of GDP in 2017 (World Bank, forthcoming). Relative to other

Figure 4.13 Tax as Share of GDP, by Country Income Group

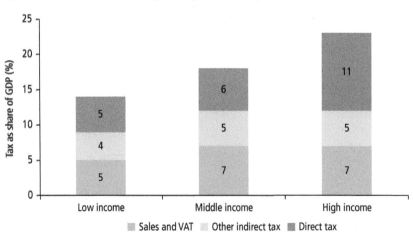

Source: World Bank 2019b.
Note: GDP = gross domestic product; VAT = value added tax.

Figure 4.14 Revenues in Sub-Saharan Africa, Non-Oil-Rich Countries versus Oil-Rich Countries

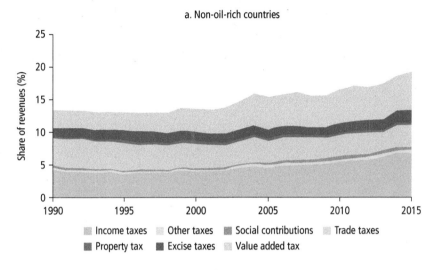

a. Non-oil-rich countries

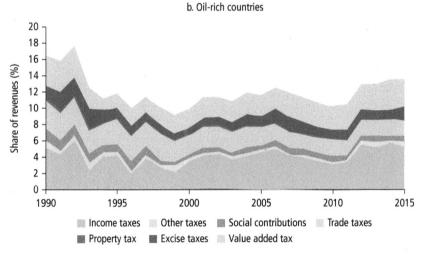

b. Oil-rich countries

Source: World Bank calculations based on internal data and United Nations University World Institute for Development Economics Research data.

regions, Sub-Saharan Africa continues to have the most economies with DRM below a minimum threshold of 15 percent (IMF et al. 2016) and the lowest tax-to-GDP ratio globally.

The reasons underlying weak revenue collection in Sub-Saharan Africa are multifaceted[10] and linked to tax policy and administration challenges. Low tax collection is correlated with low tax effort (see figure 4.15).[11]

Figure 4.15 **Tax Performance and Revenue Generation, Sub-Saharan Africa versus Selected Countries**

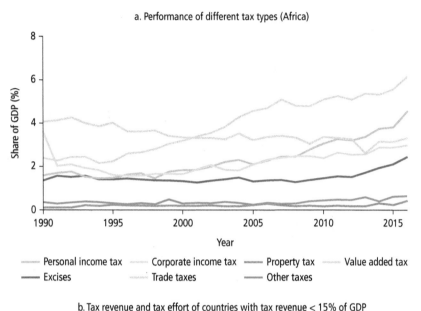

a. Performance of different tax types (Africa)

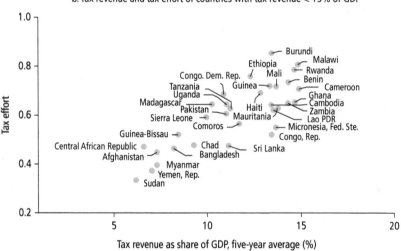

b. Tax revenue and tax effort of countries with tax revenue < 15% of GDP

Source: World Bank calculations based on internal data and United Nations University World Institute for Development Economics Research data.
Note: Tax effort (panel b) is defined as an index of the ratio between the share of the actual tax collection in gross domestic product (GDP) and taxable capacity. Taxable capacity is determined by predicting the tax-to-GDP ratio in a regression analysis. See Le, Moreno-Dodson, and Bayraktar (2012).

The effectiveness of the most important tax instruments tends to be below global averages and varies, especially among resource-rich economies (IMF 2017).[12] Although many thematic areas are relevant, four are worth highlighting. First, tax exemptions and other fiscal incentives limit resource mobilization. Differential tax treatment of specific sectors, activities, or regions is common and has wide-ranging implications for the fairness, efficiency, and effectiveness of tax regimes. Country-level estimates of tax expenditures are about 2–7 percent of national output.[13] In Mauritania, tax expenditures amount to an estimated 4.9 percent of GDP, or 30 percent of total nonextractive tax revenues. Tax exemptions are also administratively burdensome[14] and once granted prove difficult to eliminate, because beneficiaries lobby for their continued application. Research at the global and regional levels, however, suggests that, although taxes matter for investment, the effects tend to be less important in developing economies.[15] In several Sub-Saharan African economies, tax holidays have been shown to have no positive effect on investment.[16]

Second, international taxation challenges can undermine DRM efforts in Sub-Saharan Africa.[17] Several studies find that developing countries are relatively more exposed to profit shifting by multinationals[18] in an environment where revenue collection is often concentrated around a few firms.[19] Additionally, tax treaties that allocate taxing rights between countries can be a major source of revenue losses for Sub-Saharan African economies. As figure 4.16 shows, several countries have concluded highly unbalanced tax treaties, some of which reduce corporate income tax revenues by about 15 percent (Beer and Loeprick 2018).

Third, indirect taxation continues to account for the largest share of revenues in most countries in the region. Value added tax (VAT) remains the workhorse of DRM and has often allowed increasing the tax-to-GDP ratio. Given the importance of VAT in the revenue mix, it is important to maintain an efficient and administrable policy and have appropriate administrative capacity in place. Exemptions often narrow the tax base[20] and complicate administration but may sometimes be required to get the VAT accepted. In the Democratic Republic of Congo, for instance, the expansion of exemptions and lack of appropriate administrative systems undermine the effectiveness of the VAT, which was introduced in 2012 (World Bank 2019a). Restrictions on VAT refunds and administrative constraints are also common and act as an Achilles' heel for the functioning of the VAT. Pressures on a proper refund system can result from a lack of state resources, with governments effectively borrowing from taxpayers through the refund system, with real and perceived inability to guard against refund fraud, essentially an administrative challenge (see Bird and Gendron 2011).

Figure 4.16 Withholding Rates in Sub-Saharan Africa, 2016

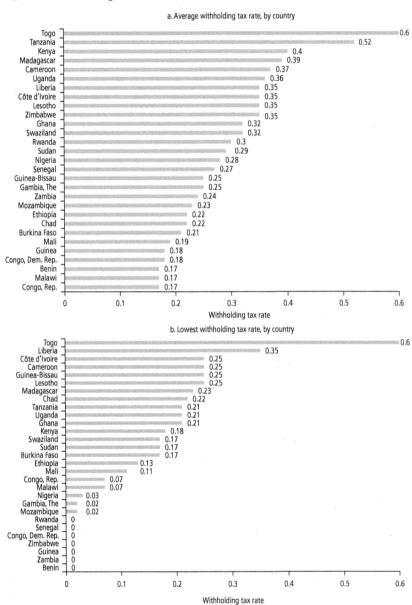

a. Average withholding tax rate, by country

Country	Rate
Togo	0.6
Tanzania	0.52
Kenya	0.4
Madagascar	0.39
Cameroon	0.37
Uganda	0.36
Liberia	0.35
Côte d'Ivoire	0.35
Lesotho	0.35
Zimbabwe	0.35
Ghana	0.32
Swaziland	0.32
Rwanda	0.3
Sudan	0.29
Nigeria	0.28
Senegal	0.27
Guinea-Bissau	0.25
Gambia, The	0.25
Zambia	0.24
Mozambique	0.23
Ethiopia	0.22
Chad	0.22
Burkina Faso	0.21
Mali	0.19
Guinea	0.18
Congo, Dem. Rep.	0.18
Benin	0.17
Malawi	0.17
Congo, Rep.	0.17

Withholding tax rate

b. Lowest withholding tax rate, by country

Country	Rate
Togo	0.6
Liberia	0.35
Côte d'Ivoire	0.25
Cameroon	0.25
Guinea-Bissau	0.25
Lesotho	0.25
Madagascar	0.23
Chad	0.22
Tanzania	0.21
Uganda	0.21
Ghana	0.21
Kenya	0.18
Swaziland	0.17
Sudan	0.17
Burkina Faso	0.17
Ethiopia	0.13
Mali	0.11
Congo, Rep.	0.07
Malawi	0.07
Nigeria	0.03
Gambia, The	0.02
Mozambique	0.02
Rwanda	0
Senegal	0
Congo, Dem. Rep.	0
Zimbabwe	0
Guinea	0
Zambia	0
Benin	0

Withholding tax rate

Source: World Bank calculations based on data from Hearson (2016).
Note: A higher value means a higher share of taxing rights for the source country. The WHT Rate Index provides an average of a linear score for the withholding rate on dividends, interest, and royalties. The name Swaziland was officially changed to Eswatini in April 2018.

Fourth, countries underuse several tax instruments. These instruments include excise duties, which often amount to less than 1 percent of GDP despite their comparative ease of administration, and property taxes, which can be an important source of local revenues and can be equitable when assessed on the basis of wealth criteria. Property taxes can be relevant in resource-exporting countries, where Dutch disease effects could lead to a property boom.

Competing Priorities for Public Investments and Policy Trade-Offs

The competing policy priorities for public investments in many countries in Sub-Saharan Africa can affect public investments in SPL systems. Many countries grapple with poor infrastructure, inefficient health systems, low educational attainment, and security and environmental challenges, all of which require government attention. Recent estimates suggest that the region's infrastructure needs amount to US$130 billion to US$170 billion per year, with a financing gap in the range of US$68 billion to US$108 billion (AfDB 2018). Thus, SPL expenditure broadly tends to be much lower than public investments in other sectors, including public sector wages and capital expenditure (figure 4.17). On average, Sub-Saharan Africa devotes 4.6 percent of total government spending to SSN programs (Beegle, Coudouel, and Monsalve 2018), which is lower than expenditures on energy subsidies, health care, education, and, in some cases, the military. In West Africa and the Sahel, many countries face severe security threats from violent extremism alongside high rates of poverty and vulnerability. Spending on energy subsidies—often cited as a means of supporting vulnerable households but largely regressive in practice—is greater than spending on SSN programs, with particularly high levels in Central and Eastern Africa and in low-income countries. Therefore, resources exist to rebalance available fiscal

Figure 4.17 Social Protection and Labor Expenditures and Other Public Investments, Selected Countries

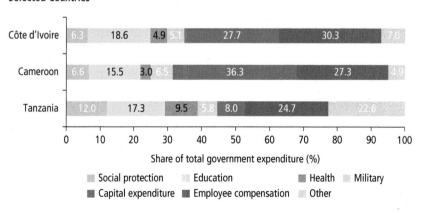

Source: World Bank calculations based on public expenditure reviews.

resources toward SPL interventions, although decisions will not be easy, given these competing demands.

Certain political economy factors also relate to perceptions of SSN programs and expectations for public investments. In several African countries, some surveys show that most of the population declares it is humiliating to receive money without having to work for it (figure 4.18) (Beegle, Coudouel, and Monsalve 2018). Among many households, the ability to provide for the needs of one's family is considered an aspect of human dignity. This attitude fits the view in many countries that recipients of SSN programs are undeserving of assistance and may become dependent on handouts—although investments in human capital are investments in the region's most precious asset.

There are also perceptions that SSN programs do not have productive impacts and are therefore a waste of public resources. In a study on cash transfers in five countries, individual beneficiaries saw few if any links between the cash transfer program and other sustainable livelihood options, and stated that it could increase dependency.[21] Although a minority of beneficiaries said they felt stigmatized by cash transfers, experiencing a loss of dignity, many said that cash transfers had increased their sense of self-worth and given them more control over their lives. In the same vein, a recent study finds that cash transfers have positive impacts on various development indicators, including monetary

Figure 4.18 Attitudes among Africans toward Receiving Money without Working for It

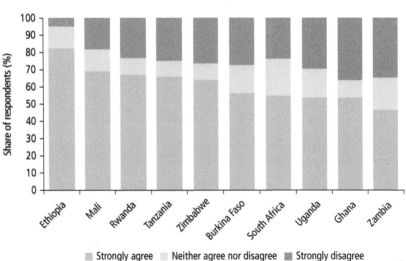

Source: Beegle, Coudouel, and Monsalve (2018) based on World Values Survey database.
Note: Respondents were asked to agree/disagree with the statement that receiving cash transfers without working is humiliating.

poverty, education, health, savings and investments, employment, and empowerment; but it also finds that these impacts depend on the programs' design and implementation features, including payment mechanisms, conditionality and complementary interventions, and supply-side services.[22]

Importance of Managing Risks, Leveraging Opportunities, and Optimizing Resources

This chapter builds on WDR 2019's recommendation for a social protection system that is progressive and starts with the most vulnerable (World Bank 2019b). For Sub-Saharan Africa, these SPL systems should aim for directly addressing shocks and risks from disruptions in labor markets (World Bank 2012). Given the low levels of DRM in the region, SPL systems need to be fiscally sustainable and balance policy trade-offs. SPL solutions will thus have three dimensions. One dimension strengthens traditional social protection systems to focus on workers in transition, especially those in the informal sector. The second dimension leverages new and innovative solutions for social protection that turn risks into opportunities. The third addresses fiscal and policy constraints by optimizing resources and navigating the political economy of policy making. In all three dimensions, digital technologies can be useful. Some examples of policy solutions are highlighted in the following subsections (see also annex 4C).[23]

Extending Traditional SPL Programs to Workers in Transition

Mitigating disruptions from technological change as well as the adjustment costs of trade integration will entail managing the uncertainty of employment transitions. Given the size of the informal economy, as discussed in chapter 3, a key priority for Sub-Saharan Africa to manage such transitions is to extend social protection coverage to the informal sector including those in urban areas and in the "gig" economy.

As many parts of Africa urbanize and workers move to cities, it is necessary to provide social protection to the urban labor force, which is often active in the informal sector. SSN programs, except for fee waivers and universal social pensions, in Africa have typically been designed with a rural focus (Beegle, Coudouel, and Monsalve 2018). A few programs have recently been launched in urban areas, however, such as the voucher system in Burkina Faso, the program to supply free access to water in urban Madagascar, the urban cash-for-work program in Mali, and the National Family Scholarship Program (Programme National de Bourses de Sécurité Familiale, PNBSF) cash transfer program in Senegal. Governments are now considering adjustments in design and implementation arrangements to identify and cover the urban poor more effectively.

The challenges to this endeavor include identification and targeting of the poor in informal urban settlements, communication campaigns, and high population mobility, which could result in low program uptake and enrollment—digital technologies can in principle help address all these challenges.

A recent World Bank study proposes a gradual realistic approach to laying the foundations of a pension scheme for the informal sector that could potentially be scaled up to become a mandatory, universal system (Guven 2019). The starting point for policy makers in Africa is to identify and understand the characteristics of the informal sector in their countries in order to design the appropriate scheme. Figure 4.19 presents the typical characteristics of informal sector workers and provides a summary of how these characteristics may be addressed when designing and operationalizing an appropriate pension scheme. Overall, three main principles need to be addressed, as follows (see also box 4.2): (1) minimizing administrative costs through reliance on technology such as digital payment systems; (2) leveraging stakeholders, such as informal sector associations, microfinance institutions, and so on, so that the institutional structure relied on for managing the scheme can identify informal sector

Figure 4.19 Addressing the Challenges of the Informal Sector

Challenges in the informal sector

| Informal sector is heterogeneous | Incomes and savings may not be regular | Sector is more susceptible to short-term shocks | Mobile and geographically distributed workers are hard to reach | Workers use other informal savings mechanisms | Informal sector is organized |

How these challenges can be addressed

| Allow for deposits made in different periods and amounts | Include behavioral economics and financial inclusion mechanisms | Allow for partial withdrawals | Build trust and links to other services in scheme |

| Allow population to use different channels to contribute remotely | Create a database to track individual contributions | Ensure transparency in services for population |

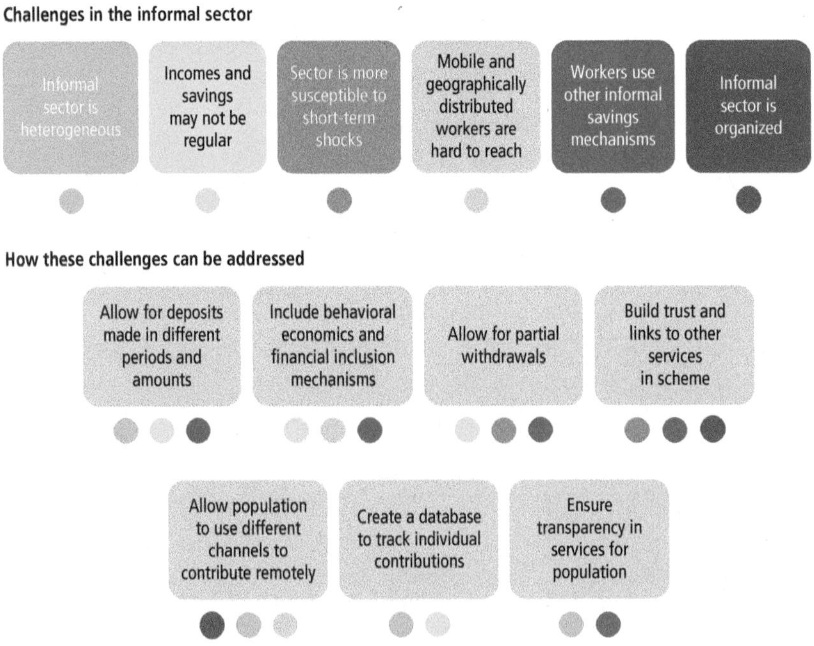

Source: Guven 2019.

workers who are able to save; and (3) instituting professional management of informal sector workers' savings to optimize returns and to minimize asset management costs. Although these principles apply to all pension schemes, they are particularly important in building trust and encouraging people to contribute in the case of voluntary pension schemes for the informal sector. Efficient administration and investment would avoid the erosion of the relatively small amount of savings by minimizing administrative and asset management costs. To manage expectations, programs must clearly communicate what people may expect to receive as a pension depending on what they contribute.

Despite the existence of several initiatives in the region, the experience of African countries (and the world) in extending pension coverage to the informal sector is limited. The governments of Ghana and Kenya were the first in the region to introduce specific schemes to cover the informal sector. Given the persistent low coverage and the realization that existing schemes do not respond to the needs of the informal sector, more governments are undertaking initiatives, although most efforts are incipient. The countries involved include Benin, Côte d'Ivoire, Mali, Nigeria, Rwanda, Senegal, Sierra Leone, Uganda, Zambia, and Zimbabwe.

These pioneering countries employ different approaches. In Rwanda, the formal sector pension administrator is also the central administrator for the informal sector pension scheme, which involves matching contributions from the government. Kenya launched the first mobile money scheme in the region, which leveraged the National Federation of Jua Kali Associations, an informal sector association, with the involvement of the Retirement Benefits Authority, a strong regulator, but struggled to attain scale. It initially reached only 100,000 individuals. Administrative costs have thus become a problem. The government plans to relaunch the Mbao Pension Plan and address the administrative challenges. In Uganda, the approach has relied on a more classic microfinance type scheme, but reaching scale has been a struggle. The government is considering a centralized approach to address the scale issue. The government of Ghana has been trying a combination of the above approaches. There, the Social Security and National Insurance Trust and other commercial providers operate in the market, but scale might be an issue. Other examples abound. Some countries in Latin America have extended coverage to small enterprises and the self-employed by a subsidy combined with a simplified tax and social security contribution mechanism called a mono-tax (Gentilini 2018; Ortiz 2018).

Recognizing these challenges, African governments are seeking innovative pension solutions that respond to the distinct needs of the informal sector. No one-size-fits-all program design can be implemented across the informal sector throughout Africa. Box 4.2 discusses several general principles that policy makers and technicians may consider.

BOX 4.2

Principles to Guide the Design of Informal Sector Pension Schemes

The general principles to guide policy makers in the design of pension schemes for the informal sector in African countries include the following.

- African governments can benefit from modern technology for improved outreach and reduced costs. Today, Africa is a global leader in the use of mobile money. Mobile network services are expanding rapidly across the region, which provides an opportunity to use mobile network operators in the collection of pension contributions from a widely dispersed informal sector. The cost of using mobile phones in the collection of contributions, including in remote areas, is likely to decline with scale.

- A communication strategy should be designed and implemented to raise awareness and build trust regarding the benefits of informal sector pension schemes. Governments should seek collaboration with potential public and private stakeholders—including microfinance institutions, mobile network operators, and associations among informal sector workers—in the implementation of a relevant communication strategy. A financial literacy training program during the implementation of the strategy could help informal sector workers make informed decisions.

- The design of pension products offered by an informal sector pension scheme should reflect the characteristics of the informal sector. A survey of these characteristics suggests that a voluntary defined contribution scheme involving a combination of short- and long-term savings accounts may be one possible product. The amounts and frequency of contributions, pension scheme rules, the payout requirements, and synergies with other services, such as health care, microfinance, training, and so on, should be carefully considered in the design of products and communicated to the public at the outset.

- An administrative platform needs to be established for the scheme. The platform should be able to maintain records on contributions, withdrawals, and account balances, while minimizing administrative costs. Creating the platform would require financing as part of the start-up costs. The administration of the pension scheme should ideally be linked to the national identification system. Central administration of the informal sector pension scheme can help on the costs front. Custodian and fund management services can also be aggregated under a central system to reduce costs.

- To improve the success of the scheme, the contributions should be invested by professionals to maximize returns and minimize asset management costs. Proper regulations must also be developed and implemented. The identity of the administrator of the pension scheme depends on the country context. It might range from the current pension administrator in the formal sector to a private sector operator or any other institution with the appropriate capacity. To be successful, these schemes must reach scale while minimizing the costs of asset management and operations.

(continued next page)

Box 4.2 (continued)

- The various approaches to realizing a scheme should be pilot tested before a national scale-up to evaluate methods and processes, including behavioral nudges, the role of various stakeholders, synergies with other products, the amount of contributions, subsidies, and so on. Although several broad approaches may work, the country-specific lessons learned through pilot testing should inform national design and implementation arrangements.

Source: Guven 2019.

Leveraging Innovative Solutions around Social Protection

As Africa experiences profound demographic changes, SPL programs should adapt and respond to the needs of people in transition. At least two solutions are worth highlighting here. First, interventions that combine short-term SSN programs with complementary active labor market policies that leverage economic activities targeted to youth can pave a pathway to productive employment (Newfarmer, Page, and Finn 2018). This support comes at a critical period when young people may be completing their education, making the transition to work, or engaging in low-productivity occupations (Filmer and Fox 2014). Remedial education and training programs, which aim to bridge the skills gap affecting youth employment prospects, combine training with internships, apprenticeships, and other labor market insertion initiatives (Arias, Evans, and Santos 2019, 315–21). Such programs tend to have modest impacts unless they are well designed and adapted to local contexts.

Second, rising migration provides the opportunity to better leverage migrant remittances for social protection. Migrant remittances help smooth household consumption and act as a form of insurance for African households facing shocks to their income and livelihood caused by natural disasters (Mohapatra and Ratha 2011). Globally, remittances seem to have stronger poverty-reducing impacts than formal cash transfers. Studies in Moldova and Vietnam show that remittances reach a greater share of poorer households, are often higher in value than cash transfers, and may be used particularly for productive investments.[24] Ethiopian households that receive international remittances are less likely than other households to sell their productive assets, such as livestock, to cope with food shortages (Ratha et al. 2011). Remittances in many low- and middle-income countries now represent the largest source of foreign exchange earnings—larger than official development assistance (ODA) (Mohapatra and Ratha 2011; World Bank 2019a). In Sub-Saharan Africa, they have grown by 9.6 percent, from US$42 billion in 2017 to US$46 billion in 2018 (World Bank 2018b, 2019a). Nigeria, which receives the highest amount of

Figure 4.20 **Migrant Remittances and Official Development Assistance, Selected African Countries**

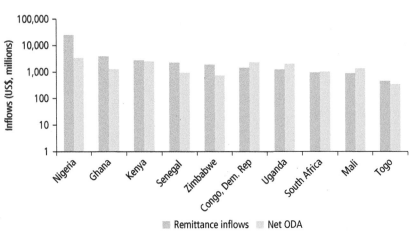

Sources: World Bank calculations using World Development Indicators data on official development assistance (2017) and migrants and remittances (2018).
Note: ODA = official development assistance; US$ = US dollar.

remittances in the region and the sixth-highest amount among lower-middle-income countries, received more than US$24.3 billion in official remittances in 2018 (figure 4.20). Similarly, in Cabo Verde, Comoros, Lesotho, Zimbabwe, and other countries, remittances are far larger than ODA receipts.

Reducing remittance costs can better enable African countries to reap the benefits of migration by channeling diaspora remittances toward social protection for poor households. The average cost of sending US$200 to Sub-Saharan African countries was 9.3 percent in 2019, the highest in the world (figure 4.21). Despite a declining trend, this cost is higher than the average 7 percent for lower-middle-income countries and more than triple the Sustainable Development Goal target of 3 percent by 2030 (World Bank 2019a). Remittance costs across many African corridors remain greater than 10 percent, the highest in the world (figure 4.21). Because of policy incoherence, remittance costs tend to include a premium, or cost markup, when national post offices have exclusive partnership arrangements with a dominant money transfer operator. The high costs involved in money transfers along many remittance corridors, particularly for poor workers who lack adequate access to banking services, reduce the benefits of migration, especially for poor households in origin countries. At the national level, opening national post offices, banks, and telecommunications companies to partnerships with other money transfer operators could remove entry barriers and increase competition in remittance markets (World Bank 2019a).

Figure 4.21 Cost of Sending Money and Cost Corridors in Sub-Saharan Africa, 2018

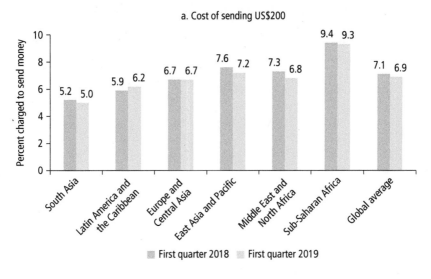

a. Cost of sending US$200

b. Highest-cost corridors

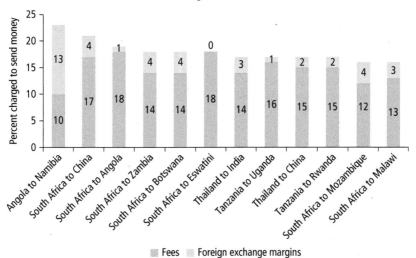

Source: Adapted from World Bank 2019a.
Note: Eswatini was previously named Swaziland. It was officially changed in April 2018. US$ = US dollar.

At the international policy level, reviewing financial regulations that deal with anti-money laundering (AML) and combating the financing of terrorism (CFT) measures can help reduce remittance costs. These AML/CFT measures have played an important role in de-risking strategies by global banks, which restrict business relations with whole categories of high-risk clients (World Bank 2019a). These banks indicate that risks to their reputation from AML/CFT and possible sanctions deter them from having correspondent bank accounts with MTOs. Mobile money services and digital payment systems can also help remittance transfers arrive faster and can potentially reduce costs.

Optimizing Resources for Investments in Social Protection

The optimization of resources can help address the fiscal and policy constraints to expanding social protection coverage. This section discusses three approaches: mobilizing sustainable resources, increasing the efficiency of current social protection expenditure, and managing policy trade-offs in allocating public investments.

Sustainable Resource Mobilization to Extend Social Protection Coverage

The fiscal space of Sub-Saharan African economies can be broadened by reallocating public expenditure toward social investments (Ortiz, Cummins, and Karunanethy 2017). Such reallocation could entail assessing ongoing budget allocations through Public Expenditure Reviews and other types of thematic budget analyses, and replacing high-cost, low-impact investments with those that have larger socioeconomic impacts. The social impacts of some large infrastructure projects, such as airports in third-tier cities and large sports stadiums, and public sector wages tend to be limited, but they consume large quantities of public resources. Budget items with large recurrent costs but small social impacts should also be reconsidered. For example, Costa Rica and Thailand reduced military spending to finance needed social investments (Ortiz, Cummins, and Karunanethy 2017). Countercyclical fiscal policies in resource-rich economies that are dependent on oil and mineral rents for government revenues can help mitigate the volatility of these rents and prevent a disruption in social spending.

Eliminating spending inefficiencies and tackling corruption can also create the fiscal space for social protection. The African Union estimates that 25 percent of the GDP of African states, amounting to US$148 billion, is lost to corruption every year. Global initiatives to return laundered resources back to developing countries, such as the Stolen Assets Recovery Initiative, should be a source of finance for social protection.

Tax reforms can generate additional revenue for sustainable investments in social protection. Estimates suggest that Sub-Saharan African countries could raise between 3 percent and 5 percent of GDP (US$50 billion to US$80 billion) from tax reforms, more than the US$36 billion the region receives each year through international aid (IMF 2018c). At least four solutions can help address the DRM challenges in Sub-Saharan Africa. First, eliminating or dramatically reducing cost-ineffective tax incentives through a systematic and transparent approach could result in significant additional revenues.[25] To help reduce race-to-the-bottom pressures among countries, coordination at a subregional level can provide boundaries and common targets. Notably, the West African Economic and Monetary Union (WAEMU) provides its members target corridors for VAT rates (15–20 percent), corporate income taxes (25–20 percent), and excise taxes (set by product); however, the effectiveness of WAEMU's de jure measures has been mixed.[26] Second, international tax rules need to be simpler and more responsive to match developing country needs. Priorities include appropriate unilateral or regional measures to help protect tax bases. Such measures include solutions to address challenges of asymmetrical information,[27] the revision of unbalanced tax treaties, and the adoption of wider antiabuse measures.[28] Third, countries need to pursue other tax policy opportunities, such as improving VAT efficiency and strengthening underused instruments. Excise taxes, which tend to be comparatively low in the region, hold large revenue potential (figure 4.22). They include socially desirable "sin taxes" (cigarettes, alcohol, sugar-sweetened beverages), "green taxes" (on fossil fuels and even carbon emissions), taxes on luxury goods consumed by high-income individuals, and other forms of taxation to help achieve progressivity and address negative externalities. Property taxes also can be increased as an important revenue source (figure 4.23).

Figure 4.22 Excise Tax Trends, Sub-Saharan Africa versus the Rest of the World

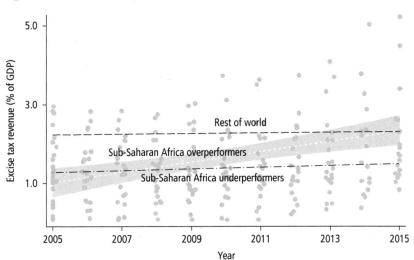

Source: World Bank calculations based on internal data and United Nations University World Institute for Development Economics Research data.
Note: Each dot represents a different country. The yellow band shows the 95 percent confidence interval around the mean. GDP = gross domestic product.

Figure 4.23 Property Tax Collections in Sub-Saharan Africa

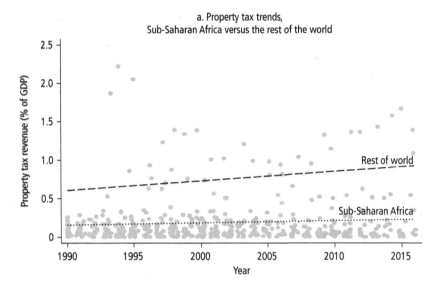

a. Property tax trends,
Sub-Saharan Africa versus the rest of the world

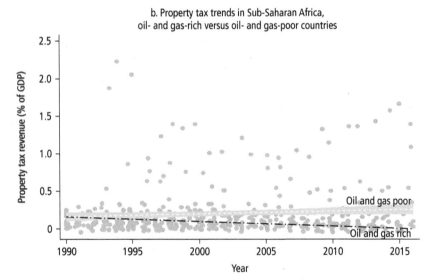

b. Property tax trends in Sub-Saharan Africa,
oil- and gas-rich versus oil- and gas-poor countries

Source: World Bank calculations based on internal data and United Nations University World Institute for Development Economics Research data.
Note: Each dot represents a different country. The yellow band shows the 95 percent confidence interval around the mean. GDP = gross domestic product.

Fourth, major opportunities exist to leverage digital technologies to address common technical revenue administration challenges. Reviewing existing information and communication technology systems and processes to deepen the computerization of operations can bear fruit. Basic and meaningful initial steps include investing in (1) obtaining and expanding relevant information available to tax and customs administrations, (2) instituting better mechanisms for effectively sharing information across institutions, and (3) filling capacity gaps in core functions such as data analysis, modeling, and audit selection. Extending e-filing options can bring important benefits in improving the business environment and help generate revenue,[29] and so can the promotion of electronic cash registers (see Awasthi and Engelschalk 2018). A recent simulation analysis suggests that reducing the distance to the digitization frontier by one-half can raise median VAT revenue by 1.7 percent (and median tariff revenue by 0.5 percent) in low-income developing countries (IMF 2018a).

Diaspora bonds could enable the direct use of remittances to provide social protection. These bonds are debt instruments issued by a government to raise financing from its overseas diaspora (Ketkar and Ratha 2004). Investors who purchase such bonds are usually motivated by a desire to contribute to the development of their home countries (Beegle, Coudouel, and Monsalve 2018). India, Israel, and Nigeria have successfully introduced diaspora bonds. Through such bonds, the State Bank of India raised more than US$11 billion by 2007, and Nigeria issued US$100 million in diaspora bonds in 2013 (Ketkar and Ratha 2004). Diaspora bonds are one component of using development impact bonds for social investments (Coleman 2016).

Finally, African governments can involve the private sector in innovative ways for sustainable resource mobilization to expand social protection coverage. Some governments in the region and elsewhere have made strides in leveraging corporate social responsibility (CSR) initiatives to fund their social development priorities (Beegle, Coudouel, and Monsalve 2018). In El Salvador, multinational companies have supported the creation of two major foundations in education and broader socioeconomic development. In Mauritius, the Ministry of Finance requested that all firms spend 2 percent of their profits on CSR activities approved by the government or transfer the funds to the government to be used for social and environmental projects. Several areas to consider in leveraging CSR to fund SSN programs include placing social protection on the global business development agenda, leveraging government engagement in the development of CSR within countries, ensuring that CSR activities align with the development objectives of SSN programs to maximize synergy, and defining those components of SSN programs that can be effectively addressed by CSR activities and resources.

Increasing the Efficiency of Current Social Protection Expenditures
The efficiency of SPL programs can be enhanced through better coordination, including through the use of digital technologies. Social registries can help reduce duplication of effort for concurrent SPL programs. Through integrated social registries that harmonize multiple programs using common intake and registration gateways, citizens can gain access to a broad array of benefits and services, with far lower transactions costs (Leite et al. 2017). These registries can connect people to public services (social, health, and financial inclusion) and prioritize the poorest with the aid of digital technology platforms that save millions of dollars caused by predigital era errors (Georgieva 2018). Pakistan's social registry now includes 85 percent of the population, serves 70 different programs, and has contributed to savings of US$248 million. In South Africa, a similar harmonization of various SPL programs saved US$157 million. Similar efforts to consolidate and rationalize programs are on the policy agendas of many countries (Beegle, Coudouel, and Monsalve 2018).

Increasing and rebalancing SPL spending among population groups and instruments can have a more lasting impact on poverty reduction. In addition to the current focus of SSN programs for children (29 percent) and households (over 31 percent coverage), more of the working-age population (currently at 19 percent) should also be covered, given that they are at high risk in Sub-Saharan Africa's changing world of work. Because SPL expenditures tend to be concentrated around pensions, it will be important to accelerate efforts to expand such contributory schemes to the informal sector. SPL interventions currently skewed toward cash transfers (41 percent of the SSN budget) should do more in productivity upgrading. An illustrative, but not exhaustive, list of instruments includes economic inclusion programs that combine safety nets with productive elements (see box 4.3, for example), public works for infrastructure, and health care programs directed at boosting human capital. Governments in East Asia successfully used public works programs to mitigate the impact of the Asian financial crisis in the late 1990s (Mitra and Ranjan 2011). Presently, South Asia has the highest share of public works spending, at 25 percent of its overall SSN budget (World Bank 2018d). Countries like Bangladesh and India, with large public works programs, have also recorded tremendous progress in poverty reduction.

Although public works programs improve consumption, income, and rates of employment in the short term, their long-term impact on economic welfare is less certain and depends on program design and implementation (Mvukiyehe 2018; Subbarao et al. 2013). In a recent survey, most SSN beneficiaries chose public health and nutrition programs (86 percent) over cash transfers (13 percent) and also chose roads (over 63 percent) over cash transfers (35 percent) (Khemani, Habyarimana, and Nooruddin 2019). Such a rebalancing in coverage of SSN instruments, depending on the context and type of risk,

Productive Inclusion through the Sahel Adaptive Social Protection Program

"Economic inclusion" or "productive inclusion" programs are multisectoral interventions that support and enable households to achieve sustainable livelihoods and increase their incomes and assets, while building human capital and promoting social inclusion. The Sahel Adaptive Social Protection Program is an example of a regional safety net that has productive elements. It covers severely climate-stressed and very low-income countries in the Sahel (Burkina Faso, Chad, Mali, Mauritania, Niger, and Senegal). It aims to foster increased productivity for very poor households engaging in agriculture and nonagricultural self-employment through a "graduation-type" integrated package designed to help them manage risks and increase resilience. Selected beneficiaries receive group formation and coaching through community-level agents, access to savings (village savings and loan associations), technology training, a US$150 cash grant, and psychosocial support (life and social skills training and an aspirational video). Several variations are being tested across countries (different recipients of the programs, conditional transfer recipient or not, rural versus peri-urban, and timing at the beginning or end of the transfer cycle). Different delivery arrangements are also being tested.

Source: World Bank's Partnership for Economic Inclusion Trust Fund.

and larger aggregate sums based on improved DRM, can help respond to the disruptions to African labor markets in the changing world of work.

Finally, improved coordination is necessary among development partners. This coordination would involve having clear reporting systems and a focus on the partners' respective comparative advantages to optimize development assistance for SPL programs. Development agencies should coordinate their resources and advice (see box 4.4) to avoid contributing to fragmentation, and to help develop SPL programs to scale, rather than spending on isolated pilots (World Bank 2012). Currently, large development partners like the European Union, France, and the United Kingdom are more likely to channel their support through their own programs, whereas those with smaller ODA programs, such as Austria and Finland, channel their support through multilateral agencies like the International Labour Organization, United Nations agencies, the World Bank, and international nongovernmental organizations (OECD 2012). This fragmentation is also reflected in the diverse mechanisms for providing social protection support directly and indirectly through sectoral programs. To ensure harmonization, development partners must adjust how they report and track aid spending on social protection (*Devex* 2016). Desirable measures

BOX 4.4

Donor Collaboration through the Rapid Social Response Trust Fund

The Rapid Social Response (RSR) multidonor program was established in 2009, in partnership with the World Bank, to help the world's poorest countries build effective social protection systems. The RSR is supported by Australia, Norway, the Russian Federation, Sweden, and the United Kingdom. In its Phase 1 (2009–12), the RSR had a crisis response orientation. It assisted countries in addressing urgent social needs stemming from crises and helped them build the capacity and institutions to respond better to future crises. In Phase 2 (2012 onward), the RSR shifted toward a broader agenda of social protection and labor (SPL) systems building. Cross-sectoral by nature, the RSR embraces core SPL areas as well as priorities in other sectors, including gender, nutrition, employment, jobs, and—more recently—disaster risk management. Since 2009, RSR has been able to support the growing social protection agenda through supporting pilot programs in countries without prior SPL experience, facilitating new dialogues and partnerships, and supporting knowledge exchanges between countries and globally. Specific interventions include designing new payment modalities, creating new targeting mechanisms, strengthening management information systems, and coordinating with ministries, agencies, and subnational governments. As of December 2016, approximately 131 million people worldwide were covered by SPL programs associated with RSR funding. The RSR's role, importance, and engagement continue to evolve in response to new challenges in social protection. As new frontiers emerge in the development arena, the role of social protection is growing, along with expectations for it to become more innovative and collaborative, with new programs and systems that will be able to respond not only to shocks originating within an economy, but also to exogenous shocks such as climate change, natural disasters, and displacements.

Source: World Bank 2018c.

include explicitly providing a code for social protection in the OECD Creditor Reporting System, providing a social protection marker comparable to tracking aid for gender and climate change, and using terms such as "cash transfer," "pension," and "insurance" in social protection project descriptions. Last, better coordination can be achieved if the various development partners engaged in Africa focus on their comparative advantage. Almost 40 percent of development assistance in 2016 from the OECD Development Assistance Committee went to social sectors (education, health, water, governance, and so forth) whereas non-OECD donors like China focused more on economic sectors (energy, transport, communications, banking, and business) (figure 4.24).

Figure 4.24 Comparing OECD-DAC Bilateral Aid and Chinese Loans to Africa, 2016

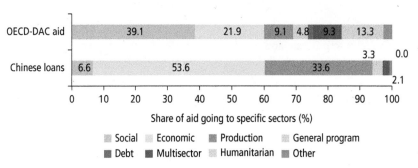

Sources: World Bank calculations based on the Johns Hopkins University School of Advanced International Studies–China-Africa Research Initiative database, (http://www.sais-cari.org/data), and Organisation for Economic Co-operation and Development Statistics, (https://www.oecd.org/dac/financing-sustainable-development/development-finance-data/Africa-Development-Aid-at-a-Glance-2019.pdf); Atkins et al. 2017; OECD 2018a.
Note: Data from the Organisation for Economic Co-operation and Development's Development Assistance Committee (OECD-DAC) include data for bilateral donors and aid by European Union institutions. Social sectors include health, education, governance and civil society support, water, and population. Economic sectors include communications, energy, business, transport, and banking. Production sectors include agriculture, forestry, industry, mining, and trade.

Managing Policy Trade-Offs

To manage policy trade-offs in allocating public investments, SPL policies should be integrated into the wider national and regional strategies of African governments. The goals of resilience, equity, and opportunity to help workers adjust and benefit from the future of work cannot be achieved with isolated programs, within a single sector, or through public mandates alone. Attaining them requires appropriate policy, legal, and institutional frameworks, as well as a portfolio of instruments and collaboration across economic sectors (World Bank 2012). The transition out of industrial era social insurance systems ideally should be linked to broader civil service reforms. This approach could be more politically feasible for rebalancing social spending that is otherwise skewed toward pensions in many countries. As the AfCFTA comes into effect, a broader discussion and review of SPL policies at the national and regional levels is necessary to minimize the negative impacts of trade liberalization on different population groups. Such discussion and review might result in specific SPL interventions targeting important regional corridors across the continent, especially in East, West, and Central Africa. Increasing public investments in social protection can be linked to a broader strategy to provide regional public goods in an era of increased integration. Managing policy trade-offs may necessitate renewing the underlying social contract between the state and citizens on where and how to allocate public resources to have the greatest welfare impacts in a changing world of work.

Conclusion

Building on the foundation of WDR 2019, this chapter examines social protection policies to mitigate and manage risks in the future of work in Africa. The following are areas in which further research can provide important insights.

- More assessments of the effectiveness of emerging SPL interventions that aim to extend social protection to the informal sector and the gig economy. This chapter highlights some interventions, including recent attempts to provide pensions to informal workers in India and across several African countries. Impact evaluations of these initiatives could help inform policy makers on whether these initiatives achieve the desired outcomes of retirement savings for the target group. Further research can help identify other emerging innovations that can be piloted and scaled up.

- Understanding ways to collaborate with the private sector, especially for active labor market policies to address urban poverty and youth unemployment. Global discussions around the role of the private sector have heavily, and rightly so, emphasized fair taxation as a means to support domestic revenue mobilization. In addition, more research is needed on how to leverage the private sector to support the provision of social protection. There can be collaboration with the private sector in areas around building skills of the poor and the vulnerable, apprenticeships, on-the-job learning, and other related labor market policies.

- How to leverage informal private transfers to serve a more effective risk-sharing and co-insurance function, especially in fragile settings. The chapter highlights how informal transfers such as remittances have grown so rapidly that they now exceed net ODA flows in several African countries. The importance of remittances is even more salient in countries or regions in conflict and fragility where public services collapse or are absent. Further research can help outline ways of further leveraging this growing source of financial flows for risk mitigation, especially among the poor and vulnerable in fragile situations.

Annex 4A. The World Bank's ASPIRE Program Classification

SPL AREA	PROGRAM CATEGORY	PROGRAM SUBCATEGORY
SOCIAL INSURANCE	Contributory pensions	Old age pension (all schemes, national, civil servants, veterans, other special)
		Survivors pension (all schemes, national, civil servants, veterans, other special)
		Disability pension (all schemes, national, civil servants, veterans, other special)
	Other social insurance	Occupational injuries benefits
		Paid sickness leave benefits
		Health
		Maternity and paternity benefits
LABOR MARKET	Labor market policy measures (active labor market programs)	Training (vocational, life skills, cash for training)
		Employment incentives and wage subsidies
		Employment measures for disabled
		Entrepreneurship support and start-up incentives (cash and in-kind grants, microcredit)
		Labor market support and intermediation through public employment services
		Other active labor market programs
	Labor market policy support (passive labor market programs)	Out-of-work income maintenance (unemployment benefits, contributory)
		Out-of-work income maintenance (unemployment benefits, noncontributory)
SOCIAL ASSISTANCE	Unconditional cash transfers	Poverty-targeted cash transfers and last resort programs
		Family, children, orphan allowance (including orphan and vulnerable children benefits)
		Noncontributory funeral grants, burial allowances
		Emergency cash support, including support to refugees and returning migrants
		Public charity, including zakat
	Conditional cash transfers	Conditional cash transfers
	Social pensions (noncontributory)	Old age social pensions
		Disability benefits and war victims noncontributory related benefits
		Survivorship
	Food and in-kind transfers	Food stamps, rations, and vouchers
		Food distribution programs
		Nutritional programs (therapeutic, supplementary feeding, PLHIV)
		In-kind and nonfood support (education supplies, free texts, uniforms)

(continued next page)

SPL AREA	PROGRAM CATEGORY	PROGRAM SUBCATEGORY
	School feeding	School feeding
	Public works, workfare, and direct job creation	Cash for work
		Food for work, including food for training, food for assets, and so forth
	Fee waivers and subsidies	Health insurance exemptions and reduced medical fees
		Education fee waivers
		Food subsidies
		Housing subsidies and allowances (and "privileges")
		Utility and electricity subsidies and allowances
		Agricultural inputs subsidies
	Other social assistance	Scholarships and education benefits
		Social care services, transfers for care givers
		What is left out from above categories
PRIVATE TRANSFERS	Domestic private transfers	Domestic transfers, interfamily in-kind gifts and monetary transfers
		Alimony (divorce, food)
		Income and support from charity and private zakat, support for churches and NGOs[a]
	International private transfers	Remittances from abroad

Source: World Bank Atlas of Social Protection Indicators of Resilience and Equity (ASPIRE) database, http://datatopics.worldbank.org/aspire/region/sub-saharan-africa.
Note: NGO = nongovernmental organization; PLHIV = people living with HIV; SPL = social protection and labor.
a. Depending on country contexts and on how NGOs are financed, transfers from NGOs may be classified as social assistance.

Annex 4B. WDR 2019 on Social Protection in the Changing World of Work

To address the risks associated with current and future labor markets, *World Development Report 2019* (WDR 2019) recommends that governments should rethink social protection systems (World Bank 2019b). It focuses on risks created by the impact of digital technologies on the business models of firms, their production processes, and their demand for skills and therefore jobs. Through the guiding principle of "progressive universalism," the report recommends an expansion of social protection coverage while giving priority to the poorest people. This bottom-up expansion can occur while navigating the fiscal, practical, and political trade-offs that incremental levels of coverage involve. Progressive universalism starts with a guaranteed social assistance minimum and eventually extends to a comprehensive system that provides social insurance and reforms industrial era labor market regulations (figure 4B.1).

Figure 4B.1 Framework for Social Protection and Labor Regulation to Manage Labor Market Challenges

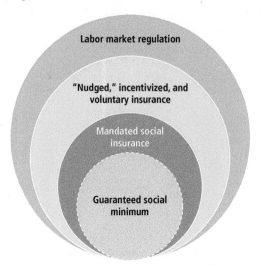

Source: World Bank 2019b.

WDR 2019 proposes the enhancement of social assistance through a guaranteed social minimum and the reform of social insurance and labor regulations. This social minimum comprises social assistance programs that provide financial support to a large share of the population. This package aims to provide adequate support regardless of an individual's employment situation and is complemented with insurance that is independent of formal wage employment. In a changing world of work characterized by new occupations in the "gig" economy, the typical Bismarckian model of social insurance systems based on a standard employer-employee relationship excludes many individuals in labor markets.[30] Additional insurance through voluntary saving schemes that are "nudged" by the state reduce the burden on labor regulation of having to deal with risk management. As people become better protected through enhanced social assistance and insurance systems, labor regulation can be made more flexible to facilitate movement between jobs. Complementary support for learning new skills, along with new arrangements for strengthening the voice of workers, becomes even more important. Taken together, the expanded coverage of social assistance and the provision of subsidized social insurance imply a stronger role for governments.

Annex 4C. Illustration of Social Protection Policies to Mitigate Risks and Leverage Opportunities

	Digitization and trade integration risks	Climate change and fragility risks	Population transition risks
Social assistance	• Public works programs (PWPs) to manage transitions and generate income for displaced workers (Mitra and Ranjan 2011). • To strengthen social assistance, mineral-rich economies can directly distribute resource revenues to host communities that could be affected by automation of mining jobs, through resource-dividend schemes (Moss, Lambert, and Majerowicz 2015). The subnational, resource-dividend schemes in Alaska and Canada are interesting examples (World Bank 2019a).	• Flexible and scalable social safety nets (SSNs) can help households mitigate shocks and enable them to respond after they occur (World Bank 2018d). Digital technology–supported social registries can help in identifying and targeting individuals and households at risk (Leite et al. 2017; World Bank 2018d). "Productive-inclusion" elements can help enhance productivity. • PWPs can increase household and climate resilience, for example, soil and water conservation and management, development of irrigation channels, food storage facilities, rainwater capture, renewable energy jobs (ILO 2017; World Bank 2018d), and emergency cash-for-work programs (Bastagli 2014; Marzo and Mori 2012; McCord 2013). • Private transfers and other informal SSNs can be leveraged to complement weak formal social protection systems in fragile situations. These include Islamic zakat, church tithings, and revolving village savings and credit associations. They could be strengthened with formal risk pooling and reinsurance solutions that offer protection for covariate and catastrophic risks.	• SSNs targeted at the urban poor can help working-age populations in transition. • Safety Nets Plus delivers complements to cash transfers to the urban poor with active labor market policies (ALMPs) such as links to financial services, access to capital or training in a range of skills including microenterprise development, and technical and life skills (Filmer and Fox 2014).

(continued next page)

	Digitization and trade integration risks	Climate change and fragility risks	Population transition risks
Social insurance	• Social insurance reforms should expand insurance coverage beyond formal employer-employee contracts, especially to the informal sector (Guven 2019).	• Governments can facilitate and strengthen private sector solutions to insurance and risk sharing.	
Labor market policies	• ALMPs can facilitate the transition to new jobs of workers displaced by trade liberalization or automation and minimize the costs of trade adjustment. These policies include training and job search programs, formal and vocational education, and skills-job matching programs (Abebe et al. 2016; World Bank 2018a).		• ALMPs, remedial training programs, and employment, entrepreneurial and business support in collaboration with the private sector, especially in the digital economy. Some initiatives across the continent include the Microsoft tech hubs for software engineers in East and West Africa; business training for tech entrepreneurs by Alibaba in collaboration with the Rwandan government (Abayateye 2018; *East African* 2017; *Business Daily* 2017; *Quartz Africa* 2019) and by the Tony Elumelu Foundation Entrepreneurship Program (*PM News* 2019).[a]
Other	• Investments in regional public goods, including early warning systems for natural disasters and epidemics, regional centers of excellence on research and training, development of private markets for risk-sharing (Beegle and Christiaensen 2019; Beegle, Coudouel, and Monsalve 2018, 67), and a regional approach to reduce remittance costs.		

Note: ALMP = active labor market program; PWP = public works program; SSN = social safety net.
a. On remedial education and training, see Arias, Evans, and Santos (2019); on collaborating with the private sector, see Filmer and Fox (2014). For more information on The Tony Elumelu Foundation in Nigeria, see https://tonyelumelufoundation.org/.

Notes

1. The term "shocks" used here refers to the "covariate" type that affect communities or whole societies, rather than the "idiosyncratic" type that affect individual households, such as life-cycle events like births, illnesses, or deaths. Further discussion is available in Bastagli (2014) and McCord (2013).
2. This definition is comparable to definitions from the International Labour Organization (see ILO 2019) and the Organisation for Economic Co-operation and Development (see Social Spending Indicators web page, https://www.oecd-ilibrary.org/social-issues-migration-health/social-spending/indicator/english_7497563b-en).

3. These trends and disruptors are adapted from ILO (2017), Packard et al. (2019), and WEF (2016).

4. These efforts include the Southern African Development Community, the Economic Community of West African States, and the Common Market for Eastern and Southern Africa, among others.

5. The agreement came into effect in May 2019, after 52 countries signed the agreement, and 22 countries had ratified it, the minimum needed to activate the AfCFTA.

6. This result was driven by imperfect labor mobility and declining labor demand. Slow interregional labor mobility happened because entrepreneurs waited for their capital investments to depreciate fully before closing their firms, and because negative regional agglomeration effects amplified the fall of labor income in regions adversely affected by import competition relative to other regions.

7. Data from the United Nations High Commissioner for Refugees' Operational Portal: Refugee Situations, https://data2.unhcr.org/en/situations.

8. The analysis in this section is largely but not exclusively drawn from Beegle, Coudouel, and Monsalve (2018), World Bank (2019b), and World Bank (2018d).

9. Other options considered in this debate include programs that guarantee jobs or "public works programs." The report notes that a UBI may be an alternative to public works when their overwhelming function is mere income support. When more meaningful activity is envisioned, however, public works emerge as a complementary instrument for those who are fit and able to work (World Bank 2019b).

10. Structurally, agriculture remains the main economic activity in the region, with the sector commonly providing for most employment opportunities; however, the sector tends to be only lightly taxed, and revenue potential among smallholders and subsistence agriculture is limited. Collection efforts often risk not being cost-effective.

11. Tax effort is defined as an index of the ratio between the share of the actual tax collection in GDP and taxable capacity. Taxable capacity is determined by predicting the tax-to-GDP ratio in a regression analysis. See Le, Moreno-Dodson, and Bayraktar (2012).

12. For a discussion of the literature and methodological challenges, see LaPorte and de Quatrebarbes (2015).

13. For example, tax expenditures are estimated at 4.5 percent of Cabo Verde's GDP (World Bank 2018d), 7.8 percent of Senegal's GDP in 2014 (Senegal 2016), and 5.2 percent of Ghana's (World Bank 2017).

14. In the region, the determination of eligibility for special tax and customs exemptions often follows a discretionary negotiation and approval process that is sometimes outside the scope of oversight by the legislature. It is not uncommon for taxpayer-specific conventions to be negotiated on a project-by-project basis, generating high ex ante screening and ex post monitoring costs, while jeopardizing a level playing field among competing projects in the same industry. Monitoring of the use of incentives and associated abuse risk also results in significant administrative effort. For instance, tax planning to move profits from higher to lower taxed affiliates in the same firm can create challenges that are difficult to monitor in reviewing domestic transfer pricing arrangements (see Beer and Loeprick 2018; Cooper et al. 2016).

15. Surveys suggest that tax incentives do not feature among investor priorities in developing countries (IMF et al. 2015). Similarly, household survey data often reveal that

VAT exemptions, especially for food and utilities, are not well targeted to poor households in Africa (Harris et al. 2018).

16. In francophone Africa, Van Parys and James (2010) find no robust positive relationship between tax holidays and investment.

17. The revenue at stake can indeed be substantial but depends on country specifics and does not always exceed other DRM priorities. In Sub-Saharan Africa, corporate tax tends to account for a larger share of revenue and the sums at stake in specific cases involving international tax issues can be large compared with overall revenues.

18. Estimates based on microdata are limited for developing countries (Beer, De Mooji, and Liu 2018). Relying on publicly available firm-level information on 26,000 multinational enterprises in 94 low- and middle-income countries (but only including 170 firms in Sub-Saharan Africa), Johannessen, Tørsløv, and Wier (2016) find relatively more exposure to profit shifting in developing countries. Similarly, Beer and Loeprick (2015) find more exposure of non-OECD countries when estimating profit shifting in the oil and gas sector. In an assessment of taxpayer data in South Africa, Reynolds and Wier (2016) find a higher profit shifting response among South African subsidiaries than in more developed countries; however, their findings also suggest that the income at stake may only be moderate.

19. In Togo, in 2016, the five largest companies accounted for 66 percent of total direct tax revenue from businesses and around 50 companies accounted for more than 90 percent of the receipts (World Bank 2018d).

20. A critical dimension for the policy discussion is the VAT treatment of the agriculture sector in Sub-Saharan Africa, which is frequently exempted. Crops and livestock are often exempt from VAT because of equity concerns. These general exemptions tend to also exclude large farmers from the tax base. In absolute terms, the level of support provided to these larger operators can significantly exceed the support provided to small farmers. A reasonable general VAT exemption threshold would normally still allow the vast majority of small farmers to remain outside the scope of the tax.

21. The economies are Kenya, Mozambique, Uganda, the Republic of Yemen, and West Bank and Gaza (Jones, Samuels, and Malachowska 2013).

22. The study reviews evidence from 165 studies, covering 56 programs, on the impact of cash transfers on monetary poverty; education; health and nutrition; savings, investment, and production; and employment and empowerment (Bastagli et al. 2016).

23. Discussion on targeting, program design, and delivery systems, although important, goes beyond the scope of this chapter. Suggested further reading includes del Ninno and Mills (2015).

24. On Vietnam, see Van den Berg and Cuong (2011); on Moldova, see Waidler et al. (2017). For a literature review on remittances having a stronger poverty-reducing effect than cash transfers, see Hagen-Zanker and Himmelstine (2014).

25. For a detailed summary and methodological guidance, see IMF et al. (2015).

26. For a detailed discussion, including remaining scope for competition via derogatory regimes outside the main tax legislation, see Mansour and Rota-Graziosi (2013).

27. For detailed discussion, see IMF et al. (2017).

28. These include minimum taxes on turnover, already commonly used in about 20 African countries (Durst 2018; see also Leigh Pemberton and Loeprick 2019; OECD 2019).

29. Using cross-country data from World Bank Enterprise Surveys, Kochanova, Hasnain, and Larson (2018) find that adopting e-filing systems reduces tax compliance costs, the likelihood and frequency of firms being visited by a tax official, and the perception of tax administration as an obstacle to firms' operation and growth. In their sample, e-filing is also associated with a moderate increase in the ratio of income tax revenue to GDP.

30. The "Bismarckian model" refers to the industrial era social insurance system that provides benefits to workers in the formal sector financed by dedicated taxes on wages. Otto von Bismarck, Germany's chancellor in the nineteenth century, is widely recognized as the inventor of this model (World Bank 2019b).

References

Abayateye, M. D. 2018. "Ghana: Huawei Launches ICT Training Centre." *Allafrica*, December 5. https://allafrica.com/stories/201812060479.html.

Abebe, G., S. Caria, M. Fafchamps, P. Falco, S. Franklin, and S. Quinn. 2016. "Curse of Anonymity or Tyranny of Distance? The Impacts of Job-Search Support in Urban Ethiopia." Working Paper 22409, National Bureau of Economic Research, Cambridge, MA.

AfDB (African Development Bank). 2018. *African Economic Outlook 2018*. Abidjan: African Development Bank.

Alfani, F., A. Dabalen, P. Fisker, and V. Molini. 2015. "Can We Measure Resilience? A Proposed Method and Evidence from Countries in the Sahel." Policy Research Working Paper 7170, World Bank, Washington, DC.

Arias, O., D. K. Evans, and I. Santos. 2019. *The Skills Balancing Act in Sub-Saharan Africa: Investing in Skills for Productivity, Inclusivity and Adaptability*. Africa Development Forum Series. Washington, DC: World Bank.

Atkins, L., D. Brautigam, Y. Chen, and J. Hwang. 2017. "China-Africa Economic Challenges of and Opportunities from the Commodity Price Slump." Economic Bulletin 01/2017, China Africa Research Initiative, Johns Hopkins University, Washington, DC.

Awasthi, R., and M. Engelschalk. 2018. "Taxation and the Shadow Economy: How the Tax System Can Stimulate and Enforce the Formalization of Business Activities." Policy Research Working Paper 8391, World Bank, Washington, DC.

Bastagli, F. 2014. "Responding to a Crisis: The Design and Delivery of Social Protection." Briefing Paper 90, Overseas Development Institute, London.

Bastagli, F., J. Hagen-Zanker, L. Harman, V. Barca, G. Sturge, T. Schmidt, and L. Pellerano. 2016. "Cash Transfers: What Does the Evidence Say?" Overseas Development Institute, London.

Beegle, K., and L. Christiaensen, eds. 2019. *Accelerating Poverty Reduction in Africa*. Washington, DC: World Bank.

Beegle, K., A. Coudouel, and E. Monsalve, eds. 2018. *Realizing the Full Potential of Social Safety Nets in Africa*. Africa Development Forum Series. Washington, DC: World Bank.

Beer, S., R. A. De Mooji, and L. Liu. 2018. "International Corporate Tax Avoidance: A Review of the Channels, Magnitudes, and Blind Spots." Working Paper 18/168, International Monetary Fund, Washington, DC.

Beer, S., and J. Loeprick. 2015. "Profit-Shifting: Drivers of Transfer (Mis)Pricing and the Potential of Countermeasures." *International Tax and Public Finance* 22 (3): 426–51.

———. 2018. "The Costs and Benefits of Tax Treaties with Investment Hubs: Findings from Sub-Saharan Africa." Policy Research Working Paper 8623, World Bank, Washington, DC.

Bird, R. M., and P.-P. Gendron. 2011. *The VAT in Developing and Transitional Countries*. New York: Cambridge University Press.

Brixiová, Z., Q. Meng, and M. Ncube. 2015. "Can Intra-Regional Trade Act as a Global Shock Absorber in Africa?" Discussion Paper 9205, Institute of Labor Economics, Bonn.

Business Daily (A. Njanja). 2017. "Huawei Opens Training Centre to Bridge Local ICT Skills Gap." December 7. https://www.businessdailyafrica.com/corporate/companies /Huawei-opens-training-centre-to-bridge-local-ICT-skills-gap/4003102-4219146-5dc8jpz /index.html.

Coleman, D. 2016. "Variations on the Impact Bond Concept: Remittances as a Funding Source for Impact Bonds in Low- and Middle-Income Countries." Education Plus Development, Impact Bonds Series, Brookings Institution, Washington, DC. https:// www.brookings.edu/blog/education-plus-development/2016/09/27/variations-on-the -impact-bond-concept-remittances-as-a-funding-source-for-impact-bonds-in-low-and -middle-income-countries/.

Cooper, J., R. Fox, J. Loeprick, and K. Mohindra. 2016. *Transfer Pricing and Developing Economies: A Handbook for Policy Makers and Practitioners*. Directions in Development Series. Washington, DC: World Bank.

del Ninno, C., and B. Mills, eds. 2015. *Safety Nets in Africa: Effective Mechanisms to Reach the Poor and Most Vulnerable*. Washington, DC: World Bank.

Devex (J. L. Ravelo). 2016. "3 Alternative Sources of Financing for Social Protection." August 22. https://www.devex.com/news/3-alternative-sources-of-financing-for -social-protection-88667.

DFID (Department for International Development). 2011. "Defining Disaster Resilience: A DFID Approach Paper." DFID, London.

Dix-Carneiro, R. 2014. "Trade Liberalization and Labor Market Dynamics." *Econometrica* 82 (3): 825–85.

Dix-Carneiro, R., and B. K. Kovak. 2017. "Trade Liberalization and Regional Dynamics." *American Economic Review* 107 (10): 2908–46.

Durst, M. C. 2018. "A Corproate Tax Policy Agenda for Lower-Income Countries." *Tax Notes International* 91 (3): 255.

East African (V. Kirpop). 2017. "500 African Youth to Learn E-Commerce in China." July 22. https://www.theeastafrican.co.ke/business/500-African-youth-to-learn -ecommerce-in-China/2560-4027810-1556amwz/index.html.

Filmer, D., and L. Fox. 2014. *Youth Employment in Sub-Saharan Africa*. Africa Development Series. Washington, DC: World Bank.

Francois, J., M. Jansen, and R. Peters. 2011. "Trade Adjustment Costs and Assistance: The Labour Market Dynamics." In *Trade and Employment: From Myths to Facts*, edited by M. Jansen, 213–52. Geneva: International Labour Organization Office for the European Union.

Gentilini, U. 2018. "What Lessons for Social Protection from Universal Health Coverage?" *Let's Talk Development* (blog), August 8. http://blogs.worldbank.org /developmenttalk/what-lessons-social-protection-universal-health-coverage.

Georgieva, K. 2018. "Technology Works for Getting Poor People's Problems Fixed— We Just Have to Get It Right." *Voices* (blog), June 27. http://blogs.worldbank.org /voices/technology-works-for-getting-poor-people-s-problems-fixed-we-just-have-to -get-it-right.

Guven, M. 2019. "Extending Pension Coverage to the Informal Sector in Africa." Social Protection and Jobs Discussion Paper 1933, World Bank, Washington, DC.

Hagen-Zanker, J., and C. L. Himmelstine. 2014. "What Is the State of Evidence on the Impacts of Cash Transfers on Poverty, as Compared to Remittances?" Working Paper, Overseas Development Institute, London.

Harris, T., D. Phillips, R. Warwick, M. Goldman, J. Jellema, K. Goraus, and G. Inchauste. 2018. "Redistribution via VAT and Cash Transfers: An Assessment in Four Low and Middle Income Countries." Working Paper W18/11, Institute for Fiscal Studies, London.

Hearson, M. 2016. ActionAid Tax Treaties Dataset, International Centre for Tax and Development, Institute of Development Studies, Brighton, UK, http://ictd.ac/datasets /action-aid-tax-treaties-datasets.

Hommann, K., and S. Lall. 2019. *Which Way to Liveable and Productive Cities? A Road Map for Sub-Saharan Africa*. International Development in Focus Series. Washington, DC: World Bank.

ILO (International Labour Organization). 2017. *Inception Report for the Global Commission on the Future of Work*. Geneva: ILO.

———. 2018. *World Employment and Social Outlook—Trends 2018*. Geneva: ILO.

———. 2019. *World Social Protection Report: Universal Social Protection to Achieve the Sustainable Development Goals*. Geneva: ILO.

IMF (International Monetary Fund). 2017. "The Effects of Weather Shocks on Economic Activity: How Can Low Income Countries Cope?" In *World Economic Outlook 2017— Seeking Sustainable Growth: Short-Term Recovery, Long-Term Challenges*, 117–83. Washington, DC: IMF.

———. 2018a. *Fiscal Monitor: Capitalizing on Good Times*. Washington, DC: IMF.

———. 2018b. *Regional Economic Outlook: Sub-Saharan Africa—Capital Flows and the Future of Work*. Washington, DC: IMF.

———. 2018c. *Regional Economic Outlook: Sub-Saharan Africa—Domestic Revenue Mobilization and Private Investment*. Washington, DC: IMF.

———. 2019. *Regional Economic Outlook: Sub-Saharan Africa—Recovery Amid Elevated Uncertainty*. Washington, DC: IMF.

IMF, OECD, UN, and WBG (International Monetary Fund, Organisation for Economic Co-operation and Development, United Nations, and World Bank Group). 2015. "Options for Low Income Countries' Effective and Efficient Use of Tax Incentives for Investment." A Report to the G-20 Development Working Group, World Bank, Washington, DC.

————. 2016. "Enhancing the Effectiveness of External Support in Building Tax Capacity in Developing Countries." Report prepared for submission to G-20 Finance Ministers. World Bank, Washington, DC.

————. 2017. "A Toolkit for Addressing Difficulties in Accessing Comparables Data for Transfer Pricing Analyses." Platform for Collaboration on Tax. World Bank, Washington, DC.

Johannesen, N., T. Tørsløv, and L. Wier. 2016. "Are Less Developed Countries More Exposed to Multinational Tax Avoidance? Method and Evidence from Micro-Data." Working Paper 2016/10, United Nations University World Institute for Development Economics Research, Helsinki, Finland.

Jones, N., F. Samuels, and A. Malachowska. 2013. "Holding Cash Transfers to Account: Beneficiary and Community Perspectives." Overseas Development Institute, London.

Ketkar, S. L., and D. Ratha. 2004. "Development Finance via Diaspora Bonds: Track Record and Potential." Policy Research Working Paper 4311, World Bank, Washington, DC.

Khemani, S., J. Habyarimana, and I. Nooruddin. 2019. "What Do Poor People Think about Cash Transfers?" *Future Development* (blog), April 8. https://www.brookings .edu/blog/future-development/2019/04/08/what-do-poor-people-think-about-direct -cash-transfers/.

Kochanova, A., Z. Hasnain, and B. Larson. 2018. "Does E-Government Improve Government Capacity? Evidence from Tax Compliance Costs, Tax Revenue, and Public Procurement Competitiveness." *World Bank Economic Review* 34 (1): 101–20. https://academic.oup.com/wber/advance-article-abstract/doi/10.1093/wber/lhx024 /5025102?redirectedFrom=fulltext.

LaPorte, B., and C. de Quatrebarbes. 2015. "What Do We Know about the Sharing of Mineral Resource Rents in Africa?" *Resources Policy* 46 (Part 2): 239–49.

Le, T. M., B. Moreno-Dodson, and N. Bayraktar. 2012. "Tax Capacity and Tax Effort: Extended Cross-Country Analysis from 1994 to 2009." Policy Research Working Paper 6252, World Bank, Washington, DC.

Leigh Pemberton, J., and J. Loeprick. 2019. "Low Tax Jurisdictions and Preferential Regimes: Policy Gaps in Developing Economies." Policy Research Working Paper 8778, World Bank, Washington, DC.

Leite, P. G., T. George, C. Sun, T. Jones, and K. A. Lindert. 2017. "Social Registries for Social Assistance and Beyond: A Guidance Note and Assessment Tool." Social Protection and Labor Discussion Paper 1704, World Bank, Washington, DC.

Lundgren, C. J., A. H. Thomas, and R. C. York. 2013. *Boom, Bust or Prosperity? Managing Sub-Saharan Africa's Natural Resource Wealth.* African Department. Washington, DC: International Monetary Fund.

Mansour, M., and G. Rota-Graziosi. 2013. "Tax Coordination, Tax Competition, and Revenue Mobilisation in the West African Economic and Monetary Union." Working Paper 13/163, International Monetary Fund, Washington, DC.

Marzo, F., and H. Mori. 2012. "Crisis Response in Social Protection." Social Protection and Labor Discussion Paper 1205, World Bank, Washington, DC.

McCord, A. 2013. "Shockwatch and Social Protection: Shock Response Readiness Appraisal Toolkit." Overseas Development Institute, London.

Mitra, D., and P. Ranjan. 2011. "Social Protection in Labour Markets Exposed." In *Making Globalization Socially Sustainable*, edited by M. Bacchetta and M. Jansen, 199–231. Geneva: International Labour Organization.

Mohapatra, S., and D. Ratha, eds. 2011. *Remittance Markets in Africa*. Directions in Development Series. Washington, DC: World Bank.

Mo Ibrahim Foundation. 2019. "Africa's Youth: Jobs or Migration? 2019 Ibrahim Forum Report." Mo Ibrahim Foundation, London. http://mo.ibrahim.foundation/forum /downloads/.

Moss, T., C. Lambert, and S. Majerowicz. 2015. *Oil to Cash: Fighting the Resource Curse through Cash Transfers*. Washington, DC: Center for Global Development.

Mvukiyehe, E. 2018. "What Are We Learning about the Impacts of Public Works Programs on Employment and Violence? Early Findings from Ongoing Evaluations in Fragile States." *Development Impact* (blog), April 16. https://blogs.worldbank.org /impactevaluations/what-are-we-learning-about-impacts-public-works-programs -employment-and-violence-early-findings.

Newfarmer, R. S., J. Page, and T. Finn. 2018. *Industries without Smokestacks: Industrialization in Africa Reconsidered*. Oxford: Oxford University Press.

Ng'weno, A., and D. Porteous. 2018. "Let's Be Real: The Informal Sector and the Gig Economy Are the Future, and the Present, of Work in Africa." CGD Note, Center for Global Development, Washington, DC. https://www.cgdev.org/publication/lets -be-real-informal-sector-and-gig-economy-are-future-and-present-work-africa.

OECD (Organisation for Economic Co-operation and Development). 2012. "Evolution of ODA for Social Protection." OECD Publishing, Paris.

———. 2018a. "Development Aid at a Glance: Statistics by Region—Africa, 2018 Edition." OECD Publishing, Paris.

———. 2018b. *States of Fragility 2018: Highlights*. Paris: OECD Publishing.

———. 2019. "Addressing the Tax Challenges of the Digitalization of the Economy: Policy Note." OECD/G20 Base Erosion and Profit Shifting Project. OECD Publishing, Paris.

Ortiz, I. 2018. "The Case for Universal Social Protection: Everyone Faces Vulnerabilities in Their Lifetime." *Finance & Development* 55 (4): 32–34.

Ortiz, I., M. Cummins, and K. Karunanethy. 2017. "Fiscal Space for Social Protection and the SDGs: Options to Expand Social Investments in 187 Countries." ESS Working Paper 48, International Labour Organization, Geneva.

Packard, T., U. Gentilini, M. Grosh, P. O'Keefe, R. Palacios, D. Robalino, and I. Santos. 2019. *Protecting All: Risk-Sharing for a Diverse and Diversifying World of Work*. Human Development Perspectives Series. Washington, DC: World Bank.

PM News. 2019. "AfDB, Elumelu Foundation, Partner on Youth Entrepreneurship in Africa." March 26. https://www.pmnewsnigeria.com/2019/03/26/afdb-elumelu -foundation-partner-on-youth-entrepreneurship-in-africa/.

Quartz Africa (T. Shapshak). 2019. "South Africa Is Now a Major Hub for Big Tech's Cloud Datacenters." March 20. https://qz.com/africa/1576890/amazon-microsoft -huawei-building-south-africa-data-hubs/.

Ratha, D. K., S. Mohapatra, C. Ozden, S. Plaza, W. Shaw, and A. Shimeles. 2011. *Leveraging Migration for Africa: Remittances, Skills, and Investments*. Washington, DC: World Bank.

Reynolds, H., and L. Wier. 2016. "Estimating Profit Shifting in South Africa Using Firm-Level Tax Returns." Working Paper 2016/128, United Nations University World Institute for Development Economics Research, Helsinki, Finland.

Senegal, Ministry of the Economy, Finance and Planning. 2016. "Rapport d'Evaluation des Desponses Fiscales." Ministry of the Economy, Finance and Planning, Dakar. http://www.impotsetdomaines.gouv.sn/sites/default/files/Actualites/rapport_depenses _fiscales_2014.pdf.

Subbarao, K., C. del Ninno, C. Andrews, and C. Rodriguez-Alas. 2013. *Public Works as a Safety Net: Design, Evidence and Implementation*. Directions in Development– Human Development Series. Washington, DC: World Bank.

UN DESA (United Nations Department of Economic and Social Affairs). 2017. *World Population Prospects: The 2017 Revision*. New York: UN DESA.

UNECA (United Nations Economic Commission for Africa), African Union, and African Development Bank. 2017. *Assessing Regional Integration in Africa VIII: Bringing the Continental Free Trade About*. Addis Ababa: UNECA, African Union, and African Development Bank.

United Nations and World Bank. 2018. *Pathways for Peace: Inclusive Approaches to Preventing Violent Conflict*. Washington, DC: World Bank.

Usman, Zainab, N. Oppong, N. Nwogu, and A. Henry. Forthcoming. "Digital Technologies and the Future of Work in Africa's Mining Sector." World Bank, Washington, DC.

Van den Berg, M., and N. V. Cuong. 2011. "Impact of Public and Private Cash Transfers on Poverty and Inequality: Evidence from Vietnam." *Development Policy Review* 29 (6): 689–728.

Van Parys, J., and S. James. 2010. "The Effectiveness of Tax Incentives in Attracting Investment: Panel Data Evidence from the CFA Franc Zone." *International Tax and Public Finance* 17 (4): 400–29.

Waidler, J., J. Hagen-Zanker, F. Gassman, and M. Siegel. 2017. "Do Remittances and Social Assistance Have Different Impacts on Expenditure Patterns of Recipient Households? The Moldovan Case." *Migration and Development* 6 (3): 355–75.

WEF (World Economic Forum). 2016. "The Future of Jobs: Employment, Skills and Workforce Strategy for the Fourth Industrial Revolution." Global Challenge Insight Report, World Economic Forum, Geneva.

WEF and Accenture. 2017. "Digital Transformation Initiative: Mining and Metals Industry." World Economic Forum and Accenture, Geneva. http://reports.weforum .org/digital-transformation/wp-content/blogs.dir/94/mp/files/pages/files/wef-dti-mining -and-metals-white-paper.pdf.

World Bank. 2012. "Resilience, Equity, and Opportunity: The World Bank's Social Protection and Labor Strategy 2012–2022." World Bank, Washington, DC.

———. 2016. "Africa Region—Accelerating Climate-Resilient and Low-Carbon Development: Progress Report on the Implementation of the Africa Climate Business Plan." World Bank, Washington, DC.

———. 2018a. "Managing Coal Mine Closure: Achieving a Just Transition for All." World Bank, Washington, DC.

———. 2018b. "The Market for Remittance Services in Southern Africa." Finance, Competitiveness & Innovation Insight, World Bank Group, Washington, DC.

———. 2018c. "Rapid Social Response Program Progress Report 2016–17." World Bank, Washington, DC.

———. 2018d. *The State of Social Safety Nets 2018*. Washington, DC: World Bank.

———. 2019a. "Migration and Remittances: Recent Developments and Outlook." Migration and Development Brief 31, World Bank, Washington, DC.

———. 2019b. *World Development Report 2019: The Changing Nature of Work*. Washington, DC: World Bank.

———. Forthcoming. *Democratic Republic of Congo Country Economic Update*. Washington, DC: World Bank.

World Bank and China Development Bank. 2017. "Leapfrogging: The Key to Africa's Development? From Constraints to Investments in New Opportunities." World Bank, Washington, DC.